BETWEEN
EARTHQUAKES
AND
VOLCANOES

BETWEEN EARTHQUAKES AND VOLCANOES

Market, State,
and the Revolutions
in Central America

Carlos M. Vilas
Translated by Ted Kuster

Monthly Review Press
New York

Library of Congress Cataloging-in-Publication Data
Vilas, Carlos Maria
    Between earthquakes and volcanoes ; market, state, and the
revolutions in Central America / by Carlos M. Vilas ; translated by
Ted Kuster.
        p.   cm.
    Includes index.
    ISBN 0-85345-902-9 : $36.00. — ISBN 0-85345-903-7 (pbk.) : $18.00
    1. Central America — Politics and government — 1979– 2.
Revolutions — Central America — History — 20th century. 3.
Central America — Economic conditions. 4. Democracy — Central
America.
    I. Title.
F1439.5.V55 1994   94-31721
972.805'3 — dc20   CIP

Monthly Review Press
122 West 27th Street
New York NY 10001

Manufactured in the United States of America
10 9 8 7 6 5 4 3 2 1

Contents

Preface

For thousands of years the volcanoes of Central America have spewed ash over the isthmus's western plains, bequeathing an extraordinary fertility to the soil. Forests of immense trees and generous orchards sheltered the sparse indigenous populations that decided to settle in the region after migrations that spanned several millennia. Corn was the basis and the expression of their cultures, the symbol of life and fertility, of nourishment and identity. After hundreds of years, the middle of the twentieth century witnessed the replacement of corn by new crops, brought from other parts of the world to be shipped out again to other parts of the world, signaling the disappearance of the forests, the death of their fauna, the flight of their inhabitants. It brought the rise of new identities, with new behaviors, attitudes, possibilities. In the shadow of the volcanoes, the idea began to emerge that these men and women were capable of setting out to redesign the world they called home, and more: that they had a right to make of this world a world of their own.

Geological volcanoes had already sparked the social volcanoes of revolution when the earth shook in Managua in 1972, in Guatemala in 1976, and in San Salvador in 1986. The social earthquakes of the insurgent peoples found an echo in the movements of the soil on which they lived. The seismic fissures laid open the complete rapacity of the regimes against the people in rebellion; geology added its own arguments and judgments to the popular critique.

And so, between volcanoes and earthquakes, Central America underwent a process of revolutionary agitation between the mid-1970s and the beginning of the 1990s that threw its social structure, its political institutions, and its ties to the international system into turmoil, with severe effects on the lives and destinies of millions of Central Americans. More than 300,000 people died in the violence, most of them executed by state or parastate forces. Insurgent processes with broad popular support emerged in El Salvador, Guatemala, and Nicaragua. Nor were Costa Rica and Honduras spared; while not directly involved, they too were locked into the polarization of the region's political scene, and in time took up significant roles of their own in counterrevolutionary strategies, or in redirecting revolutionary conflict along less radical lines.

Open war, with the explicit involvement of the United States, broke out on the isthmus. Societies that for more than fifty years had gone unnoticed by international public opinion, receiving only as much attention as is customarily accorded the picturesque, plunged full-force into the hemispheric debate. The revolutionary storm blew the region into the center of what we now know was the final phase of the cold war system.

Yet the revolutionary period that so intensely stirred the region now belongs to the past. The Sandinistas practice parliamentary politics, in their own fashion; the Salvadoran revolutionaries have become a political party and run for office; the Guatemalan revolutionaries are working toward peace negotiations with the government and the armed forces. Under the circumstances, then, what is the point of paying any more attention to the Central American revolutions?

The question itself reveals a certain ingenuousness, to say the least. To presume that there will be no more social revolutions is as frivolous as to claim that revolutions are always the order of the day. Social revolutions are not a very frequent phenomenon in human history, but there have nevertheless been a good many of them, in an enormous variety of societies and historical moments. Since the market assumed a determining role in people's lives, each century has witnessed at least a couple of great social revolutions. There is no reason to suppose that the next century will be unusual in that regard. Social earthquakes and popular eruptions are like their geological counterparts: we can never safely say we have seen the last of them.

Revolutions are not inevitable, although neither are they accidents. The conditions that fuel and finally ignite a revolutionary process are always particular to each situation, but analysis at the proper level of abstraction brings out recurring elements in the specifics of each case; a significant organizational component is to be seen in even the most spontaneous phenomena. It is also possible to act on these conditions, whether to accelerate the process or to prevent or redirect it. To study the recent revolutionary movements in Central America today, therefore, is to do more than simply fill in the historical record.

The revolutionary cycle that opened in the early 1960s has closed at the ballot box and the negotiating table, but the socioeconomic factors that set off the cycle are still present, many of them more oppressive and widespread today than they have been in thirty years: the spread of urban slums, deep social inequities, massive poverty. It is therefore fashionable—in good taste, even—to speak of the failure of the Central American revolutions. However, from the point of view of the elites, things are no better. The guerrillas did not succeed in gaining power—or, in Nicaragua's case, keeping it—but the Central America of today is not the place it was in the 1950s and 1960s. The social and political order of today bears little resemblance to the *pax oligarchica* of those days. Revolution did not triumph, but the traditional order did not escape the winds of change.

It is understandable, therefore, as this century draws to a close no one had imagined, that all of us have something at which to feel a bit disappointed: those of us who looked with hope to the promise of a better future, and those who wished to chain themselves to the past. Things turned out differently, and it is not the first time that politics has yielded such a surprise. Nevertheless, for those of us who have put some of our own efforts into the processes that this book studies, I do not think being disappointed is the same as concluding that all was in vain. If there was anything in abundance in those years, it was meaning, sense, reason, hope; there were things that were worth doing and needed to be done.

Eric Hobsbawm, in a penetrating essay, warns against separating the study of revolutions from the study of the specific periods in which they occur, or from the period in which they are studied and the researcher's own biases (Hobsbawm 1986). The former enables us to locate revolutions in a context of macrohistorical change, as moments of rupture in systems undergoing growing tensions. The latter helps identify the elements of the researcher's own system of values, elements that enter into any analysis of a phenomenon as explosive as a revolution.

With regard to Hobsbawm's first point, the Central American revolutions are grounded in the most recent phase of the process of structural change in the region, which for the most part began in the early 1950s. Their origins lie, therefore, across the "three golden decades" of worldwide economic development, and they endure throughout the entire span of the cold war. The rapid and wide-ranging transformation of Central America, launched by capitalist modernization, changed the living conditions of broad sectors of the population; it deprived them of their traditional social position without offering a new one. Any judgment of the achievements and the failings of the revolutionary experiences must take place in permanent counterpoint with this broader and longer context.

My personal biases incorporate the conviction that all humans, by virtue of being human, have an inalienable right to dignity and happiness, and a life without fear; that there can be no dignity or happiness without health, education, and decent work and shelter; that we have a right—a natural right, as it once was known, or a human right, as it is called today—to seek them; and that the best government is that which is based on the people's participation and that they are able to change. I am further convinced that for all intents and purposes, these were the real stakes in the Central American revolutions, and are still at stake in the aftermath.

This book attempts to answer a few basic questions: Why did revolutions break out in Central America? Why did they do so in some countries and not in others? What did they achieve? What did the people who joined them, or opposed them, seek? Chapter 1 discusses, on a conceptual level, the plurality of elements that go into the gestation of revolutionary situations. The next two chapters focus on the role of socioeconomic transformations and the institutional and political framework. Chapter 4 attempts to evaluate the reach and the limits, the gains and the losses, of the Central American revolutions: what are their final balance sheets, and what potential exists on that basis for a stable democratization of the societies and political regimes of the area. Finally, Chapter 5 systematizes the study's main conclusions and places them in perspective, and draws hypotheses on the outlook for democratization, development, and equality in Central America.

The comments of colleagues and students at seminars and conferences in the spring of 1993 at the Institute of Latin American and Iberian Studies and the Latin American Seminar, both at Columbia University in New York; the Center for Latin American and Caribbean Studies, New York University; the Council on Latin American Studies, Yale University; the Latin American Studies Consortium, North Carolina and Duke Universities; and Gettysburg College, helped me to formulate my ideas. I acknowledge in particular Raúl Benítez Manaut (Centro de Investigaciónes Interdisciplinarias en Humanidades/Universidad Nacional Autónoma de Mexico) and John Hammond (Hunter College, City University of New York), who read the complete manuscript with a critical eye. The failings that certainly remain are my exclusive responsibility.

ONE

Revolutions: Economics, Consciousness, and Politics

When abrupt and regressive changes in living conditions sharpen inequality and break the implicit system of reciprocities that permits people to legitimate the social order, revolutionary situations tend to arise.

Social order is built upon a set of tradeoffs, both real and symbolic but not usually explicit, that makes it possible for people to persuade themselves that their involvement in social relations and their acceptance of political institutions gives them access to returns that they regard as generally fair. When this reciprocity is broken, for reasons that can be quite varied, people begin to consider that they are contributing more in work, products, obedience, personal services, taxes, or any number of other ways, than they are receiving in exchange in the form of institutional services, security, employment, recognition.

A consciousness of injustice begins to germinate, and this, when reinforced by external agents, can eventually alter traditional patterns of collective behavior, erode existing systems of loyalties, and point the protests of the dissatisfied against those who appear to benefit from the unjust situation: the rich, the powerful, the state.

State action can redirect, suppress, or accelerate the manifestations of social unrest. Whichever course the state chooses, it will further politicize the conflict. If the choice is suppression, its failure not only helps consolidate and advance revolutionary agitation, but usually opens fractures in the bloc in power as well, as segments of the bloc abandon it to join the protest. While the state's social base narrows with its ineffective handling of the crisis, the revolutionary coalition, in contrast, emerges as a potential power center and earns the recognition of broad sectors of society.

How people become convinced that the established institutions offer no choice but to join the revolution if things are to be changed is among the central theoretical concerns in discussing social revolutions. The factors are both individual and collective, both objective (socioeconomic structures and political institutions) and subjective (psychosocial processes, ideological definitions, and attitudes). How do large portions of the population come to interpret their living conditions as unjust, turn that interpretation into a consciousness of their own political oppression, and then place their faith in the power of their own involvement in direct collective and extra-institutional confrontation with established political forces? After conspiracy theories of history or the more vulgar versions of *foquismo* are put aside, the issue can be seen in all its complexity, including elements of both spontaneity and organization. It brings with it a very broad array of particular questions, and there is not a great deal that can be said about it in general terms.

The roots of a revolutionary process are too complex to be reduced to a single element, even "in the final analysis." Such economic, political, and psychosocial elements are always present in revolutionary processes, but none alone can offer sufficient explanation. The change in people's consciousness that makes them join in revolution does not materialize from thin air; it is a response to abrupt changes in the economy and in the political regime. In the absence of such a shift in consciousness, on the other hand, economic and political changes have no transformative power.

A revolutionary situation, therefore, arises when three sets of factors converge: those that bring changes in living conditions (usually economic or political-military factors); those that lead to a negative judgment of the new situation (psychosocial or ideological factors); and institutional factors that open or close the outlook for changing adverse situations within the existing political system. Change for the worse is not by itself enough, if people can justify it. Nor is the consciousness of injustice sufficient by itself to mobilize people against institutions—modern history offers many examples of prolonged dictatorships under which most oppressed people do not rise in protest. Revolutionary situations are the combined result of this plurality of elements.

It follows that if it is important to identify the macroeconomic and macropolitical processes that contribute to sparking or blocking a revolutionary situation, it is just as important to examine how these factors operate on a microbasis in people's ordinary, everyday lives. Rising or falling international prices, the substitution of export crops for consumer crops, and an insensitive government are among the factors usually identified as the seedbeds of revolutionary situations. But the actual shape of these factors ultimately depends on the ways that they touch people's daily lives.

Global macroeconomic and macropolitical indicators sketch out, in the abstract, the stage upon which revolutions are possible. To go beyond this beginning point and describe the passage from what is possible to what is real, we must examine the ways these global factors influence the lives of the people who make revolutions. Attention to the microeffects of macrofactors makes it possible to discern the ways people construct and live out general concepts such as exploitation, corruption, injustice, order, happiness, violence, well-being, and so on.

To focus on the microfoundations of social action is not to ignore the structural factors that set the borders within which individual choices operate. Different levels of perception and analysis of social problems, in fact, always coexist within revolutionary processes. While leaders and activists emphasize the macroeconomic and macropolitical dimensions and their effects on the construction of microsocial circumstances, the "common" people privilege their own microconjunctures, through which they come to be conscious of the world that exists outside their village, their neighborhood, their factory, their community.

This duality of perspective can help invigorate revolutionary mobilization and the operation of the revolutionary regime, but can also pose problems for it. What is the legitimate history of a revolutionary process: the great developments and global structures narrated by its leaders, or the concrete daily lives of those who are led? And if it is both and neither at the same time, how can we construct a synthesis?

Economics

Collective rejection of the material conditions of life is one necessary ingredient of revolutionary situations, but it is not so to the same degree for each participant; nor is it alone sufficient. The living conditions of large portions of the Central American population have been, and remain, extremely unsatisfactory. Nevertheless, poverty in itself is not enough to prompt revolutions.

What moves people to rebel is sudden change for the worse in their living conditions: change that alters their perceptions and judgments of the world in which they live. The speed of change is as important as its magnitude, because it keeps people from adapting or generating defense mechanisms. One loses what one has faster than one can adapt, and all that remains is a feeling of enormous insecurity.

In agrarian economies, sudden economic changes are usually associated with the growth of the commercial economy and cash crops. They may emerge from the replacement of traditional crops with new ones, with the accompanying shifts in land use; from changes in the rules that regulate farmers' access to the land; from the use of new technologies; or from other factors. At other times they are linked to state action in support of agroexport capitalism: building infrastructure such as highways or dams, for example, which destroy forests, invade lands, and flood areas people have lived in for centuries.

Accelerated economic development always causes profound dislocations in people's lives. The growth of agricultural capitalism ties local economies into the international market and exposes them to often-intense fluctuations between low prices, against which peasants cannot protect themselves, and high prices, which they cannot exploit. The repercussions of the changes are magnified when they take place over a few years, in contrast to the traditional pace of rural life. Wallerstein (1980) and Walton (1984) stress the role of peripheral economies' entrance into the world system in generating these changes, pointing to shifts in global demand, new technological developments, and variations in international prices, among other things. This is also Lindenberg's thesis (1990): their small size and broad opening to the exterior make Central American economies extremely vulnerable to shifts in the world market, the effects of which in turn bring on instability and social unrest. The cycles of the world economy feed the peripheral societies' cycles of stability and instability, protest and consent.

These cycles are indeed brought on by changes in markets and the subordination of local economies to them, but their most visible aspect, on the local level, is usually political. Shifts in patterns of production, employment, and daily life are actually carried out by institutional agents directly or indirectly linked to the state: legal functionaries, official surveyors, public works companies, legislation, the repressive apparatus, and the institutional delegitimization of the complaints and demands of those affected. The intervention of an "extra-economic" power, in short, opens new spaces for market expansion and capital accumulation.

Both precapitalist and developed capitalist societies, due to their basic stability, offer few opportunities for massive revolutionary mobilization. For good or ill, the common people have an assigned place in social relations, with institutionally sanctioned systems of rewards and punishments, whatever social distribution. Social relationships and the behavior of their actors—"the rules of the game"—are predictable. The probability of revolutionary challenges is tied most closely to the dislocations, ruptures, and instabilities of the transition from one kind of society to another, of the always-conflictive passage toward an economy dominated by the market, commercial crops, agroindustry, growing globalization of economic and social processes, and a kind of authority based on the abstract rationality of "even law" (Cerroni 1972:69ff).

People lose their old modes of participation in the social order faster than they gain new ones, and the technological characteristics of the new forms of production speed this marginalizing effect: the mechanization and chemicalization of agriculture, for example, not only reduces labor demand but also demands a different kind of labor (with greater and more formal training) than did traditional agriculture. Peasants are deprived of either land or their traditional mode of access to land: as rent ceases to be payable in labor or in kind and becomes payable only in money, possession of formal title to land becomes mandatory, and communal patterns of land use are threatened.

Wage-earning work becomes a necessity when the plot of land proves incapable of providing for the family economy. The new crops impose a seasonal employment schedule with long periods of "idle time"; the itinerant nature of this work forces people to travel throughout the country from harvest to harvest, and the market economy's schedule clashes with the celebrations, rituals, and other events that shape the calendar of the traditional economy. Meanwhile, the substitution of export crops for basic consumer crops derails the nutritional patterns of the family unit. As its stock of land and equipment is reduced or lost, family income falls, and the family's structure changes: young people must leave the family unit to work and earn their own income. Distance and economic autonomy from their elders leads to a relaxation of obedience and respect, from the elders' viewpoint. New perceptions and horizons open up for the women who wash the laundry or clean the homes of well-to-do families. The picture in the cities is no different: a rigid job supply, slums, lack of personal safety, delinquency, prostitution.

Deteriorating access to resources affects every dimension of life and throws traditional reference points into crisis. But together with this deterioration comes a perception of enrichment and prosperity enjoyed by others. The issue is not merely the impoverishment of some, but its connection with the success of others. Some lose while others gain: inequality grows. This is not to say that the traditional or precapitalist order lacked injustices and inequalities. People lived badly then; they worked hard, and often for nothing—how else to interpret the multiple forms of *corvée*? But there were explanations to legitimize the system and mechanisms for adapting to it. These explanations and mechanisms are now missing.

Paige (1985, 1987), Williams (1986), Bulmer-Thomas (1987), and others emphasize the role of changes brought by agroexport capitalism in the emergence of revolutionary conditions in Central America. Other factors being constant, they argue, the erosion of traditional agrarian society over a single generation created the conditions for broad masses of the Central American population to accept the revolutionary call and imbue it with the capacity to challenge the existing order. In this view, revolution resulted from modernization and its dislocating impact on the living conditions of millions of people, both in the countryside and in the city. Weeks (1986), on the other hand, takes the reverse approach. Appealing to the Marxist hypothesis of the contradiction between the development of the productive forces and the relations of production, he concludes that the land-owning societies' structural rigidity in the face of capitalist changes delays those changes and exacerbates their social cost to the workers and peasants. The spark that set off the Central American revolutions, mobilizing both the poor of countryside and city and segments of the modernizing elites, was not the advance of capitalist modernization but the resistance to such modernization put up by the large landowners and commercial capital, protected by the "reactionary despotism" of the state.

More interesting than the conflicts between these approaches is their complementary focus on the condition of the have-nots. These people, trapped between the modernizing vigor of capitalism and the rigidity of the traditional structure, got the worst of both worlds: they were deprived of the elements—material or symbolic—that had given their old world its meaning and justification, and were given no plausible hope of fitting into the new one.

This process, fraught with tensions, overtook all five Central American republics simultaneously. But why did El Salvador, Guatemala, and Nicaragua become the scene of violent social mobilizations and fertile ground for revolutionary movements from the early 1970s on, while Costa Rica and Honduras managed to remain above the fray? The differences among them are not irrelevant, but if we try to analyze the presence or absence of revolutionary processes in each country, it is clear that socioeconomic differences do not suffice to explain the political variations.

Tables 1.1 through 1.4 give a picture of the region's marked socioeconomic homogeneity: the differences among the five Central American republics are less decisive during this period than is sometimes thought. They also indicate that the lines of socioeconomic distinction do not correspond to the political differences underlying the presence or absence of revolutionary processes.

The figures on land tenure concentration (Table 1.1) show, within a framework of relative homogeneity, some differences

Table 1.1
Central America: Land Tenure in the 1960s

| | Multi-family plot [1] | | | | Family plot[2] | | Sub-family plot [3] | |
| | a) medium | | b) large | | | | | |
	No.	%	No.	%	No.	%	No.	%
Costa Rica	68	3	20	14	1	42	11	41
El Salvador	91	22	7	21	0.5	37	1.5	20
Guatemala	88	14	9	13	1	42	2	31
Honduras	67	12	26	27	1	28	6	33
Nicaragua	51	4	27	11	2	41	20	44
Central America	79	10	15	16	0.5	38	5.5	36

Source: CEPAL et al. 1973. Some figures have been rounded.

[1] Farms generating an income above that necessary for the reproduction of one family.

[2] Farms generating an income sufficient for the reproduction of one family.

[3] Farms generating an income below that necessary for the reproduction of one family.

between El Salvador and Guatemala, on the one hand, and Nicaragua, Costa Rica, and Honduras on the other. Table 1.2 indicates some similarity in income distribution among the lower strata in Nicaragua, Guatemala, and El Salvador, but income polarization and the distance between the different income groups (Table 1.3) is smaller in those countries than in Costa Rica and Honduras.

Population density is the only measure that reflects a relatively strong dispersal, which discredits any demographic hypothesis on the Central American conflict (Table 1.4). Pressure on the land in Nicaragua was the lowest in Central America.[1]

In sum, it is clear that crude structural hypotheses apply much more closely to Costa Rica than to Nicaragua.

Consciousness

In the development of revolutionary processes, the economic, or structural, element is a necessary but not a sufficient one. Economics plays a role in generating widespread feelings of insecurity and instability, generating a powerful shift in people's expectations of the order of things. They know they are producing more and working harder than before, but they do not see this translate into an easing of their tribulations; on the contrary, life becomes even more difficult. There is a feeling of loss, even if in strictly material

Table 1.2
Central America: Income Concentration in the 1970s (by Percentage)

Percentile	Costa Rica	El Salvador	Guatemala	Honduras	Nicaragua
Top 5%	22.8	15.4	5.0	21.8	28.0
Next 15%	27.9	49.4	23.9	29.5	32.0
Middle 30%	28.5	22.8	23.8	25.2	25.0
Bottom 50%	20.8	12.4	17.3	23.5	15.0

Source: Vilas 1986.

terms some may be a little better off, or at least avoid joining in the collective deterioration to some degree.

The symbolic dimension of this process is as important as material life conditions. Symbolic elements have long offered explanation and justification for the existing social order. Whether the order that is retreating under the assault of the market was objectively better or worse than the new one, therefore, is not the issue; people perceive it as better because the symbolic elements they possess enable them to evaluate it in this way, not merely because the old way of life was objectively less unsatisfactory. Under the old regime, people knew what to expect.

The symbolic elements of culture do not exist in a vacuum: if peasant economies had not permitted people's needs to be at least minimally met, it is difficult to imagine that symbolic justifications would have remained effective for long. But the arguments that legitimize a social order tend to take on a certain autonomy from their substantive foundations. This is true of any social order and helps to explain the apparently inexplicable "tolerance" or adaptation that people can display under an oppressive or evil order.

In agrarian societies, this ingredient of consciousness (an emotional, or subjective, element) rests on the argument of custom. Economic changes and their effects convince people that their customs, and the normal order of things, are being violated. And it must be noted once again that this is above all a result of the speed of these changes, which take place so quickly that there is no time to reformulate old customs to fit the new context.

Customs are both constructed and "received." They are made up of objective practices reiterated across time, and of the representations, ideas, and meanings that people build with regard to those practices. Each generation recreates the customs on the basis

Table 1.3
Central America: Per Capita Income, 1980[a]

	Costa Rica	El Salvador	Guatemala	Honduras	Nicaragua	Central America
Poorest 20%	46	111	52	62	90	177
30% below median	155	203	102	178	228	501
30% above median	341	364	167	356	423	884
Wealthiest 20%	1535	1134	616	1200	1330	2165
Polarization[b]	33.3	10.2	11.8	19.3	14.8	12.2
Accumulated distance	60.7	25.8	28.3	40.1	32.8	28.6

Sources: Gallardo & López 1986 and author's calculations.   [a] 1970 dollars.   [b] Richest 20%/poorest 20%.

Table 1.4
Central America: Population Density 1960-1980 (Inhabitants per Square Kilometer)

	Costa Rica	El Salvador	Guatemala	Honduras	Nicaragua	Central America
Population (in thousands)						
1960	1250	2430	3960	1900	1420	9900
1970	1730	3580	5350	2640	1970	13810
1980	1970	4800	7260	3690	2730	18790
Area (thousands of sq. km)	51	21	109	112	139	355
Density (persons/sq. km)						
1960	24.5	115.9	36.3	16.9	10.2	27.9
1970	33.9	170.4	49.0	23.5	14.1	38.9
1980	43.0	228.5	66.6	32.9	19.7	52.9

Source: SIECA 1980.

of their own experience of the present and of the past, experiences that are by definition contemporary. The speed of change makes custom more difficult to reproduce and to update, and intensifies the feeling of rupture and loss. The development of new modalities of production and access to land, the mercantilization of the labor force, the dislocation of the family, all in the space of a couple of decades, creates an intergenerational break and blocks the transmission of values, attitudes, and beliefs.[2]

More than anything else, these changes weaken the peasantry's capacity to adapt and maneuver. Hobsbawm (1973) pointed out peasants' capacity for "'working the system' to its advantage—or rather to its minimum disadvantage," referring to the myriad forms of passive resistance, on the micro- and everyday level, to the laws of the market, the arbitrariness of the large landowner and the merchant, and to the arrogance of the state. This passive resistance can be merely symbolic: joking about the perceived ineptitude of the city dweller, sneaking home some of the harvest, creating "microspaces" in which an ambiguous counterhegemonic discourse can develop, such as the cantina or the carnival. These resources, limited as they are, can be interpreted as forms of both resistance and adaptation, but they endow those who practice them with a feeling of effectiveness against a more powerful adversary. The rupture of the traditional order breaks up the continuity of these practices, and leaves peasants defenseless against the new forms of domination.[3]

At the same time, the tradition of any village or region is fed by the experiences and the memories of rebellions past. Some observers have even identified "traditionally rebellious" areas, in which a history of revolt makes fertile ground for new revolutionary mobilization (Wolf 1972; Winocur 1980; Cabezas 1982; etc.).

The fact that the erosion of the traditional local way of life arises mainly from an invasion of external factors encourages a certain idealization of the former: the symbolic reality of the traditional order is reinforced at the very moment that its objective reality is vanishing. With this as a catalyst, the community's internal differentiation fades in importance before the conflict between the community as a whole and the assault of capitalist modernization. This explains why the early leaders of protest are often the members of the community with the most resources or prestige. It is also what gives the early expressions of social protest the defensive character that Womack famously described in his study of the 1910s Zapatista rebellion—"This is a book about peasants who did not want to change and who for that very reason made a revolution"—and that Moore later examined more deeply (Womack 1969:xi; Moore 1978, ch. 15).

People, in fact, do not want change—or rather, they do not want the kind of change that the market and the state wish to impose on them. Ironically, people's will to resist these processes helps to speed changes up and draws the people into the resulting whirlwind—thus transforming society overall and, in so doing, transforming people themselves.

To the extent that political institutions endorse the new situation and delegitimize complaint and protest, the conviction becomes stronger that these institutions are doing violence to the implicit pacts that sustain the relationship between the governing and the governed. This conviction is therefore rather subjective, but is based on objective and tangible facts. The advance of agrarian capitalism, the development of urbanization, and the deterioration of the local community erode client–patron relations as well as the reciprocal loyalties that derive from them: compaternity loses its content; festivities and associations lose their meaning; personal relationships are superseded by associations as impersonal and abstract as signing papers at the bank, at the notary's office, or in the courts. The network of primary relationships cannot compete with the network of the market.

This effect is felt most profoundly at the level of local power, for it is local power in its multiple manifestations that was most dependent on this network of "primary loyalties" (Geertz 1973; Alavi 1973) or "primary connections" (Mazlish 1991). After all, in the initial stages of the process, the national state is but one more abstraction; local authority is what really matters. This distinction is important, because the characteristics of the political system and its institutions on the national level can carry less weight in this process than its local expressions. The political system may be democratic, broad, and participatory in cities or at the national level, and still function arbitrarily and despotically in its local capillaries. Conversely, the concentration of despotic or dictatorial power in some aspects of national life, or in certain regions, may at certain times have no effect on other parts of the country.

Consciousness of injustice is based on comparisons between what is and the image of what was and should be. The interpretation of the past, its content more or less mythical depending on the case, becomes the criterion for judging the injustice of the present. This attitude is particularly strong in indigenous communities and in peasant societies (Scott 1977; Skocpol 1982; McClintock 1984), but it should not be simplistically identified with backwardness. All revolutionary movements legitimize their present-day struggle by emphasizing their roots in the past. The Cuban revolution bases its historical legitimacy on Martí, just as the Central American revolutions are presented as continuations of past indigenous struggles or challenges to United States intervention. The authenticity of these constructed historical lineages matters less than their construction itself, the content of truth that people project onto them, and their capacity to mobilize collective action.

Consciousness of injustice involves the conviction that power and the powerful have violated the social contract in a fashion not justified by the conduct of the ruled. It is the consciousness of arbitrariness and a shared feeling of insecurity as the reference points of reciprocity are lost. By failing to fulfill its obligations to the governed, authority delegitimizes itself and ceases to be authority. Some sources stress the growth of inequality as the material basis for these progressive changes in consciousness (Russet 1964; Sigelman and Simpson 1977). There is a breach in the proportionality of material and symbolic social tradeoffs, or, as we have seen, the system of reciprocities that synthesizes those tradeoffs breaks down, and with it, the judgments made on the basis of that system. People's expectations change: they no longer know what to hope for; anything may happen. The system becomes random and sinks into chaos. A profound collective insecurity emerges: One may be all right today, but who knows about tomorrow; today there is work, next month perhaps not; the children are who knows where.

This brings us to another constant in revolutionary mobilizations. The defense of those aspects of the traditional order through which people's existence was reproduced is closely connected with people's hope for real change beyond the limits imposed by that order (Wolf 1972; Paige 1975; Stacey 1980; Rudé 1981; Knight 1984;

Friedman 1992; etc.). This is "the appetite for innovation along with a profound nostalgia for the past" (Smith 1987:174) that so disoriented Lenin (1905) and that is captured in Womack's line quoted earlier. Social revolutions link the radical goals proposed by "vanguards"—here identified generically as "external agents"—with the defense of traditional rights, commitments, and obligations that, when violated by the elites, move the masses.

This conjunction of apparently antithetical aims and aspirations within a single case of confrontation with established power illustrates the sociological complexity of revolutionary movements in societies moving toward agroindustrial capitalism. On the one side are the masses of people, their traditional role in the economy under attack from the market and advancing globalization; their material basis and cultural references have retreated, yet still exist, serving as a support base and a rearguard for their political involvement. The community, the neighborhood, the village, are all resources to be mobilized in support of the opposition project (see, for example, Cruz Díaz 1982; Smith 1987; Kincaid 1987; Gould 1990; Mossbrucker 1990).[4]

On the other side are the leaders and activists, who are predominantly of urban petty bourgeois or middle-class origin, with higher levels of formal education, and whose integration into the new order is already relatively advanced. In multiethnic societies, this first generation of activists comes primarily from the dominant ethnic groups, or from the hispanicized (or *ladinizado*) elements whose access to educational institutions—traditional sites for the radicalization of the middle groups—has broadened their perspective beyond the borders of the village, region, or neighborhood (Vilas 1989b:130ff).

Men also predominate: not because they are more authoritarian or violence-prone than women,[5] but because of the enormous obstacles women must surpass in order to join political organizations, go underground, move to the mountains, and live among men without the traditional tutelage of elders and siblings. The cost, and the leap, is much greater for women than for men (see, for example, Randall 1980). The complexity of this sociological profile explains the particular physiognomy of revolutionary movements: like Janus, they look forward with one face, back with the other.

The living conditions of the masses reinforce this conjunction of "forward" and "backward" perspectives. These are people whose position in the traditional order has eroded but has not disappeared. They are vulnerable to new relationships and structures but still have a rearguard. They still have something to lose, and therefore something to defend. The Communist Manifesto's image of the proletarian who is revolutionary in his very essence because he has "nothing to lose but [his] chains" is historically in error. Those who rebel are not those who have lost all, but those to whom something still remains. The Bolshevik revolution provides additional evidence for this (Bonnell 1983; Fitzpatrick 1984).

Of course, once they are in motion, people's demands are not limited to recovering what has been lost. They mobilize not only to take back that which has been unjustly taken away—access to resources, control of working time, social recognition—but also to liquidate the oppressive dimensions of the old order: taxation, arbitrariness, authoritarianism, and so on. In their attempt to rebuild the old social order, they finally demolish it. Social revolutions thus tie progressive forces to archaic impulses, hope to frustration, rebellion to reaction.

Politics

Nevertheless, this feeling of injustice cannot in itself mobilize people against the established order. People's capacity to endure iniquitous conditions is not infinite, but it is often much greater than we intellectuals may surmise. As long as they are supplied with proper justification, humans can come to tolerate—and even resign themselves to—extreme hardship. Consciousness of injustice does not necessarily involve a disposition to action. For people to be driven to active rebellion, they must not only perceive their situation as negative; they must be convinced that collective action can set things right.

People's dissatisfaction with their living conditions alone, then, does not determine the political orientation of their protests. Economic and social change, and its impact on the minds and the outlook of those affected, place the latter in a position of "availability" (Deutsch 1961; Germani 1962); that is, in a position to opt for new collective behaviors and new leadership, in line with proposals that they have not themselves generated.

A revolutionary agenda is not the only possible form of collective response. Para-police bodies recruit their members from the same social groups that revolutionary organizations seek to represent: those harmed by capitalist modernization or political change. Revolution and counterrevolution compete, sociologically speaking, for the support of the same actors. The *Cristero* war in Mexico is a case in point, as are the insurrection against the Fulgencio Batista dictatorship in Cuba, the revolution in El Salvador, and the years of counterrevolutionary war in Nicaragua (O'Connor 1964; Amaro Victoria 1970; Samaniego 1980; Vilas 1988). What these collective displacements have in common is that all involve violent behaviors, both against the state and the beneficiaries of the order it protects and against those who challenge them. But there is also evasive behavior: physical evasion through migration, and inward evasion in the form of spiritualist phenomena such as fundamentalist religion and esoteric philosophies.

External agents too, as catalysts of social discontent, play a central role in the leap from consciousness to action, and in the direction that this leap ultimately takes. Until a few years ago, communism was regarded by the U.S. government as the external agent behind the Central American revolutions; the term was used so extravagantly, especially by the rulers and military forces of the area, as to lose much of its meaning (González et al. 1984; Schoultz 1987; Falcoff 1989). Nevertheless, it must be recalled that Lenin's theory of the Bolshevik party as the agent that would forge revolutionary proletarian consciousness among workers, who by themselves could not transcend the level of "reformism," is indeed one of the earliest formulations of the role of the external agent.

These agents exist in great variety: priests, preachers, teachers, journalists, students, social workers, agricultural extension trainers, and of course political activists. A new generation of priests, many of them foreigners, played a signal role in building social protest in Guatemala and El Salvador. Students and some professors at the University of San Cristóbal de Huamanga in Peru seem to have been central to the rise of the Shining Path guerrillas. In Nicaragua, "delegates of the Word" and student movement activists were instrumental in consciousness-raising and agitation. In Guatemala, the impact of Peace Corps volunteers, agricultural extension workers, and even U.S. anthropologists has been called a factor in mobilizing indigenous discontent toward confrontation with political institutions.

These agents are external primarily because they do not belong to the community or to the environment that they mobilize. They may not be totally foreign—they may be students returning to their hometowns, or provincial journalists—but their training and their experiences reach beyond the local sphere. They also hold positions that carry with them prestige and a certain kind of authority: priests are the typical case, but the same can be said of teachers or health workers. Their standing encourages people to listen to them and take them seriously. They earn credibility by trying to resolve problems: health, education, farming, people's relationship with God. "Externality" is rarely total, because the agent is fulfilling some already-existing function in the life of the community or neighborhood, in the school, the church, the health station, or some other such institution.

The role of external agents is a broad one: they communicate experiences that make it possible to link events within the area or community to happenings in the world outside; they disseminate information and knowledge; they organize. Above all, they supply arguments that delegitimize people's privations and offer reasons for change. At the same time, external agents teach people new ways of working, of adapting to the new market conditions, of trying to get ahead. It bears noting that there is nothing predetermined about the content of the changes these agents help bring about. Agricultural extension trainers, religious workers, and Peace Corps volunteers in the 1960s all preached cooperation, basic education, and hygiene; the goal was to improve the position of Latin American rural communities in capitalist development and to increase their chances for success in that context. When these efforts were thwarted by state authoritarianism, and by the exclusionary character of capitalist modernization itself, many of these external agents were moved to drastic changes in approach.

During periods of crisis and rapidly deteriorating living conditions, people become more receptive, and the external agents' field of activity tends to expand. Two additional factors often encourage a positive response from the population. Because social kinship networks supply the framework for the organization of work and decision-making, entrance into self-defense organizations, including revolutionary ones, tends to take place collectively: fathers bring along their children; one brother persuades the rest; the family becomes a support network (Warman 1980; Cabezas 1982; Reyes and Wilson 1992). Family networks traditionally loom large in agrarian societies, but they are also significant in urban environments of recent settlement (Sader 1988).

Relative spatial isolation is the second factor. Fragile ties between the peasant villages or indigenous communities on the one hand and the national order on the other, whether due to distance or the poor physical integration of the territories, favor rebellion. Hence the volatility of frontier regions, where the presence of central authority is less strongly felt: the North in the Mexican revolution, the eastern Sierra at the outset of the Cuban revolution, and the north-central region in the Sandinista revolution (Wolf 1972:398; Migdal 1974:235; CIERA 1984).

The role of external agents ought not to be viewed as simply conspiratorial or voluntaristic, for their effects are linked to changes that are already underway. Their presence in the regions and villages is itself a result of the expansion of the market, the economy's opening to the exterior, the internationalization of political processes, the new accessibility of remote regions, and greater interaction between the cities—which all of these agents have at least passed through—and the rural world. In their own way, they are but one more product of the intrusion of agro-industrial capitalism in the countryside and the mountains. Without them, however, popular frustration could scarcely become a confrontational force, or even move beyond the level of local protest.

The peasant, the artisan, or the indigenous person comes in contact with this or that merchant, this or that judge, this or that police precinct. The external agent subsumes this plurality of individual experiences into a general concept: capital, the state, the police. Only then does the Indian's and the peasant's relationship with the bosses, the Hispanics, the large landowners, come into view. Rebellion must be able to personalize the exploiter, but must also be able to locate the particular exploiter (and exploited) in a general category. Only then do we have social confrontation.

The action of external agents can be interpreted as one dimension of a growing interconnectedness between discontent in the countryside and agitation in the cities, a link on which the success of revolutionary mobilization depends to a great degree (Gugler 1982; Walton 1984). Only when rural protest connects with the popular rebellion in the cities does the political regime in fact begin to be threatened. Sooner or later, this leads to the question of the leadership of the movement as a whole. A number of factors tend to subordinate the peasant, or rural, movement to the urban one: the localism that remains a strong ingredient in the perceptions and demands of the countryside's poor and exploited; their social dispersion; and other things (Moore 1966: 479–82; Córdova 1979; Skocpol 1979:114–15). Revolutions do not come to power without rural participation, but the peasants' own leadership is not enough to carry them to victory.

The development of revolutionary activity is also linked to the skill and effectiveness of the state in mobilizing its resources to prevent social explosions, to redirect them into less confrontational areas, or to suppress them. The state's opportunities to mobilize resources, and its capacity and effectiveness in doing so, depend in turn on both technical and political factors. Technical factors are the administrative reforms that put the state apparatus and its agencies in a position to actively regulate social dynamics: improving efficiency in bureaucracies, or creating planning agencies, for example. These measures, in principle, enable the government to broaden its field of activity and its influence over the workings of society, in such areas as settlement programs, agrarian reform, tax reform, participation in domestic or foreign marketing of some products, social security systems, etc. The greater their technical effectiveness, the larger portion of the financial surplus state agencies can capture and assign to given purposes. Specifically, they can invest it in areas of heavy social impact in order to ameliorate the negative impacts of agroindustrial capitalization on broad sectors of the popular classes.

It is well known that in peripheral societies the state's capabilities of mobilizing resources have proven unsatisfactory. Thus perspectives of modernization and reform have tended to be linked to foreign intervention and cooperation. U.S. military invasions in the Caribbean and Central America in the early twentieth century included attempts to bring administrative and fiscal reforms to state agencies, to prepare them for new duties demanded by capital accumulation as conducted by U.S. firms, and to secure political governability. In the 1960s, the Alliance for Progress emphasized the need to reform state institutions and policies to adapt them to new developments in international economies as well as to deal with social demands (Vilas 1979; 1989b, ch. 2).

Political factors, however, remain decisive. The recent history of developing countries offers multiple examples of administrative reforms that enjoyed generous external support but ended in failure because of the wrong political conditions. Proper political conditions would essentially mean the effective articulation of the dominant groups with the state, which is in turn an aspect of the relations between the dominant groups and the popular classes. When market expansion and deteriorating living and working conditions strain these relationships, elites are encouraged to resort to intervention through the state apparatus in order to channel the conflict or to directly repress it.

In multiethnic societies, social and ethnic exploitation overlap: the state embodies class rule and ethnic discrimination at the same time; racism is an institutional part of the political system. As different channels of oppression and discrimination merge and reinforce each other, both the potential for conflict and that conflict's degree of violence increase. The state also institutionalizes gender inequality, but in Central America the androcentric dimension of social domination was to come into conscious focus only belatedly, in the framework of the revolutionary agitation of the 1980s.

The success of state intervention in preventing or deflecting social tensions depends above all on the stage of development of capitalism and of social protest. There is a time for reform, and there is a time for repression. When they come late, the state's reformist interventions can be counterproductive. Social reforms by definition are perceived differently by different classes and groups. For the elites, reforms earn legitimacy if they neutralize or prevent social protest and do not require too large a reduction in the surplus the elites appropriate. For the emerging classes, reforms are legitimate if they are in fact reforms; that is, if they actually change the structure of social domination. As a result, reforms heighten social confrontation over state policies, and intensify the pressure upon the state. The cross-purposes behind such pressures make it very difficult to reach even the smallest degree of consensus on the scale or the scope of state intervention.

The failure of reforms, whether it is due to their belatedness or to elite opposition, weakens the state and those who support it, and sharpens the potential for social conflict. People's sense of having been taken in usually lends power to revolutionary calls; protest takes on a mass character. The state and its agencies, once repressive action or ineffective reformism has identified them with elite interests, become a privileged target of social protest.

Thwarted reform intensifies people's radicalization and their forms of expressing it, at the same time as it narrows the state's social base. What later become known as the "final stages" of revolutionary mobilization processes are usually set off by a violation of legality by the state itself or dominant groups, and the use of electoral fraud, nonrecognition of popular candidates' voting successes, preventive military coups, etc., to close off institutional, "reformist" avenues for expressing popular discontent.

This helps explain the initial ties between many of the revolutionary organizations and already-existing political and social organizations of legal, "reformist" character. The choice of a revolutionary path generally arises within organizations that until then have acted within legal bounds: because they are subjected to repression or forced underground, or because internal fractions or tendencies opt for direct action in the face of what they regard as the ineffectiveness of the institutional route. As a result, the first generation of revolutionaries usually enjoys some previous political experience (Vilas 1989a:49ff).

In its efforts to prevent revolutionary challenges, state activity may itself contribute to the fragmentation of the ruling groups and may accelerate the process of social and political confrontation. Some segments of the power bloc may begin to blame continued conflict for damage to the country's economy, or for further radicalizing the insurrectionists. State repression can even begin to touch the ruling classes themselves. The Somoza regime's repressive policies, for example, reached some of the children of Nicaragua's traditional ruling families, and the incursions of the dictator and his followers into the business world displaced segments of the elites; both of these actions alienated segments of the prosperous classes, leading them in the end to join the Sandinista-led struggle against the dictatorship.

The division of the ruling bloc weakens the state by paring away its social base, reducing the state to a mere instrument of coercion. It also deals a further blow to the state's legitimacy, already deeply eroded by the mass character of social protest.

Nevertheless, the power of repression to break up a revolutionary movement must not be underestimated. Sufficient coercive resources, mobilized in time, may derail or at least neutralize a revolutionary challenge. Massive repression, even if it does not defeat the revolutionaries outright, can weaken their base and their sources of support, and can force changes in their strategy. The massacre of 1932 "cleansed" El Salvador of revolutionary threats for four decades; in the Dominican Republic, the 1966-to-1972 counterinsurgency program liquidated leftist political organizations. In the Sandinista insurrection, on the other hand, the combination of an intensive mobilization of the popular and middle sectors and respectable firepower neutralized the Somoza regime's repressive capacity.

But repression to the degree the dominant groups require is not always an option; nor does the choice exclusively depend on the will of state agencies. It must be backed by a consensus throughout the state's social base, as well as a favorable climate of opinion among the international actors with influence in the country in question. Moreover, massive state violence helps to polarize the situation. State terror can elicit responses of abandonment and passivity, or even drive people into the arms of the opposition: some people finally decide to heed the revolutionary call if only because they know they will be killed either way (Vilas 1986, ch. 2).

Now, repression means different things to different people. Some social groups are more likely than others to feel the effects of specific forms of repression, and to react to them. In agrarian societies with high levels of illiteracy, for example, government or military repression in the universities, repression of the student movement, and press censorship usually affect very small population groups. Urban and rural workers, in contrast, must *always* overcome innumerable restrictions and obstacles in order to organize themselves or strike, even when they enjoy the constitutional right to do either. The violence that is unleashed daily against the peasantry—the arbitrariness of the landlord, or the arrogance of the local political commander—does not necessarily disturb normal city life, or inhibit the formally democratic game of politics. In general, for those who are excluded from the effective practice of citizenship rights, as were the rural Central American populations until very recently, the repression that restricts participation in the institutions of public life—parties, unions, parliaments, universities, media—may not be immediately experienced as such, for public life happens in a faraway world that has little to do with their daily horizons and the things that matter to them.

On this mass, unorganized level, repression against what I have previously called "microspaces of counterhegemonic discourse" tends to have larger repercussions. These "microspaces"—meetings in town or neighborhood cantinas, the relatively permissive environment of the carnival, humor and mockery, among other things—permit the development of an ambiguously critical discourse that puts up a challenge, or at least an objection, to the tangible local expressions of power: the priest, the police commander, the boss, the judge. These expressions do not at first call the reproduction of the social order into question; on the contrary, they are an integral part of it in its local reflection. They are spaces staked out for voicing the dissatisfaction of the poor and the suppressed, spaces in which they can for a moment cease to feel so—pressure valves for frustration. To eliminate them is therefore more dangerous than to allow them to function; if the causes of social frustration and dissatisfaction remain, and these spaces are dismantled to boot, people have no choice but to create other spaces, outside of the informal control of traditional institutions.

Revolutionary situations and revolutionary change

The foregoing suggests that the gestation of a revolutionary situation is a possible but not an inevitable result of a complex conjunction of multiple factors, many of which take shape gradually over long historical periods. A historic break is at hand when the revolutionary situation itself emerges, not merely when one or more of its constituting ingredients appears. But in the measure that each new ingredient emerges, history accelerates, and the numerous dimensions of the process begin to feed into each other. When this moment arrives, any element can be the fuse that throws people into the streets and into battle.

The enormous mobilization of energies involved in a revolutionary situation tends to create an impression out of proportion with the revolution's actual achievements. The experience of most modern revolutionary processes shows neither a necessary correspondence nor a linear correlation between revolutionary situations and revolutionary transformations. A victorious revolution may give rise to a more democratic society, with more equitable access to resources and broader social participation, but this is not inevitable. The outcome of a revolution depends on the social forces that are mobilized and on who leads them, as well as on their organizational structures and the reaction of the other social and political actors.

From this perspective, we must distinguish between two moments in every revolutionary process: that of violence against, and finally "conquest" of, state power—what is sometimes called "political revolution"—and the socioeconomic and institutional transformation that it brings about. This is not a clear-cut distinction: some revolutionary processes (in China, for example) began to introduce social change in the territories they controlled before reaching overall state power. But it is broadly illustrative.

While the political phase features an acceleration in tempo, the transformation phase does not. The agencies of revolutionary government may produce legislation at a dizzying pace, but the transformative effects of these new rules take longer to develop, especially in the case of cultural change. It is not unusual for societies in revolution, more than a decade after the "seizure of power," to display many of the hallmarks of the previous society. This is inevitable in all revolutions, no less so in the twentieth century than in the "great revolutions" of the eighteenth: institutional change does not keep pace with changes in society, especially when such changes involve direct and active people's participation.

Finally, the outcome of a revolutionary situation depends as much on the forces that resist it, and on the international context, as on those that initiate it. Harding (1984:1–50) suggests that the political and economic transformations introduced in the USSR in the 1920s owe as much to the effects of the counterrevolutionary civil war as they do to the "revolutionary" events of 1917 to 1919 themselves.

Perry Anderson, in a polemical essay, adheres to the theory of political revolution, calling revolution "the political overthrow from below of one state order, and its replacement by another" (Anderson 1984). A revolution involves an acceleration of the political tempo; it is "a *punctual* and not a permanent process ... compressed in time and concentrated in target, that has a definite beginning—when the old state apparatus is still intact—and a finite end, when that apparatus is decisively broken and a new one erected in its stead." According to Anderson, to diffuse a revolution over time misses the point by rendering it indistinguishable from reform, while extending it into every department of social life reduces it to a mere metaphor ("cultural revolution," "technical revolution," etc.). Anderson's position, while logically coherent, obscures the social dimension of revolutionary change. In this concept of revolution there is neither space nor time for social change, and the state is reduced to a given set of government agencies. None of the great social revolutions of modern times— England, France, Russia, China, Cuba—fits easily into this analysis.

Revolutionary processes in peripheral or dependent societies display three basic dimensions of change: economic transformation and development, democratization of political institutions, and reformulation of relations with the international system. Consequently, such processes bring together a broad spectrum of classes and social groups, which accept the call to revolution for varied reasons and to uneven degrees. This plurality of forces confronting established power gives rise to a diversity of opinion as to the proper direction, depth, and scale of the transformation. The degree of leadership that any given group manages to gain over this array of actors will determine the way those basic questions are articulated and prioritized, and whether they develop sequentially or all at once.

The sociological profile of an army tells us little about the content and the political scope of the war, and the same is true of revolutions. Those who fought in the trenches of the French revolution were not bourgeois, but they fought for what became in the end a bourgeois revolution. The revolutions of the twentieth century are no different. There is nothing unanimous about social transformation; its measure depends on the meaning it is assigned by the various actors involved.

The inability of the FMLN (*Frente Farabundo Martí para la Liberación Nacional*) and the URNG (*Unión Revolucionaria Nacional Guatemalteca*) to topple the regimes they confronted has led some scholars to argue that we cannot properly speak of revolution in El Salvador and Guatemala—that the term applies only to Nicaragua. Booth (1991) offers the broader term "national revolts," as defined by Walton (1984) to encompass all three cases.

The concept of national revolt is broader than that of revolution, according to Walton, in that it includes change initiated from within the state in response to the insurgent challenge, even though such change is not the direct result of rebel power. National revolts are "protracted, intermittently violent, nonlocal struggles" involving the large-scale mobilization of classes and status groups that "become recognized claimants of rival sovereignty" and that "engage the state in responses with the effect of transforming social and state power in the development process" (Walton 1984:13).[6]

Walton's "national revolt" concept emerged from his comparative study of the historical roots of the Huk rebellion in the Philippines, *la violencia* in Colombia, and the Mau Mau revolt in Kenya, and the impact of the world system on all three societies. This is why, from a long-term historical perspective, manifestations of violence are described as "intermittent." Some historical processes of national revolt culminate in revolutions, and others do not.

Walton's approach, while useful for placing insurgency processes in perspective, risks losing sight of specific intensified concentrations of political violence in the general historical panorama, thereby missing the significance of particular outbreaks such as those in Central America in the 1970s. On a 200- or 300-year timeline, two decades of violent struggle can indeed seem "intermittent." This approach, therefore, is of disputable value, for it emphasizes the continuities at the cost of ignoring the ruptures.

Booth's approach, however, centers on the question of the armed conquest of power, an aspect that Walton does not consider especially relevant. The Sandinista revolution is a revolution because it "triumphed"—it destroyed the Somoza dictatorship and seized state power—while those in El Salvador and Guatemala are not, because they did not.

Granted, a "national revolt" is not something less than a revolution, but something different. Still, there are at least two questionable aspects to this approach: it reduces the process to a method or strategy of political struggle, and it posits too close a correlation between the "seizure of power" and socioeconomic and political change.

Reducing revolution to a strategy for political struggle is common in revolutionary organizations themselves. It arises from the close association between state power—"new" state power, in this case—and socioeconomic change. To the extent that the latter depends on political change—on the destruction of the "old regime" and its state—the nature of that change and the way it is executed are the main issue. In fact, revolutions are usually characterized by accelerated political change (Dunn 1972:12; Skocpol 1979:4), which in turn is possible only when the revolution enjoys state power. There is an interesting parallel between this approach and the conventional rhetoric of democratic regimes, which reduces political change to a method of election: the ballot. From Booth's perspective, revolution is synonymous with condensed and accelerated political violence, in the same way that democracy is synonymous with elections.

As we have shown, every revolutionary situation involves violent confrontation with established institutions, but not all violent confrontation is in itself part of a revolutionary situation. A revolution is the conjunction of certain modalities of collective action and certain kinds of socioeconomic and institutional changes; a one-dimensional focus on any of these ingredients at the expense of any other can lead to unbalanced perceptions and to false conclusions.

The connection between the armed "seizure of power" and structural change is similarly questionable. The experience of European social democracy in the early twentieth century illustrates the possibility of profoundly reforming political systems and social structures through existing institutional channels; the same is true, to a degree, for Latin American populism in the mid-twentieth century. The experience of various revolutionary processes, in contrast, suggests that political power may be a less effective vehicle for carrying out short-term structural change (Eckstein 1985; Utting 1992; Vilas 1992-93).

The timeliness of change, and particularly of subjective change—that is, in people's consciousness and in their private lives—is a matter of protracted development, largely independent of the pace of political power. This gradual tempo projects itself upon changes in people's conduct: producer and consumer habits, interpersonal relations, patterns of organization, etc. The state's promotion of change can be a factor both in accelerating development and in slowing it; which way it pulls depends above all on the fashion in which the "new" state power is exercised and on its relationship with social mobilization.

Like every attempt at social revolution, the Central American revolution aimed to seize political power in order to democratize it, to change socioeconomic relations by improving workers' access to resources—land, work, food, education, health—and to advance national sovereignty. Our assessment of the attempt should not be reduced, therefore, to the question of government or state, even though this is one of the basic dimensions of revolutionary change.

Although the Guatemalan and Salvadoran revolutionaries did not in the end reach political power, revolutionary mobilization itself cleared the way for some social transformations and for the emergence of new actors, who have certainly contributed to changing many aspects of their societies. Conversely, the Sandinista revolutionary project suffered many of its reverses while the Sandinistas were still in power.

Whether social revolutions or national revolts, events in Nicaragua, El Salvador, and Guatemala profoundly stirred the entire region. Their immediate political results—negotiations in El Salvador and Guatemala; electoral defeat and retrogression in Nicaragua—should take nothing away from the transformations that Central America underwent during this terrible stage of crisis, war, and foreign intervention.

TWO

The Modernization
of Central American Capitalism

Central America's specialization in agricultural exports has a long history, going back to the colonial days of natural dyes. Coffee crops re-articulated the region into the international market in the second half of the nineteenth century, with bananas following close afterwards. The region is also a cattle raiser and exporter of long standing, while cotton growing dates back to the decades before World War II. The transformations that came in the mid-twentieth century could hardly have been as swift and far-reaching as they were had the area's economies not been already involved in similar activities, and had their economic actors not enjoyed some experience at them. Stimuli from abroad, generated by changes in the world economy, found fertile soil in the economies and societies of the isthmus, permitting very rapid responses to the new terms of the accumulation process.

The same is true of the enormous social costs of capitalist modernization and the impoverishment and degradation of peasant economies and patterns of life. To grasp the magnitude, depth, and suddenness of the deterioration of living conditions for millions of men and women, and the new forms of subordination to capital and to capitalists, these must be viewed in the broader context of societies that were already traditionally organized around structures and processes designed for the brutal subjugation of the labor force by capital. The new modalities of oppression took shape in a social matrix that already functioned along those lines (Bulmer-Thomas 1987, ch. 1; McCreery 1990). Recent studies of the impact and scope of Central America's agroexport transformation, by focusing on the deterioration of the living conditions of the working masses, tend to give the impression that the rise of agroexport capitalism violently destroyed what had been a balanced and equitable social order. This impression is misleading. The profound economic and social changes of the 1950s through the 1970s could take place as quickly as they did only because there was already a "structural bias" in their favor. This does not minimize the magnitude of the transformations or their impact on the various social and political actors, but it helps explain their context.

The decline in the living conditions of broad sectors of the Central American population was accompanied by social transformations that enabled them to gain a growing consciousness of their rights, and finally to severely question their societies' political organization, forcing changes that in many cases have endured to the present day. This response "from below" was not among the intentions or the plans of those who pushed through capitalist modernization "from above," but without it Central America could hardly have arrived at its current condition.

1. The Transformation of Agrarian Capitalism

Central America's productive structure—cotton, cattle, sugar cane, tobacco—began to diversify rapidly in the 1950s, in response to exogenous factors: rising international cotton prices; the development of fast-food chains in the United States, in the case of cattle farming; the curtailment of the Cuban sugar export quota to the United States after the revolutionary triumph; the spread of Havana-style tobacco growing as a result of the emigration of Cuban businessmen. All of this took place in the context of the prolonged boom in the international economy and in foreign demand that took hold after World War II and the Korean conflict. To these positive factors we must add the drastic fall of world coffee prices at the end of the 1950s and problems with the production and marketing of bananas, which provided additional stimulus toward diversifying agricultural exports. Irrigated rice production also grew during this period, due to large capital investments, but it was mainly meant for domestic consumption. This accelerated diversification was carried out primarily by domestic capital. Foreign capital that participated did so mainly outside the sphere of primary production: banks, input supply, marketing. The state took an active role by building infrastructure (roads, electrical energy, communications); offering bank credit and subsidies to companies for new products; writing prodevelopment tax policy; and encouraging mechanization and technological research.

The process went further in some countries than in others. In Costa Rica, the land area used for sugar cane doubled between 1950 and 1973, and production tripled; between one-third and one-half of all sugar cane produced in the 1970s was exported. The land area under cattle doubled between 1950 and 1963 (from 630,000 to 1.2 million hectares); it occupied 24 percent of the nation's territory in 1963 and 34 percent (1.7 million hectares) in 1976. By the middle of the 1960s the country's beef exports represented between 25 and 30 percent of the region's total (Reuben Soto 1982:205; Barahona Riera 1980:55).

In Guatemala, lands planted in cotton grew tenfold between 1950 and 1963, while production grew from less than 10,000 bales a year in the early 1950s to more than 250,000 in the early 1960s, and more than 650,000 at the beginning of the 1970s. The area in sugar cane grew by a factor of twelve between 1967 and 1976. The physical volume of beef exports grew eightfold during the 1960s (Hintermeister 1982; Vilas 1989a:24).

In Nicaragua, the land surface planted in cotton grew more than tenfold between 1950 and 1973. An annual yield of slightly more than 20,000 bales at the beginning of the 1950s grew to more than 200,000 by the end of the decade, and had surpassed a half-million by the middle of the 1970s. By the late 1960s Nicaragua accounted for almost 40 percent of the region's beef exports. Lands used for cattle raising doubled between 1960 and 1975, and beef's share of the country's exports tripled between 1960 and 1970, 90 percent of the shipments being destined for the United States and Puerto Rico.

In El Salvador, cotton production jumped from some 90,000 bales a year in the mid-1950s to 375,000 a decade later, to level out since then at about 360,000 a year. Cotton farms, which numbered

654 in the 1950s, had multiplied to over 3,200 ten years later (Vilas 1986, ch. 2).

In Honduras, bananas kept their central role in production and export until the 1960s. At the beginning of that decade, bananas still represented 69 percent of the country's exports, while cotton accounted for less than five percent. Several factors explain the slower development of agroexport modernization in Honduras. Heavy specialization in bananas, in the form of foreign enclaves with a solid footing in the United States market, reduced incentives for other crops. Less domestic capital was available for new investment, and the influx of foreign capital was small. There was nothing like the cotton "boom" that developed in Nicaragua and Guatemala. Only beef shows a comparable dynamic: Honduras accounted for almost 20 percent of Central American beef exports between 1966 and 1980 (Slutzky 1979a; Williams 1986:206).

Exports versus internal markets

In apparent contrast with this vertiginous growth, but in fact as a byproduct of it, production for internal consumption slowed markedly. The extensive nature of agroexport development involved a drastic process of crop substitution and the displacement of subsistence crops toward marginal areas, while basic grains began to be imported for domestic consumption.

Nevertheless, agricultural export development was not a zerosum process in which the more land area was turned over to export crops, the less was available to crops for internal consumption. The displacement of some domestic-consumption crops by agroexport crops took place alongside a growth in the land area dedicated to the former, although this growth was on other lands, usually of lower quality and farther from its markets (Vilas 1989a:22).

The divergent growth rates in the lands devoted to different crops dictated a relative decline in the area dedicated to basic grains. To this we must add the rate of population growth, and the wide differences in the evolution of crop yields, which were much higher and more dynamic in agroexport than in production for internal consumption (Ruiz Granadino 1986:24–35). The result of this set of factors was a smaller domestic food supply, and a progressive increase in basic grain imports. Central America ceased to be a net exporter of basic grains at the beginning of the 1950s, and has been a net importer ever since (Quirós 1973).

Slower growth in food-producing land also meant a relative decline in food crops' share of the total cultivated land area. This share shrank from 63 percent across the region in the early 1950s to little more than 52 percent in the years 1976 to 1978. The steepest declines took place in Nicaragua (from almost 57 percent to 44 percent), Guatemala (from almost 75 percent to 58 percent), and Costa Rica (from 55 percent to 42 percent). The decline was relatively small in El Salvador, while Honduras showed no significant change.

In line with standard theories of international commerce, this shift might be expected to produce an advantage for Central America: the economy ceases to utilize land to produce food, instead producing exportable goods that generate income in foreign exchange which is freely convertible for several times the value of the displaced production, enabling imports to be used to supply the goods that are no longer produced. But Central America's high level of income concentration works against this model: the import profile of these countries reflects the demand characteristics of the higher-income groups much more closely than the general population's food needs, and their internal market structures block basic foodstuffs from reaching rural areas. Consequently, the majority of Central American peasants who stopped producing corn in order to grow cotton or sugar cane did not switch over to eating imported corn: they simply began to eat less.

During the three decades of extraordinary agroexport growth between 1948 and 1978, food production per capita shrank by 17 percent across Central America. Basic grain imports at the end of the 1970s represented 41 percent of total consumption in Costa Rica, 20 percent in El Salvador, 14 percent in Guatemala, 19 percent in Honduras, and 24 percent in Nicaragua (Brockett 1988:78–80). In the latter country, which before the agroexport boom had been self-sufficient in basic grains, production for the internal market declined during the 1950s and per-capita production of corn and beans stagnated after 1960, notwithstanding increases in the land area under cultivation. During the 1970s the food supply (production + inventory + imports) represented 36 percent of national demand for dairy products, 73 percent of that for meat and fish, 88 percent for beans, 21 percent for vegetables and 61 percent for eggs (Vilas 1986, ch. 2; Enríquez 1991:46). In El Salvador, the expulsion of peasants to poorer land in favor of cotton expansion generated a basic-grain deficit and a demand for imports. El Salvador shows a strong positive correlation between the expansion of cotton lands and the growth of corn imports at least since the 1930s (Durham 1979:32; Cabarrús 1983:68).

Growth of cattle ranching was accompanied by a steep decline in per-capita beef consumption. In Costa Rica, consumption shrank at an average of 13 percent a year throughout the 1960s, and in El Salvador at 35 percent a year between 1961 to 1963 and 1971 to 1973. In Nicaragua, the daily supply of proteins per inhabitant fell by almost 15 percent during the 1970s, the decade of greatest growth in beef exports (Barahona Riera 1980:55; IICA/FLACSO 1991:157). These changes seem all the more drastic in light of the scant absolute level of consumption of this staple: in El Salvador, per capita meat consumption fell from 18.6 grams a day to 12 grams between the early 1960s and the early 1970s.

The outcome of this tension between the growth of export agriculture and the production of basic foodstuffs, given the heavy dependence of most of the Central American population on basic grains, was a decline in nutritional conditions. Corn, rice, and beans together represent between two-fifths and two-thirds of the isthmus's food basket (PREALC 1983b).

Basic grain imports were channeled mainly through the United States government's PL–480 program, which allows imports to be paid for in local currencies. This device, while it helps solve the traditional problem of grain surpluses for Midwestern farmers in the United States and saves the receiving governments foreign exchange and balance of payments trouble, also works to dismantle domestic production and nutrition systems. Moreover, food price inflation was greater than the general growth in prices of consumer goods, with the sole exception of Honduras (IICA/FLACSO 1991:tables 3.1, 3.3). As a result, neither the export bias of modernization, nor increased imports of basic grains had a relevant positive impact in the countryside.

Internal imbalances

The growth of the new agroexport categories placed additional pressure on the Central American economies' external sector. The revenue benefits from the new exports were partly counterbalanced by the heavy proportion of inputs for the new crops that were themselves imported: agrochemicals, machinery and equipment, fuel, and other things.[1] Agricultural exports therefore had a smaller net impact on the balance of payments than is suggested when looking only at export revenues.

Agroexport growth was limited to a few crops and a small number of growers. Unequal productivity growth sharpened the structural heterogeneity of agriculture, as most small producers remained outside the reach of modernization. Not all lands were appropriate for the new crops, and the technological formulas involved called for massive imports, making them too expensive or too complicated for many producers. The result was a stark differentiation between agriculture for export and agriculture for domestic use, both geographically and in terms of production units, labor markets, and access to resources.

Guatemala's agroexport boom was concentrated on the country's southern coast: with only 13 percent of the nation's land, the area generated 40 percent of the country's agricultural production by the end of the 1970s. Production of basic grains, on the other hand, was concentrated in the western highlands, where small farms predominate: 50 percent of the land in this region belonged to farms of less than ten manzanas, while only 19 percent of all farms were that small at the national level (Hintermeister 1982:18).

In Nicaragua, the agroexport "heartland" by the end of the 1970s comprised less than 500,000 manzanas, about 7 percent of the country's farmland: 130,000 manzanas in coffee, 250,000 in cotton, and 60,000 in sugar cane. Cotton and coffee crops were concentrated in the Pacific region, displacing peasant basic grain production (in the departments of Nueva Segovia and Zelaya and parts of Boaco, Chontales, and Río San Juan) toward the agricultural frontiers—the mountains and the tropical rain forest—from which they were in turn expelled by export-oriented cattle ranching.

A marked distinction thus emerged between the high-productivity export sector and the sector growing foodstuffs for the internal market. Agroexport tended to be concentrated on medium and large farms, while production for domestic consumption remained the province of small and very small peasant farms. During the 1970s, 69 percent of Central America's corn, 78 percent of its beans, and 96 percent of its wheat came from farms of less than ten manzanas, and only irrigated rice, because of its capital and technology requirements, was produced in significant amounts on larger farms. In contrast, 98 percent of Central America's cotton, 85 percent of its sugar cane, 68 percent of its coffee, and all of its bananas were generated by medium and large farms (PREALC 1986:155; Hall 1984:217; Martínez et al. 1987).

Agroexport had a corrosive impact on the region's ecology. Between 1948 and 1978, tropical forests lost 50 percent of their area in Nicaragua, mainly to cattle ranching. The southern Honduras pine forest receded by 44 percent between 1950 and 1970, and fallow lands were reduced by 55 percent, while grazing lands grew by 53 percent (Stonich 1992). Between 1963 and 1984 the area dedicated to cattle almost doubled in Costa Rica, covering more than half the country's territory, at the cost of the destruction of the forests and the erosion of the soil as ever more fragile lands were pressed into service. Copious and ever-growing applications of agrochemicals (fertilizers, herbicides, pesticides), especially in cotton, polluted farming areas and hastened the desertification of the soil (Carriére 1990; Faber 1992).

Central American fertilizer consumption quintupled between the beginning of the 1960s and the mid-1970s, as part of a rapid opening of Central American agriculture to technologies spreading from the developed world. The development of aerial application techniques facilitated large-scale fumigation, which in turn required technical personnel and sparked the emergence of a certain number of specialized small businesses. Mechanization of agriculture proceeded quickly. Between 1965 and 1975, the average amount of arable land per tractor fell from 2,197 hectares to 457 hectares in Central America as a whole (Ruiz Granadino 1986:22). Since tractors, trucks, and airplanes run on oil, the introduction of this new technology further deepened the export sector's reliance on imports, weakened its net capacity to generate foreign exchange, and weighed heavily on the Central American economies' trade balances, especially after the oil shock of 1973.

Forms of organization of production varied from country to

country, within a certain range. The large hacienda very energetically spearheaded Guatemalan and Salvadoran agroexport development, embarking on a rapid process of modernization. In Honduras, agrarian reform enterprises, cattle haciendas, and transnational corporations developed in concert, while medium-sized property played the foremost role in Nicaragua.

From 1957–1958 to 1965–1966, the average size of all cotton farms in Guatemala grew from 285 to 399 manzanas, but the average size of farms of over 100 manzanas grew from 299 to 423 manzanas. These over-100-manzana farms represented 87.5 percent of all cotton farms in 1957–1958 and 93 percent in 1965–1966 (Adams 1970:366). Growers numbered only 161 at the beginning of the 1970s (Baumeister 1985). El Salvador combined a broad productive base and the decisive weight of large-scale growers through their control of the Salvadoran Cotton Cooperative (COPAL). Created to promote cotton growing and to centralize marketing, COPAL swiftly became the owner of cotton processing plants and later came to control credit and foreign marketing as well, establishing a degree of vertical integration that maximized the influence of the large producers (Thielen 1989). Cotton's production base in El Salvador (1,634 growers in 1971) was ten times larger than that in Guatemala. In 1972 and 1973, only nineteen Salvadoran families controlled a fourth of the country's cotton production, most of them also having investments in coffee, sugar cane, the textile industry, and agricultural inputs (Colindres 1977, fig. 67).

In Honduras, self-managed "associative enterprises" created under the agrarian reform of the 1960s and 1970s, tied into the marketing networks of transnational corporations, played the leading role (Slutzky 1979b; Slutzky and Alonso 1980). Direct production remained in the hands of the associative enterprises, while transnational capital reserved the preindustrial processing and marketing for itself. In Nicaragua, medium-sized production played the main role in the form of a sort of agrarian bourgeoisie, seated atop the mass of peasants but subordinated to the large landowners and to commercial, banking, and industrial capital. The solid vertical integration that was evident since the beginning of modernization in El Salvador, and to a lesser extent in Guatemala, was practically nonexistent in Nicaragua. In that country a clear separation emerged between export-oriented agricultural producers and financial, commercial, and industrial capital, to which the former must submit to a greater or lesser degree. Before 1979, almost 3,000 cotton producers did business with only twenty-eight processing plants, eleven exporting firms, and three banks, all under the firm control of Somoza capital. The relatively close alliance between the state and these urban fractions of capital set the stage for many agrarian producers to be pushed into opposition to the dictatorship, in pursuit of their own demands for better prices, market conditions, access to credit, and related issues.

State intervention

Government policies played an important role in these changes. It was the ability of the Central American states to adapt to the new context, by helping to retarget local markets toward the new opportunities for accumulation, that enabled them to exploit the demand conditions created by the international market. Business initiatives and government promotion worked effectively in concert to this end.

Public spending was steered toward the new activities and the lands on which they were located. Per-capita public investment in Guatemala's chiefly agroexport departments was 55 percent higher than the national average, and almost 350 percent higher than public investment in the typically peasant departments of the Western Highlands, where crops for internal consumption predominated (Hintermeister 1982). In Honduras's northern banana-growing region, per-capita public spending was almost twice the national average (Membreño Cedillo 1985). Salvadoran tax policy showed a similar tilt (Lazo 1987).

Bank credit also promoted agroexport development and discriminated against basic grain production. El Salvador's agroexport sector received 96 percent of all bank credit issued in 1960–1961, 68 percent in 1968–1969, 64 percent in 1974–1975, and 81 percent in 1979, while a maximum of 10 percent was granted to basic grain production (Cabarrús 1983:68). Guatemalan coffee, cotton, and sugar crops together received 68.5 percent of all credit from 1966 to 1970, and 87 percent of all agriculture credit. From 1971 to 1975 they received 60.6 percent and 76.3 percent, respectively, and for the years 1976 to 1980 the figures were 61.7 percent and 75.6 percent (Hintermeister 1982, figure 7). Nicaragua's agroexport sector received more than 90 percent of all bank credit during the first half of the 1960s, even though it represented less than half of all cultivated land; the minuscule remainder was granted to growers for the internal market, for whom private lenders—wholesalers, warehouses, and the like—were the principal source of financing, usually on quite onerous terms (Enríquez and Spalding 1989).

Dispossession and transformation of the peasantry

The extensive character of the new staples—especially cotton, sugar cane, and cattle ranching—and the consequent competition for land, along with the aforementioned bias in government incentive policies, all worked to displace domestically-oriented agriculture toward poorer-quality or marginal lands. Since peasant farming units were so closely associated with production for the domestic market, this shift took the form of fierce competition between capitalist agroexport enterprises and peasant farms. The dispossession of small farmers, combined with population growth, changed the peasantry's land/people ratio for the worse, as the number of small farmers with insufficient land grew sharply.

The term *peasant* describes a variety of situations—family farms, subfamily plots, microplots, landless workers—and refers not only to insufficient land availability but also to the relationship between land and other forces of production, especially the labor force. The impact of agroexport was felt unevenly at the various strata of this overall category. In general, both the number of family farms and their land allotment shrank, while the number of landless peasants, or peasants with insufficient access to land, grew—either because of the conditions for access or the declining total amount of land available. Part of the family labor force became redundant, and had to seek employment on larger farms, or outside the rural world altogether. It must be noted here once again that this process did not originate with the post-1950s agroexport boom. This was a dramatic acceleration in forces and trends already in existence, the most significant roots of which probably lie in the brutal dispossession of indigenous communities that followed the liberal reforms of the second half of the nineteenth century (Feder 1971).

The Guatemalan peasantry grew from 300,000 farms to more than one-half million between 1950 and 1980. The number of microplots (less than one hectare) grew more than any other category: in 1979 there were 240 percent more than in 1950. The increase took place mostly between 1964 and 1979, the period of greatest agricultural growth, and it accompanied a marked deterioration in the foundation of the peasant economy—the land (Hintermeister 1982:20, 24, 35). With the heavy concentration of indigenous farmers in the western highlands, the decrease in available land in this area dealt a drastic blow to the material basis for those farmers' identity. In the 1950s, indigenous agricultural producers owned 69 percent of all microplots, 67 percent of subfamily plots, and 50 percent of family farms. Ninety-four percent of all microplots and subfamily plots were in the departments of Sololá and Totonicapán, in the Quetzaltenango highlands, in Huehuetenango, and in Quiché (CIDA/EFCE 1971:173–75).

The loss of land to the advancing cattle ranches damaged the indigenous village economy, especially handicrafts. Furthermore, the crisis in the peasant economy forced many people to reduce or curtail their participation in traditional rituals, leading in turn to their increasing exclusion from celebrations and other traditional mechanisms of solidarity.

In Nicaragua, a country with an ample agricultural frontier and low population density, the Gini index of land concentration grew from .74 in 1950 (Central America's lowest) to .81 in 1963 (Vilas 1986:50). In that same period, the number of farms considered to be subfamily plots grew from 35 percent to 50 percent of the total number of farms, while the proportion of family farms shrank from 37 percent to 28 percent. This means that a large portion of family-sized farms were reduced to subfamily plots, losing the capacity to sustain the reproduction of the family nucleus. Here too, the increase in the proportion of the rural population without sufficient land was closely associated with the growth in land area under the control of large capitalist farms. Land under cultivation grew by 162 percent between the beginning of the 1950s and the end of the 1970s, but the number of farms grew by only 62 percent. Land under the control of farms between 10 and 99.9 manzanas (seven to 70 hectares) shrank by 14 percent, and land in farms of under ten manzanas decreased by almost 50 percent (Barraclough 1982:52).

Insufficient land forces the small-farming peasant to intensify use of the soil beyond the levels at which its productive potential can be sustained. The progressive exhaustion of the land generates decreasing yields, forcing the peasant into even more intensive use. The fact that a relatively high proportion of small farmers do not own the land they work but are linked to it in a relatively unstable fashion—they often have the right to work the land for only one harvest—only aggravates this situation. In general, the smaller the farm, the less property relations are diffused.[2] Under these precarious, unstable conditions, the small farmer is not concerned with the regeneration of the soil; in his situation, "rational use" is that which extracts the maximum product in the minimum time. The large landholder, in contrast, uses land extensively, with low production per surface unit but a very high overall yield.

The degradation of the soil in small plots expresses a contradiction between the peasant's economic rationality and the maintenance of ecological balance. It should be interpreted as the result of the *latifundio* structure of land tenure and use: by underutilizing land under the control of large farms, this structure forces peasants to overutilize their own in order to survive. The peasant strategy works in the short run, but in the medium term it is self-defeating.

The peasantry's precarious situation is not solely a function of insufficient land and insecure tenure; these in turn damage the small farmer's negotiating power with collection and marketing networks, further reducing his income. Since the marketing network functions in both directions—buying the basic-grain surplus while selling industrial products and inputs for production—price manipulation keeps the peasant in a permanent state of indebtedness to commercial capital.

The uneven process of proletarianization, understood as the progressive loss of access to land, developed most quickly in El Salvador and in Costa Rica. High demographic pressure on the land in El Salvador had given the process some momentum even before the agroexport boom, and the Costa Rican banana enclave's heavy presence on the Atlantic Coast appears to have had a similar effect. The degree of labor proletarianization in Costa Rica's banana enclave is markedly higher than in coffee production on the central plateau. The presence of a large agricultural frontier in Honduras and Nicaragua, in contrast, translated into easier land availability even for farmers driven off their lands by the new crops. The pattern was reinforced in Honduras both by the persistence of the *ejido* system, which represented almost 30 percent of the arable land until the 1970s, and by the expulsion of Salvadoran peasants after the 1969 war.

In the context of Central American capitalism, proletarianization of the labor force does not necessarily mean a parallel flow of land-deprived peasants into wage labor. Increase in peasant dispossession was not accompanied by an equivalent growth in rural wage labor. On the contrary, the agricultural economically active populations (EAPs) of Costa Rica, El Salvador, and Nicaragua all showed decreases in the percentage of wage laborers between 1950 and 1980, and the proportion grew very slightly in Guatemala and Honduras (Dierckxens 1990). As a consequence, the rate of under-utilization of rural labor grew, with the urban economy unable to compensate for it.

Proletarianization of the labor force generated a vast "semi-proletariat" of landless peasants and seasonal and itinerant workers, a group whose class affiliation has always been controversial. Although it was significant in all five countries, this contingent was particularly large in Nicaragua and Guatemala, perhaps because of the larger role of cotton growing, which requires huge annual influxes of seasonal labor. Guatemala and Nicaragua together accounted for more than 62 percent of the region's seasonal jobs in cotton harvesting during the 1950s, 70 percent in the 1960s, and 76 percent in the 1970s.

Appealing to seasonal employment permits the capitalist sector to transfer most of its unemployment to the peasant sector, in which, as we have seen, scarce resources mean thin margins of productive activity. At the beginning of the 1960s, 56.5 percent of El Salvador's agricultural work force was unemployed, most of it concentrated in small-holding areas (Alonso and Slutzky 1971:254). In the mid-1970s it was estimated that fewer than 20 percent of Nicaraguan agricultural workers had a permanent wage (Enríquez 1991:47).

Working conditions and workers' lives were unsatisfactory to say the least, with low wages, precarious housing, and scant and poor-quality nutrition. By the end of the 1970s, the agricultural minimum wage in Guatemala was 60 percent lower in real terms than it had been at the beginning of the decade. It was 24 percent lower in Honduras and 17 percent lower in Nicaragua, while it remained steady in El Salvador and more than doubled in Costa Rica (IICA/FLACSO 1991:133; López 1986; Pérez 1986; Ruiz Granadino 1986:40-42). Wages were set at levels that often were below labor's cost of reproduction not only because of the labor supply coming out of the broad small-holding sector, but also due to the capitalist sector's recourse to legal proceedings and coercion. The absence of rural unions further reduced workers' negotiating power. By the middle of the 1960s, for example, the total incomes of the workers on 81 percent of Guatemala's agroexport farms failed to cover their food needs (Figueroa Ibarra 1980:187, 233ff; CEPAL et al. 1973:112ff), and the country's worst housing conditions were found on the cotton plantations (Adams 1970:370).

Even if they did not completely lose access to their own land, the impoverished peasants came to depend more and more on whatever income they could earn elsewhere—the smaller the parcel owned the greater the dependence—or on land rented from others.[3] The seasonal nature of wage labor, and the draconian rental conditions that landholders imposed, further aggravated precarious living conditions. In the resulting process of proletarianization, workers did not lose their direct connection with the land but were forced to seek wage work during certain seasons, determined by labor demand peaks in the agroexport sector. The consequence was a structure in which the small-holding sector absorbs the unemployment that reappears after the period of wage labor is over, and sets the conditions for the reproduction of labor. The size of this seasonal-wage proletariat, with its rearguard in the small-holding sector, varied from country to country but in every case represented a high proportion of the rural EAP.[4]

Under such conditions, the family economy becomes an essential element in reproducing the productive system, and an important cost-reduction factor for capitalist firms. Keeping peasant economies at low productivity levels and in precarious conditions tended to discourage the production of basic grains for domestic consumption and limited the development of an internal market, but this was not a problem for large landowners, since their production was targeted at international markets and their surplus was basically realized through imports.

There are notable parallels between the seasonal wage-earners' case, rotating from farming their own plot to the plantation's seasonal wage labor, and the precarious situation of landless workers. The landless worker—a farmer who subsists by renting small parcels for very short periods to produce basic grains for his own consumption—was most conspicuous in El Salvador. The number of rented farms of less than one hectare (microplots) increased by 220 percent between 1950 and 1971. By the latter year, 91 percent of all rented farmland consisted of parcels smaller than one hectare (Colindres 1977:43ff). These farmers' shaky condition derived not only from their obligation to return the land after harvesting it, but also from the customarily draconian rental conditions. In neighboring Honduras, on the contrary, two-thirds of all farmers had a relatively secure, or at least stable, access to land: about a third worked their own parcels, while another third farmed in communal lands (Ruhl 1984).

Agroexport and migration

Changes in landholding, production, and income structures sparked massive migratory processes, both seasonal and permanent. Farmers displaced by the new crops and shifting labor markets migrated toward the agricultural frontier, where it remained open (as in Nicaragua and Honduras), and to the cities. Others were drawn into government resettlement projects, while still others swelled the seasonal flow of labor into agroexport areas. The new crops simultaneously repelled and attracted population. Farmers who for generations had lived in their vicinity, growing crops for local and national consumption, were progressively pushed onto other lands or into the cities. At the same time, a massive current of seasonal labor migration came from the food-growing regions, and from the urban periphery, into the agroexport areas. The departments of Usulután in El Salvador, Chinandega in Nicaragua, and Escuintla, Retalhuleu, and Suchitepéquez in Guatemala are typical cases.

In El Salvador, migration shifted poor peasant populations from the coffee-growing departments of Ahuachapán, Sonsonate, and Santa Ana, and the cotton-growing southern region of La Paz toward the poorer areas to the north and east. Cotton expansion on Nicaragua's Pacific coast expelled peasants toward Jinotega, Nueva Segovia, Río San Juan, Zelaya, and Managua. In Costa Rica's Guanacaste department, the shift in land use from farming to cattle-ranching, with its smaller labor demand, forced people to migrate toward the central plateau and San José. In Guatemala, all of the mainly indigenous departments lost population, while the capitalist-dominated departments of the southern coast, the department of Guatemala, and such border areas as Izábal and El Petén grew.

Between 1945–1950 and 1964, the number of seasonal migrants in Guatemala grew from more than 120,000 to about 580,000 a year (CSUCA 1978a:32–37; CEPAL et al. 1973:117–18). The flow came principally from the departments of Huehuetenango, Quiché, and San Marcos: areas that would see intense insurgent activity in the decades to follow. Between 200,000 and 300,000 indigenous people a year descended from the highlands to the agroexport farms on the Pacific coast throughout the 1970s. Seasonal workers in El Salvador numbered some 250,000 between 1961 and 1971. In 1975 an estimated 30 percent of the rural EAP had less than two months of work a year, and another 19 percent had two to six months—that is, almost half the rural work force was profoundly underemployed, and itinerant as well (CSUCA 1978a and b). In Nicaragua, seasonal migrations moved some 100,000 to 120,000 workers at the beginning of the 1960s, a number that multiplied by the middle of the next decade (CEPAL et al. 1973:118). In 1975 an estimated 200,000 workers (a third of the rural EAP) were employed three months of the year at most.

International migration currents also grew, especially from densely populated El Salvador to Honduras, Nicaragua, and Guatemala. Salvadorans had been moving to Honduras in large numbers at least since the 1920s: a flow of between 25,000 and 30,000 in the 1930s swelled to 100,000 in 1949 and to some 350,000 during the 1960s, the vast majority undocumented (Alonso and Slutzky 1971:294; Durham 1979:124–25) That figure was equivalent to something over 12 percent of Honduras' population, almost 20 percent of its agricultural EAP, and about 15 percent of all rural

Table 2.1
Central America: Urbanization Growth

	Percentage of total population			
	1950	1960	1970	1980
Costa Rica	34	37	40	43
El Salvador	36	38	39	41
Guatemala	30	33	36	39
Honduras	18	23	29	36
Nicaragua	36	41	47	53

Source: United Nations 1980: Table 50.

families. Between 60 and 70 percent were poor peasants, most of them arriving after the beginning of the agroexport boom in their country, and originating mostly in the impoverished departments of Chalatenango and Cabañas. After the 1969 war with Honduras, some 100,000 to 130,000 of these Salvadorans returned to El Salvador.[5]

Rapid urban growth

High unemployment and underemployment in the countryside, combined with migration to the cities, altered the rural-urban population distribution within a few years. As a result, urbanization and metropolization accelerated rapidly, especially in Honduras and Nicaragua (Tables 2.1 and 2.2).

Although societies were increasingly urbanized, the urban economies' limited capacity to generate employment for the new cohorts of labor gave rise to huge slums and extreme poverty and marginality, especially in the cities. Peripheral shantytowns, a relatively new phenomenon for Central America, began to spread. The proportion of urban inhabitants with access to drinking water and sewer networks shrank throughout the 1970s, with an especially dramatic decline in El Salvador, where the population with drinking water fell from almost 80 percent to 67 percent between 1969 and 1979, and the population with sewer service declined from 74 percent to 47 percent (IICA/FLACSO 1991:179–80).

Central American cities had been the product of a different configuration of the socioeconomic structure, with its own distinct spatial patterns of population distribution. The rise of great con-

Table 2.2
Central America: Population in Capital Cities, 1950 and 1980
(In Thousands and in Percentage of Total Population)

	1950		1980		1950-1980
	Thousands	%	Thousands	%	% Increase
San José	146	18	508	22	248
San Salvador	213	11	858	18	303
Guatemala City	337	11	1143	21	324
Tegucigalpa	72	5	406	11	464
Managua	109	10	662	25	507

Source: IADB 1987: Table 5.

centrations of people without jobs or stable incomes created
challenges to institutional control. The political systems predating
the 1950s reflected an arrangement under which the masses, deprived of citizenship rights, lived in the countryside, while those
with access to those rights lived in the cities. The increasing mass
character of the cities, where accelerated population growth was
reducing the physical distance between classes and social groups
increasingly polarized by the economy, now placed new city-
dwellers in almost physical contact with the state agencies and the
actors competing for their control. The contrast between those who
won and those who lost—or ceased to win—was that much more
marked and frontal in the cities.

2. Industrialization and change in the urban economy

The Central American Common Market (CACM), created in the
late 1950s, provided a framework in which industrial production
could grow. From a total U.S. dollar value of $254 million in 1950,
industrial volume grew to $432 million in 1960 (in real terms), $992
million in 1970, and $1.305 billion in 1975. Although the real impact
of the CACM on industrial growth has been the subject of debate
(Weeks 1985; Bulmer-Thomas 1987; Guerra-Borges 1988), there is
no doubt that the greater part of industrial development in the
1960s was linked to integration. It must be remembered, however,
that this growth was built upon an agrarian structure on which it
could not—or did not want to—impose significant changes, in
contrast to the classical process of capitalist industrialization or, to

a lesser degree, Mexican and South American import-substitution industrialization. The endurance of traditional power structures, owing either to the weakness of the groups pushing industrialization or to the fact that the impetus for it came from within traditional society itself, meant that such development was destined from the outset to rest on investment and financing from abroad. Business groups linked to the new industrialization were unable to get the state to steer any of the financial fruits of the foreign-trade surplus into manufacturing production, and tax and credit policy continued to favor agroexport groups.

The advent of the CACM and industrialization did not change the pattern of regional concentration of productive resources that prevailed before integration. Industrial growth tended to be concentrated in Guatemala and El Salvador, as before. In 1950 the two countries' joint industrial production represented almost 65 percent of the value of all Central American industrial production; in 1960 it was 62 percent, and by the mid-1970s it was something over 65 percent.

Production, investment, and industrial exports among the economies of the isthmus flourished under the CACM in the 1960s, but stagnated in the following decade and later began to fall off. The combination of agroexport development and industrial growth set up a contrast within the export sector: while industrial exports grew between the countries of the region, the region's traditional profile as an agricultural exporter to the rest of the world remained unchanged. Food, drink, and tobacco, with textiles in a secondary role, were the branches that accounted for most industrial production—from one-half to two-thirds, depending on the country.

Industry's heavy reliance on imports was to cancel out most of its contribution to integrating the region's productive structure; industry actually became a drag on the balance of trade. The case of textiles is a particularly graphic one. Itself a large cotton producer, Central America nevertheless developed a textile industry heavily dependent on imported synthetic fibers, while natural fibers continued to be exported in bales. Due to its specialization in consumer and end-use goods, Central American manufacturing relied strongly on imported raw materials and capital goods from outside the region. About 75 percent of all imported raw materials and almost all imported capital goods were bought outside the region; the value of these imports came to represent between 55 and 74 percent of the value of exports outside the isthmus (Bulmer-Thomas 1987:193). Dependence on imported inputs also weakened the industry's contribution to processing raw materials from within the region, which put further pressure on the balance of trade with the outside world.

High levels of idle capacity and the use of obsolete technologies generated a need for protectionist trade policies, which only added to the difficulty of exporting manufactured goods outside the region. Protectionism encouraged the production of consumer goods over other industrial branches, while fiscal incentives promoted imports of capital goods on a scale far beyond the needs of regional production, further contributing to overcapacity and raising production costs. At the beginning of the 1970s, an estimated 50 percent of Central American industrial capacity was idle. A large proportion of industrial products made in Central America was sold within the region at higher prices than competitive imports from outside the isthmus (Bulmer-Thomas 1987:183–84, 192–93).

Under these conditions, access to markets outside the region was problematic, to say the least. The greater part of each country's industrial production was shipped not to the CACM but into its own small national market: an obvious negation of the logic and discourse of integration. In 1970, after a decade of experience in integration, little more than 20 percent of Central America's industrial production, by value, was being exported—11.6 percent to the CACM and 9.7 percent to the rest of the world—and at the end of the 1970s the figure still was less than 25 percent. This means that almost four-fifths of the region's industrial production was sold within the same economy that generated it (Guerra Borge 1988:55). El Salvador and Guatemala, the two economies with the greatest weight in Central American manufacturing, were also the two most sharply oriented toward exports.

The traditional commercial relationship (agricultural exports/industrial imports) now also had to finance the new industrial sector targeted at the region itself. This mechanism worked only as long as international prices for Central American exports were favorable, and as long as domestic production costs in the export sector could be kept very low—meaning that workers' wages and peasant incomes must remain at a subsistence level. The small scope of such attempts at industrialization becomes clear when we consider the limiting effect of low wages and high rates of property and income concentration on an industry that mainly produces consumer and other end-use goods for domestic markets.

A faster influx of capital from outside the region was one of the earliest effects of Central American industrial development. Foreign investment in the region, stimulated by industrialization, almost doubled between the end of the 1950s and the end of the 1960s (from $388 million to $756 million). Foreign industrial capital was practically nonexistent in Central America before the CACM, except in Nicaragua. Ten years later it represented a third of foreign investment in the region, and much more in Guatemala and Nicaragua (Membreño Cedillo 1985). United States firms took the lead, representing two-thirds to four-fifths of all foreign firms by the mid-1970s, with the sole exception of El Salvador, where they were fewer than a third.

With its heavy dependence on imported inputs and its focus on narrow markets, industrialization showed little job-generating capacity. The Central American industrial labor force did grow, but at a rate barely above the rate of growth of the total active population. Between the beginning of the 1960s and the middle of the next decade, industrial employment grew at an average rate of less than five percent a year, with an average annual gain of fewer than 17,000 jobs, while the total EAP grew at a average rate of 4 percent a year. As a result, the share of the industrial work force in the EAP remained around 10 percent throughout. In the 1960s, a period of rapid production growth, the formal sector created an average of only 3,000 new jobs a year across the whole region.

It was the informal sector that absorbed the rapid growth of the urban labor force. Between 1950 and 1980, Central America's so-called urban informal sector (UIS) grew by an estimated 900,000 persons (PREALC 1986:106). At the beginning of the 1970s, 40 percent of the nonagricultural labor force in El Salvador was in the informal sector, while open unemployment stood at 10 percent. The descent from secondary to tertiary status brought on by the process of informalization was particularly dizzying in Nicaragua, the country whose rates of urbanization and metropolization grew

Table 2.3
Central America: Economic Growth, 1950-79
(Annual Median Rate of GDP Growth)

	1950-60	1960-70	1970-79
Costa Rica	7.2	6.2	6.4
El Salvador	4.7	5.5	6.4
Guatemala	3.8	5.5	5.8
Honduras	3.4	5.6	5.4
Nicaragua	5.4	7.3	5.3[1]
Central America	4.6	6.5	5.9[1]

Source: CEPAL 1982.
[1] 1970-78 period.

the most in this period; it is estimated that almost half of the country's urban EAP belonged to the informal sector by the end of the 1970s.

3. Gains and losses in a boom economy

It is important to point out that these profound changes took place during a period of sustained economic boom (Table 2.3). In that same period, Central America's total population grew from 8 million inhabitants in 1950 to more than 20 million in 1980; the overall rate of urbanization went from 31 percent in 1950 to 37 percent in 1970 and 43 percent in 1980.

Social differentiation—most importantly, the impoverishment of broad masses of peasants and wage-earners—was not part of some even-handed recession, with everybody losing in one way or another—even if some lost more than others. On the contrary: the deterioration of the working and living conditions of most of the rural populations of El Salvador, Guatemala, and Nicaragua, and the spread of urban poverty, were part of a rapid process of economic growth and modernization that made the objective differences between the winners and the losers all the more notorious.

The diversification of production and of agricultural exports was one aspect of the accelerated dynamism of the Central American economies, and in turn helped fuel it. Between 1950 and 1980 the Central American GDP grew at an average rate of 4.9 percent a year, and increased to 6.5 percent a year during the 1960s. Per capita Central American GDP in 1980 was almost 67 percent higher than in 1950, in real terms, even though the region's population had doubled between 1960 and 1980. The faster growth of industrial production than that of overall production (7.9 percent in the 1960s and 6.1 percent in the 1970s), together with agroexport differentiation, altered the traditional profile of the economies' foreign orientation. Central American exports grew at an annual pace of more than 8 percent in the 1960s and more than 5 percent the next decade. Between 1960 and 1980, Costa Rican, Nicaraguan, and Guatemalan exports tripled in value, while El Salvador's more than tripled, and those of Honduras more than quadrupled. Total exports from all five countries, which came to $250 million in 1950, had grown to almost $5 billion by the end of the 1970s.

Modernization was not limited to the strictly economic. Productive differentiation sparked a similarly speedy process of social differentiation. New fractions of the bourgeoisie appeared, linked to the new productive sectors. While these new sectors mainly owed their existence to growing investment by the traditional groups of landowners and agrarian capitalists, they also reflected the increasing access of some urban middle-class groups—professionals and public officials, for example—to the new and growing areas of the economy. New business skills also developed, and new urban groupings emerged or expanded along the new axes of growth.

The growth in the functions of the state cleared the way for expanded public employment and for a growing number of pettybourgeois wage earners. The demand for new labor skills led governments to carry out some reforms of their educational systems, broadening the urban middle sectors' opportunities and feeding their expectations for career and social advancement. Teachers, public employees, and university and high school students led significant political mobilizations, and became the most dynamic social actors of those years.

Capitalist development and agroexport modernization threw the traditional model of social relations into crisis. Relations of patron-client reciprocity began to erode as the custom of rent in the form of labor, or in kind, gave way to rent in money, and then to the expulsion of those peasants who could not adapt to this shift.

The pressure toward proletarianization of the work force broke up peasant family structures. The traditional mechanisms of agrarian authority, which combined power with paternalism, along with the traditional system of acquired rights, disappeared before the uneven but relentless advance of the market. The growth of a wage-earning population created the conditions for union organization and labor activism to spread. People in poorer neighborhoods accumulated organizational experience as they responded to overcrowding by demanding basic services, better housing conditions, and the like. Taken together, these new elements stimulated state activism, leadership abilities, and new criteria of rationality.

"Additive development" is the term CEPAL coined to identify this juxtaposition of new economic and social strata with already-existing ones, in a process of change and modernization that does not threaten the previous socioeconomic structure (CEPAL 1983, 1986). Agroexport modernization was superimposed on the traditional export sector, while industrial development within the regional integration scheme was founded on an agrarian structure on which it could not or did not intend to impose significant changes.

This style of development is evidence of the compromise that was built between the dominant groups in traditional agroexport society and the new bourgeois groupings that had emerged from it, with distinct interests and demands for access to resources and social conditions of production (financing, prices, exchange rates, labor management, worker training, etc.). The growth of the new categories of economic dynamism required questioning the traditional order, but internal negotiations and a reformulation of the relationship with foreign countries moderated this process before it came to the displacement of the traditional groups.

The developmentalist style that state agencies of the region assumed during the 1950s and 1960s, which is analyzed in the next chapter—writing state policy to regulate and promote private activity, broadening the sphere of public-sector intervention, reforming educational and administrative systems, and enlisting the active cooperation of the United States government—reflects the operative terms and the contours of the usually implicit agreements that were reached between the new and the old fractions of the Central American elites, and their interconnection with the new modalities of United States expansion into the region.

At the same time, the export sector remained the dynamic axis of the economy, and the regional integration scheme continued to depend on traditional exports out of the region; the groups that controlled the export sector therefore retained their ultimate primacy. Given this reality, there was little chance that any "spillover" of the dynamic effects of the new alliance into the work force—and, more broadly, all the subordinate laboring classes and groups— might reshape the matrix of social relations. In South America and Mexico, rebuilt alliances between the industrial bourgeoisie and the traditional export sectors (the agreements that provided the basis for the development of import substitution) also enabled workers to scale up their demands for better working conditions, higher wages, union rights, access to social services, higher consumption levels, etc. (Vilas 1992-93). In Central America, however, capitalist modernization and the rebuilding of relations among the dominant fractions was grounded in the reproduction of the traditional relationships with the subordinate classes: intense exploitation of the labor force and repression of all efforts to organize.

What Central America experienced was, consequently, a *socially restrictive* form of development. At the beginning of the 1970s, unemployment was estimated at 10 to 12 percent in Honduras, around 13 percent in Guatemala and El Salvador, and almost 19 percent in Nicaragua. But by 1980 the total underutilization (unemployment and underemployment) of labor represented more than 42 percent of the EAP in Honduras and El Salvador, more than one-third in Guatemala, and more than one-fifth in Nicaragua (PREALC 1986:62). In 1980, 61 percent of the Central American population lived below the poverty line, and 42 percent were in extreme poverty. In the countryside the figures were 69 percent and 56 percent, respectively (Table 2.4).

One of the most sustained runs of capitalist growth in the entire postwar period generated some of the period's most widespread and acute impoverishment. In other words, it was not the *failure* of capitalist development that provided the economic ingredient for revolution—it was its success.

Income distribution among broad population aggregates, with its sharp polarization between the great share of income going to

Table 2.4
Central America: Population Living in Poverty, 1980
(Percentage of Total Population)

	Total	Urban	Rural
Costa Rica	25	14	34
El Salvador	68	58	76
Guatemala	63	58	66
Honduras	68	44	80
Nicaragua	62	46	80
Central America	61	48	69

Source: CEPAL 1992a.

the wealthiest groups and the minimal share of the poorest, remained significantly unchanged (Table 2.5). El Salvador is without a doubt the most extreme case. In a decade in which the GDP grew at an average of almost 6 percent a year, the top 20 percent increased its large portion of income while all other groups experienced a decline, even the small share captured by the bottom 50 percent. Only Honduras showed any progress in distribution: the top group's share shrank while the share of the bottom 50 percent of the pyramid improved slightly. (The next chapter examines the impact of the emerging peasant movement and agrarian reform on these trends.) In the other countries the decade's burst of economic growth had no significant impact on income distribution.

The fact that urban income distribution changed even less than did the national picture, even in Honduras (Table 2.6), suggests that the transformations shown in Table 2.5 mostly reflect the social and economic changes that were taking place in the countryside, rather than in the cities. The figures do, however, point to changes in the relative shares of the two top segments, which hypothetically correspond to different fractions of the dominant groups. Everywhere but in Guatemala, these changes were to the benefit of the middle strata of the income pyramid.

The striking persistence of a large relative share of income in the hands of the uppermost groups supports the claim of some political actors that industrialization and the other economic changes of these decades did not moderate social inequalities, but aggravated them. There was in this sense a process of *poverty production* as well as wealth production, and the modernization of the capitalist

Table 2.5

Central America: National Income Distribution, 1970 and 1980 (Percentage of Total Income Received by Each Stratum)

	1970				1980			
	Poorest 20%	30% below med.	30% above med.	Wealthiest 20%	Poorest 20%	30% below med.	30% above med.	Wealthiest 20%
Costa Rica	5.4	15.5	28.5	50.6	4.0	17.0	30.0	49.0
El Salvador	3.7	14.9	30.6	50.8	2.0	10.0	22.0	66.0
Guatemala	4.9	12.5	23.8	58.8	5.3	14.5	26.1	54.1
Honduras	3.0	7.7	21.6	67.7	4.3	12.7	23.7	59.3
Nicaragua	3.0	12.0	25.0	60.0	3.0	13.0	26.0	58.0
Central America	3.4	13.1	25.9	57.6	3.7	13.4	25.6	57.3

Source: 1970: CEPAL 1982; 1980: IICA/FLACSO 1991: 117.

Table 2.6

Central America: Urban Income Distribution, 1970 and 1980 (Percentage of Total Income Received by Each Stratum)

	1970				1980			
	Poorest 20%	30% below med.	30% above med.	Wealthiest 20%	Poorest 20%	30% below med.	30% above med.	Wealthiest 20%
Costa Rica	5.0	15.4	28.5	51.1	4.2	17.5	30.6	47.7
El Salvador	2.0	9.6	22.0	66.0	n/a	n/a	n/a	n/a
Guatemala	5.8	16.1	29.6	48.5	4.5	13.3	26.2	56.0
Honduras	4.0	13.4	27.8	54.8	4.0	15.0	28.0	53.0
Nicaragua	n/a	n/a	n/a	n/a	3.9	14.2	27.4	54.5

Source: IICA/FLACSO 1991: 118.

economy—new production technologies, new methods of factory organization, infrastructure development, expansion of market relations, development of financial services—far from reducing inequality, actually deepened it.

It should be noted that, however dramatic the Central American situation, it is not qualitatively different from the picture that prevailed in most of the hemisphere.[6] What is distinctive about Central America is that inequalities in income distribution corresponded more closely than in the rest of the continent with inequalities in access to basic resources, generating living conditions that were much more precarious. For example, a Central American in the mid-1970s had a life expectancy at birth of 59 years, while the average Latin American's life expectancy was 65 years; 57 percent of Central America's adult population could read and write, versus 80 percent across Latin America; high-school enrollment covered 18 percent and 42 percent of the population, respectively (Vega Carballo 1984; Weeks 1985:46). The naked depravity of this income concentration curve can be traced to the absence of moderating institutional mechanisms and, in general, of any compensatory state intervention.

Taken together, Central American societies did experience some significant changes in social conditions. Although the conventional indicators of social development gave the region unsatisfactory marks at the end of the 1970s, it should be recognized that some progress had been made, particularly in the areas of basic education and health. Life expectancy at birth grew by ten years between 1960 and 1975, and illiteracy was reduced from 61 percent to 59 percent in the same period. The infant mortality rate fell from 104.8 per thousand live births in 1965–1970 to 77.8 in 1975–1980; the availability of medical personnel increased, as did hospital services and, to a lesser degree, social security coverage. Elementary school enrollment grew by 50 percent in the 1970s, and access to mass media loosened up. Some consumer durable goods saw a degree of improvement in distribution, especially in the cities (IICA/FLACSO 1991:155ff; Carcanholo 1981:279–81).

Although no information is available on the effective social appropriation of these advances, income distribution figures make it reasonable to surmise that some groups benefited more than others. Tables 2.5 and 2.6 support the hypothesis that middle groups consolidated their position in Costa Rica and Honduras, while those in El Salvador and Guatemala received setbacks. In general, the middle groups behaved ambivalently: if on the one hand they suffered from unequal competition with the traditionally dominant sectors for access to resources, on the other hand they participated wholeheartedly in the accumulation that took place at the expense of the lower-income sectors.[7] Workers, at least those in the more modern pole of the economy, also made a degree of progress. The spreading activities of government agencies and the growth of public investment, which generally reproduced the productive structure's territorial imbalances by showing a preference for the areas of greatest business development, nevertheless brought modest social advances.[8]

In sum, then, agroexport development and industrialization transformed many aspects of the Central American societies, even as they reinforced others. Very high growth rates persisted for three decades, despite a slowing trend toward the end of the period. Real per capita GDP grew at an average of more than 3 percent a year for more than twenty-five years, with even higher sustained rates in Costa Rica and Nicaragua. The production structure was differentiated; the regional economy ceased to be synonymous with coffee and bananas. The population nearly tripled. Nevertheless, the benefits and costs of such dynamism and modernization were unequally distributed among social classes. Middle groups took advantage of mass dissatisfaction to better their position in the income structure in Costa Rica and Honduras, while urban and rural workers and the peasantry saw their living conditions and access to resources deteriorate sharply, as did middle groups in Guatemala, El Salvador, and Nicaragua.

This underscores the emergence of Central America's revolutionary processes precisely in the three countries in which the economic position of the middle groups was weakened in the course of accelerated capitalist development. The heavy presence of elements from these middle groups in the revolutionary leadership, which several studies have pointed out (Vilas 1986, 1988; Wickham-Crowley 1992), can be interpreted as an effect of the relative decline of their share of resources and of successful competition by the government-backed traditional sectors and parvenus. The very fragility of these middle groups, along with their exposure to some exogenous agents and the political culture spreading from the universities, equipped them to challenge the state and the traditional elites and to gain leadership of masses in a similar process of transformation.

Permanence and change in the oligarchy

Modernization and its fruits were generated at very high and exclusionary levels of concentration by the Central American economies. From a Marxist point of view, this is not a surprise: capitalism by definition leads to growing levels of concentration and centralization of capital, and to the dispossession and impoverishment of workers. Even from this perspective, however, it is unquestionable that capitalism develops in the countryside via different modalities, and that the Central American case contrasts markedly in this respect with other experiences of capitalist modernization, even within Latin American agriculture.

The deepened inequalities brought on by three decades of capitalism in Central America are an effect of its "top-down" mode of development, as are the very limits of that system. Capitalist modernization in Central America had much more to do with the traditionally dominant groups' adaptation to new international market conditions than with a push by emerging groups "from below."[9] These emerging groups did exist and were active, but they developed in the shadow of the traditional power structure, building off of the conditions of production imposed by that structure. Their ability to change the style of development or the rules of the game was small. The deep structure of the Central American economies remained unaltered by crop diversification, new technologies, the opening of bank financing, the accelerated growth of the cities, or any other such transformation. Society and its classes did grow more urban, but the center of gravity of the social matrix and of political power remained rooted in the agrarian structure— the close and dynamic interlocking relationship between *latifundio* and *minifundio*, and the matrix of social and political relations among traditional large landholders and impoverished peasants (landless peasants, or semiproletarians)—that formed the strategic power base of the landholding groups. Capitalist modernization did not involve significant shifts in the power relations among social classes, especially in El Salvador, Guatemala, and Nicaragua. Challenges to the traditional oligarchy's rule by segments of the new business groups were tenuous and not very effective.

It was the Central American landholding oligarchy, therefore, that began introducing into the region the new terms of the world economy, thus defining the modalities and the reach, and consequently the limits, of that entry. If this can be taken as proof of the backwardness of the Central American landholding elites, it may also be a sign of adaptability to new economic conditions: testimony to their ability to maintain control over society in the midst of the upheavals of change. Both may be partially the case. In any event, it must be acknowledged that by virtue of the traditional dominant groups' ability to preserve their decisive grip on the state, landholding society was in a position to accept the new challenges and at the same time to administer their impact.

The unremitting grasp of Central America's traditional ruling groups in the midst of rapid economic growth is most starkly apparent in El Salvador. What sets this country apart, aside from the unusually high concentration of property and economic power in the hands of its dominant groups, is how ubiquitous those groups are. A few powerful coffee-growing families came to control both the new agroexport categories and their preindustrial processing (coffee and cotton mills) and marketing, plus the principal manufacturing industries, retail, and finance (Colindres 1977, esp. table 67). Table 2.7 shows the concentration of property and of profits that had been achieved in El Salvador by the end of the 1970s. Guatemala presents a similar case, though on a smaller scale. In Nicaragua, in contrast, oligarchic groups were forced to coexist with new business segments organized around the Somoza holdings, in a complex matrix of alliances, competition, and tension. In all three countries, society was modernized without significant challenge to oligarchic domination, particularly the rule of large landowners.

The picture was somewhat different in Honduras and Costa Rica. The Honduran oligarchy lacked the solid and dynamic role in the international economy of its peers in El Salvador and Guatemala: it had little opportunity to participate in the coffee boom, and the enclave character of the banana economy condemned the local oligarchy to a vassal relationship with the North American

Table 2.7
El Salvador: Economic Concentration, 1978-1979

	Gini Coeff.	% of profits received by firms representing:		
		Largest 1%	Smallest 50%	No. of firms
Manufacturing	.91	71.95	3.72	9874
Retail	.70	54.48	14.20	39491
Sugar mills	.52	23.83	10.36	12
Coffee mills	.46	3.60*	15.20	73
Coffee (Pulp Extraction)	.60	12.86	11.78	102
Transportation	.40	11.61	23.90	304
Services	.43	36.70	27.86	10262
Construction	.64	9.20*	12.59	76
Electricity	.65	75.22	8.97	9
Agriculture				272,343
Coffee	.87	34.88	1.25	—
Cotton	.70	10.05	8.41	—
Basic grains	.60	25.94	11.78	—
Livestock	.93	50.83	0.20	—

Source: Sevilla 1985.
* Figure represents a single company.

companies.[10] As mining declined, internal trade and the capture of some minor customs duties came to constitute the material basis for Honduras's fragile bourgeoisie. Furthermore, the dynamism radiating from the North Coast banana plantations enabled groups of immigrant Middle Eastern entrepreneurs gradually to become the nucleus of a vigorous industrial and financial bourgeoisie, making San Pedro Sula the country's real economic capital (Euraque 1990, 1991b; Molina Chocano 1980; Murga Frasinetti 1985). Traditional extensive landowners without significant economic diversification were poorly equipped to resist the military reformism of the 1970s and the activism of the peasant and labor organizing movements. Capitalist modernization in Costa Rica, in contrast, involved significant political and economic transformations in the landholding groups and the traditional exporters, which are discussed in the next chapter.

A complex system of kinship relations gave the traditionally dominant groups at once solidity and the flexibility to adapt to, or redirect, efforts at change. Their community of material interests and political projects—that is, their consciousness of class identity—was solidified by a sense of caste that helped make their exercise of power all the more exclusive. Surnames of the *criollo* lineage, with its origins in Spain, reappear through the centuries in control of political power and the economy, particularly in Guatemala, Costa Rica, and Nicaragua (Casaus Arzú 1992b). Of the forty-four presidents of Costa Rica between 1821 and 1970, thirty-three were descendants of three original sixteenth-century settlers. Of the 1,300 deputies to the national Legislative Assembly during the same period, 350 were descended from four colonists (Stone 1975). A handful of families runs through Guatemala's political history since colonial times in a practically uninterrupted exercise of political power and oligopolistic control of the most important sectors of the economy. In the 1980s a group of eighteen families in Guatemalan high society was woven together by 155 kinship relations (Casaus Arzú 1992a:191ff). In Nicaragua, the networks on which the oligarchic groups are founded enabled them to hold onto their decisive political power through all the recent political twists and turns and economic ups and downs (Vilas 1992a).

The term "oligarchy" remains relevant for conceptualizing these traditional but economically highly dynamic groups, insofar as it synthesizes the broad arc of dimensions that make up class identity: economics, certainly—especially land-owning status—but also politics, ideology, education, lifestyles, historical continuity; the embedment of class identity within the practice of patron-client relationships; business organizations built on kinship networks. This complex set of material and cultural factors helps explain the Central American ruling groups' simultaneous solidity and malleability, and their peculiar conception of politics and the state. In the oligarchic perspective, the issue is the endurance of a supremacy that is not merely economic and political but even more importantly historical, cultural, and racial; the exercise of political power derives from that superiority and is legitimized by it.

Structural rigidity

Strict control over productive resources—especially land, the most important resource—and over a structure of production based on a mass of semiproletarianized peasants and landless

Table 2.8
Shares of the Five Primary Products in
the Total Value of Central American Exports

	1960-64	1975-79
Costa Rica	83%	63%
El Salvador	79%	64%
Guatemala	84%	56%
Honduras	66%	61%
Nicaragua	68%	66%
Central America	77%	62%

Source: SIECA 1980, 1981.
Note: The five primary products are coffee, cotton, bananas, sugar, and beef.

workers—blocked the development of an internal market. It also reduced the reach of technological modernization and the potential for industrialization. Profits were realized either in sales abroad or in the form of imports from those foreign markets. This deepened the division, and heightened the tensions, between a relatively high-yield export sector and the backward domestic production upon whose reproduction the export sector was built. The preservation of the region's traditional exporting profile, the small size of its economies, and their marginality to the world market meant Central America's character as a price taker, with the very limited options that derive from that status, would not change.

Three decades of economic transformations and productive diversification failed to alter Central America's traditional exporting profile. At the end of the 1970s, five agricultural products still accounted for two-thirds of Central America's foreign sales (Table 2.8).

Moreover, Central America's already quite limited share of world exports has declined over the long term, even in comparison with exports from other underdeveloped economies (Table 2.9).

A price taker economy is not in a position to influence the world prices of its exports, which restricts its margin for action. By nature, a price taker economy has very scant maneuvering room to increase export revenues or reduce export costs. Its capacity to cut production costs is also limited, because a high proportion of the productive inputs, fuels, and the raw materials for its export pro-

Table 2.9
Central America: Export Share of the World Market (in Millions of Dollars)

	1970	1975	1980
1. World exports	313,651	875,113	1,992,507
2. Developing countries	56,832	213,530	564,012
3. Central America	1,105	2,309	4,875
4. Percentage 3:1	0.35	0.26	0.24
5. Percentage 3:2	1.90	1.10	0.86

Source: United Nations 1986.

duction comes from abroad. Consequently, only local production costs are subject to action, and those costs can be reduced to one: labor. Accordingly, the economy's international competitiveness and the reproduction of the export system depend on an intense compression of the working and living conditions of the direct producers: low wages for workers, low prices for peasants. To the extent that almost all economies with these characteristics have a large and inexpensive labor supply, and that some of the Central American export staples are also produced by more developed economies with higher wage levels, there is a limit to this comparative advantage in labor costs. This limit forces the Central American economies to seek enough technological progress to lift their yields in export production. That in turn raises production costs, requiring even greater pressure on the labor force. The result is that workers are remunerated not according to their marginal productivity but according to their cost of reproduction, and in extreme cases, even below that.

The export sector's realization of profit via imports—not to mention the sector's own dependence on a stable import flow—removes incentives to develop the internal market and keeps the productive apparatus from integrating agriculture with industry. As long as products are not aimed at the internal market, or do not use domestic inputs, business must target the labor force as a cost to be reduced, rather than as a profit-generating component of capital. A production structure of this kind tends, by its own logic, to give rise to authoritarian political regimes and repressive governments; to deprive broad segments of the working classes of citizenship rights, especially in the countryside; to outlaw unions and other popular organizations; to resort to extra-economic compulsion of the labor force; etc. Under such conditions, any institutional shift toward political democratization will threaten to change the social conditions of production to the detriment of the accumulation process, the economy's external profitability, and the political terms of oligarchic rule. It is easy to understand, then, that every proposal for political reform, from the timid to the most radical, is therefore understood to imply a challenge to the economic and social structure. Conversely, any more or less profound change in the central characteristics of such a production structure will have repercussions on power relations and on the configuration of the state, and therefore must face resistance from those who hold political power.

It was the Central American societies' structural design itself, much more than the ideology of the challenging sectors, that would give the proposals for change that arose during the 1960s and the 1970s their enormously conflictive character.

THREE

Political Regimes, the State, and Social Mobilization

The dislocations that capitalist modernization brought to Central America, beginning in the 1950s, are often assumed to be the key factor behind the revolutionary strains that emerged in the following decades. However, all five of the region's countries were swept up, if unevenly, in those economic changes. That revolutionary processes broke out only in some countries, even though economic change was a factor across the region, suggests that the disorders of capitalist modernization are not a sufficient explanation for the emergence of radical political challenges. The political conditions and institutions that framed those structural changes and their negative impacts on particular groups and classes must also be considered. Capitalist modernization developed in a variety of political contexts: repressive states in Guatemala, El Salvador, and Nicaragua, and political systems more open to popular pressure and social reform in Honduras and Costa Rica. The interplay between these two sets of economic and political factors, rather than either one by itself, may explain the divergent paths that the two groups of countries followed.

1. Economic modernization and dictatorial regimes

Socioeconomic change in El Salvador, Guatemala, and Nicaragua was framed and led by authoritarian regimes. The occasional call to elections changes nothing about the character of the regime: arbitrary proceedings, no effective constitutional enforcement, limited ranges of choice, prohibition of alternatives to the political rule of traditional groups, fraud, and the nullification of adverse voting results were common currency in the political systems of all three countries. These measures have themselves, in fact, been strategic tools for advancing economic change (Wheelock 1976; McClintock 1985; Figueroa Ibarra 1991). Political institutions acted as instruments of the groups propelling capitalist modernization, using proscription, repression, and violence to ratify substantive changes.

Yet states occasionally did attempt to reform some of the more critical aspects of inequality and social exploitation. Designed as they were to prevent the explosion of social tensions, however, and corresponding to a logic not proper to the ruling classes themselves, these reforms frustrated the very expectations that they aroused, and earned the immovable opposition of elites not at all disposed to concessions. State reformism proved too little, too late; far from preventing social protest, it helped feed it.

El Salvador

El Salvador had lived under military governments ever since a Communist-led rural and indigenous insurrection was violently crushed in 1932: every president of the country until 1979 was a high-ranking army officer. Elections were invariably won by the military candidate, who, once in office, conducted public business in line with the outlook of the land-owning class. The 1932 popular defeat laid the basis for a political formula that relieved the economic elite of the need to be directly involved in unprofitable public affairs, and at the same time guaranteed the institutional marginalization of peasants, workers, and the middle groups.

The new wind that the Alliance for Progress breathed into inter-American politics, along with the social differentiation that arose from economic growth, brought elements of tension into this political formula. Urbanization and economic development accelerated the growth of middle sectors that did not feel represented by the political regime. After the Cuban revolution came to power, the United States government resolved to promote certain reforms in order to head off potential social conflict. The 1960s, consequently, saw a succession of tensions as modest political openings and government economic reform initiatives—such as state regulation of some aspects of credit and production—confronted the rigidity of the economy and the oligarchic groups.

Following the 1963 electoral reform, the Christian Democratic Party (PDC) surfaced as a rallying point for dissatisfied middle groups and the emerging urban sectors. By 1964 the party had gained a significant foothold in parliament, and in 1968 it elected the mayor of San Salvador. The PDC's vote was predominantly urban; the security forces made it enormously difficult for the opposition to recruit in the countryside. The reforms, limited as they were, nevertheless aroused resistance among sectors of the military and the oligarchy. This, combined with what many activists saw as the Christian Democratic leaders' reluctance to push for broader fields of action, encouraged some sectors of the opposition to turn progressively more radical. The government's reluctance to recognize the newly emerging peasant organizations, its repression against organizers, and the demand for effective political and economic reforms brought on splits in the PDC and the Communist Party in 1970 when growing numbers of militant youth, critical of their parties' compromises with the regime, left to join the incipient guerrilla organizations.

Labor protest also picked up. The number of trade unions grew by 50 percent between the 1960s and the mid-1970s, while membership grew by 150 percent (North 1985: 55; Menjívar 1985). Teachers' and public employees' unions were particularly active.

The unprecedented mobilization of the migration-swollen marginal urban population and social activism in the countryside were especially important factors in the gathering political tension. The new organizations that were beginning to spread in poor Salvadoran shantytowns in the 1960s and 1970s, like those in the countryside, fell largely outside the reach of the unions and the traditional parties. New practices among the Catholic clergy encouraged the formation of rural unions, even though legal prohibitions forced the new organizations to exist only as associations for mutual interest rather than for collective bargaining or other labor-related activities.

The February 20, 1972 presidential elections marked the end of a decade of military experiments with cautious openings in the political system. The elections were won by a very broad coalition of the PDC, the social-democratic *Movimiento Nacionalista Revolucionario* (MNR), and the *Unión Democrática Nacionalista* (UDN, the Communist Party's electoral front). The military regime refused to recognize their victory. The repression of protests against this fraud left more than 300 dead and wounded that day alone. Discontent even made itself felt within the army itself, in the form of an abortive military coup by young officers aiming to put the winning candidates in office.[1]

This launched a phase of state terrorism meant to destroy the opposition. Murders of rural workers, peasants, union organizers, and neighborhood activists became everyday events throughout the 1970s. The parapolitical groups dedicated to repression and annihilation (Orden, Falange) that had first seen action during the 1968 teachers' strike were openly incorporated into the operation of the political system.

The radical intensification of state repression provoked a response from among the popular classes. The *Fuerzas Populares de Liberación* (Popular Liberation Forces, FPL), founded a year earlier by Communist Party dissidents, began to operate as a guerrilla organization immediately after the 1972 election fraud. The *Ejército Revolucionario del Pueblo* (People's Revolutionary Army, ERP) was formed soon after. A dissident group within the ERP founded the *Fuerzas Armadas de Resistencia Nacional* (Armed Forces of National Resistance, FARN) in 1975, and the *Partido Revolucionario de los Trabajadores Centroamericanos* (Central American Revolutionary Workers Party, PRTC) emerged as a political-military organization the next year.

Mass organizations also consolidated and stepped up their activities. The *Frente de Acción Popular Unificada* (Unified People's Action Front, FAPU) was created in 1974, followed by the *Bloque Popular Revolucionario* (People's Revolutionary Bloc, BPR), the *Unión de Pobladores de Tugurios* (Shantytown Dwellers' Union, UPT), and others.

Col. Arturo Armando Molina—the president installed by the

1972 election fraud—essayed a halfhearted agrarian reform project in mid-1976 to eliminate some of the most primitive aspects of agriculture and to defuse social tension in the countryside. Landless workers and poor peasants responded by organizing still further and pushing for land redistribution and better farming conditions. Notwithstanding its limited scope—about 150,000 hectares were to be distributed among some 12,000 families—the project was finally overcome by an intensive business mobilization led by the *Asociación Nacional de la Empresa Privada* (National Private Enterprise Association, ANEP).

After Gen. Carlos Humberto Romero, the government party's candidate, won the February 28, 1977 presidential elections, protests against fraud were met with great violence. Several opposition leaders were forced to leave the country, and a wave of kidnapping, torture and assassination heralded the beginning of a veritable slaughter of the opposition. With the political parties no longer seen as an alternative to the regime, urban unions and peasant organizations threw their energies into the mass popular front. By the time the *Ligas Populares 28 de Febrero* (February 28 People's Leagues, LP-28) were formed as a new mass front in 1978, mass groups had already mobilized an estimated 100,000 people (McClintock 1985 I:187).

Following the 1977 election fraud and massacre, the Communist Party shifted its own approach. In 1979 the party created the *Fuerzas Armadas de Liberación* (Liberation Armed Forces, FAL) and joined the guerrilla struggle. Table 3.1 maps the relationships between political-military organizations, mass fronts, and military organizations up to 1979.

Functioning separately, and with a less radical outlook, was the *Unión Comunal Salvadoreña* (UCS), which from its inception in the late 1960s had had close ties with the American Institute for Free Labor Development (AIFLD). From 1980 on, the UCS was El Salvador's main peasant organization, with an estimated 60,000 members (Prosterman and Riedinger 1987:148).[2]

The role of women in popular mobilizations, already growing, accelerated in 1975 to 1976. Women were initially concentrated in teachers' movements and in shantytown organizing; they made up a very large proportion of the activists and leadership of ANDES, the teachers' union, and of the Unión de Pobladores de Tugurios.

Table 3.1
El Salvador: Revolutionary Organizations, 1979

Political-military organization: Fuerzas Populares de Liberación (FPL)
Mass organization: Bloque Popular Revolucionario (BPR)
Guerilla organization: FPL

Political-military organization: Resistencia Nacional (RN)
Mass organization: Frente de Acción Popular Unificada (FAPU)
Guerilla organization: Fuerzas Armadas de la Resistencia Nacional (FARN)

Political-military organization: Partido de la Revolución Salvadoreña (PRS)
Mass organization: Ligas Populares 28 de Febrero (LP-28)
Guerilla organization: Ejército Revolucionario del Pueblo (ERP)

Political-military organization: Partido Comunista de El Salvador (PCES)
Mass organization: Unión Democrática Nacional (UDN)
Guerilla organization: Fuerzas Armadas de Liberación (FAL)

Political-military organization: Partido Revolucionario de los Trabajadores
    Centroamericanos (PRTC)
Mass organization: Movimiento de Liberación Popular (MLP)
Guerilla organization: PRTC

The Asociación de Mujeres Progresistas de El Salvador (AMPES), founded in mid-decade, focused at first on workers' rights and later extended its reach to more direct political mobilization. COM-ADRES (Salvadoran Committee of Mothers and Relatives of Political Prisoners and Victims of Disappearance and Murder) was founded in 1977 and earned early distinction for its militant human rights work. It was followed a year later by the Asociación de Mujeres de El Salvador (Association of Salvadoran Women, AMES), with ties to the BPR. The Asociación de Trabajadores y Usuarios de Mercados de El Salvador (Association of Market Workers and Vendors of El Salvador, ASUTRAMES), whose membership was 75 percent women, was founded in 1979 (García and Gomáriz 1989 II: 207-208). Government repression and increasing political violence forced this group to cease functioning in 1982 to 1983.

With the economic deterioration brought on by the climate of general violence, along with the political system's obvious ungovernability and the corrosive impact of human rights violations on the country's international image, fissures began to appear in the armed forces. After several failed attempts to force Gen. Humberto Romero to resign, a group of young officers removed him in an October 15, 1979 coup d'état, with the support of segments of the modernizing business class and of professionals in the PDC and the MNR associated with the Jesuit-run *Universidad Centroamericana José Simeón Cañas*. They also apparently enjoyed the consent of the United States Embassy.

The October coup had a twofold political goal: to put a stop to the bloodbath into which the country had been plunged, and to offer economic and social reforms as a peaceful alternative to the guerrillas' call for revolution. The coup, which took both the guerrillas and the extreme right by surprise, intensified and brought into public view the split within the army. However, the new military government's lack of a social base and its internal divisions conspired against its reformist intentions. After an initial crisis in January 1980, the PDC formally stepped into the government by virtue of a "PDC-Armed Forces pact" designed by United States Embassy officers to exclude the most progressive civilians and officers from the new governing junta.

The increasing violence against popular leaders—even leaders of the organizations that made up the government—quickly exhausted the new junta's potential. Paramilitary groups backed by the most recalcitrant sectors of the army assassinated PDC leader Mario Zamora in February 1980. The next month they assassinated the Archbishop of San Salvador, Oscar Arnulfo Romero, as he held mass. The impunity of the terror compelled several junta members to resign, setting off a second government crisis that now spread into the PDC itself. A number of the party's first-line leaders left to found the *Movimiento Popular Socialcristiano* (MPSC), and many were forced into exile to save their lives.

State terrorism in its most brutal incarnations, already widespread in 1979, now became completely unrestrained. More than 8,000 extrajudicial executions for political reasons of civilian noncombatants were recorded in 1980, and the figure grew to more than 13,000 in 1981. Almost 61 percent of these were committed by combined military and security bodies, and 35 percent by paramilitary groups. The remaining 14 percent were the work of the "death squads" (Benítez Manaut 1989a:342). In the three years between 1980 and the end of 1982, 71 percent of the victims were peasants, 10 percent were workers, and another 10 percent were students (White 1984:44).

The critical role of reunification in the FSLN's victory in Nicaragua, and the challenge posed by the military coup, led the Salvadoran revolutionary groups to seek unity among themselves. The *Coordinadora Revolucionaria de Masas* (Revolutionary Mass Coordinating Committee, CRM), combining the five mass fronts, was formed in January 1980. That March, the five political-military groups formed the *Dirección Revolucionaria Unificada* (Unified Revolutionary Leadership, DRU). The *Frente Democrático*, a coalition of small parties and social organizations including the MPSC, the MNR, the *Movimiento Independiente de Profesionales y Técnicos* (Independent Professionals' and Technicians' Movement, MIPTES), student organizations, and small to medium businesses, was founded in April.

The Frente Democrático and the CRM soon merged to create the *Frente Democrático Revolucionario* (FDR). Its first president was Enrique Alvarez Córdoba, who as Minister of Agriculture in 1976 had launched the thwarted attempt at agrarian reform. The FDR's "Platform of the Revolutionary Democratic Government" focused on independent development, popular liberation, and creating the economic basis for the development of socialism, among other points (CDR 1980).

In October 1980, the five guerrilla organizations founded the *Frente Farabundo Martí de Liberación Nacional*, although they remained strictly autonomous in operation. The failure of reform "from above," the ceiling reached by mass mobilization, and the exacerbation of state terrorism had now shifted the struggle from the sphere of politics into that of war. In the following month, a death squad killed Alvarez Córdoba and several other FDR leaders.

Guatemala

The 1954 counterrevolution and a succession of openly repressive regimes provided the political framework for capitalist transformation in Guatemala. The overthrow of Col. Jacobo Arbenz's popularly elected reformist government by a United States-backed military invasion opened the door to a prolonged period of intense political repression by a series of military or military-controlled governments arising from coups and fraudulent elections (McClintock 1985 II:28ff).

After Arbenz was overthrown, beneficiaries of agrarian reform were stripped of their lands. Peasant organizations and agricultural unions were dissolved and their leaders and activists hunted down, imprisoned and murdered (CIDA/ESFE 1971:103ff; Figueroa Ibarra 1980:98ff; 126ff). The same fate befell the urban labor movement, whose membership fell from some 100,000 (about 10 percent of the EAP) on the eve of Arbenz's overthrow to slightly over 27,000 in 1975 (less than 2 percent of the EAP).

Presidents Julio César Méndez Montenegro (1966 to 1970) and Gen. Carlos Arana Osorio (1970 to 1974) oversaw a colonization program to move indigenous peasants into El Petén. The idea of relocation was not a new one; it had first appeared in the early 1950s on a list of World Bank recommendations for reactivating Guatemala's economy. The World Bank proposed moving indigenous farmers to zones better suited to more modern agriculture, where they could improve their production and profit levels and their living conditions, and where they could find new agricultural occupations and industries that were more productive "than present inefficient cultivation of highland corn" (IBRD 1951:28). The Jacobo Arbenz government had accepted the report, but had opted instead for agrarian reform. The politics of resettlement combined verticalism and violence. Decisions as to which communities were to be relocated and where were made by the state without consultation. Destinations were based on considerations that were foreign to the communities but in line with the military and civilian bureaucrats' own land speculation interests. Not surprisingly, many peasants were worse off after relocation than they had been already.

Nevertheless, quite incidentally to the government's intentions, these programs did create a certain amount of space for rural organizing by younger elements in the Catholic Church. A few priests began to build cooperatives in the departments of Huehuetenango and Quiché, especially in the newly populated areas to which resettlement programs had moved highland peasants. These cooperatives were a source of community development (health centers, schools, housewives' clubs, job-training and literacy workshops, rural radio stations, etc.), and played a central role in developing trade networks and power centers independent of the local elites and caudillos. By the mid-1970s, some 20 percent of the highland Indians were organized into cooperatives of some kind (Handy 1989).

The *Acción Católica* activities, combined with the growth of literacy, the economic independence that cooperatives offered, and the organizing work of the *Partido Demócrata Cristiano* (PDC) planted the seeds for significant change in the indigenous communities. Traditional indigenous religious authority persisted in many villages, under a dual system of government in which an indigenous local government structure was subordinated to the official Ladino structure. Almost every community saw the emergence of groups that either fought the traditional hierarchy or forced it to join them in the fight for political and economic independence through the local indigenous-controlled cooperatives and political parties. The very young began to reject their submission to local Ladino authority, and even to the national government altogether. Greater local political and economic independence encouraged a rediscovery of ethnic identity and a spirit of differentiation from and opposition to the Ladino culture and structures that subordinated indigenous people. The work of U.S. anthropologists in some communities was another important factor behind this new attitude.

Although *Acción Católica* and the Church hierarchy did not intend the cooperatives and the other organizational forms to take their challenge to the status quo too far, conflict with government policies was inevitable. Between 1976 and 1978, 168 leaders of cooperatives and villages were murdered. The government of Gen. Romeo Lucas García (1978 to 1982) voided the registration of more than 250 cooperatives accused of Marxism and communism. Still, there were 510 cooperatives in the country by the end of the 1970s, 57 percent of them in the highlands (Brockett 1988:110–12).

A few guerrilla organizations had emerged in the 1960s, in response to growing dissatisfaction with the antipopular and repressive character of the military governments, the helplessness of the official political institutions, and the influence of the Cuban revolution. Their principal field of activity had been on the Pacific coast, the site of important capitalist agribusiness and the highest concentration of wage workers. However, internal splits and the lack of indigenous peasant support condemned these organizations to isolation and, in the end, military defeat.

More successful guerrilla organizations appeared in the western highlands in the 1970s. The climate was more favorable there, thanks to a profound and generalized social discontent with the greed of the monopolistic landowners and the miserable wages they paid; local Ladino caudillos and their arbitrary authority over indigenous people; and small-town military and police chiefs and their abuse, repression, and murder. A decade of pastoral work by young priests from the United States and Spain, community action by the Peace Corps and USAID, and the work of various U.S. anthropologists had revived or recreated ethnic consciousness among highland farmers. The guerrillas were forced to adapt to the new conditions. Once they had done so, however—in a process that was not untouched by difficulties and tensions—they earned an unprecedented degree of support, in stark contrast with the guerrilla experience of the previous decade.

After the first actions of the *Ejército Guerrillero de los Pobres* (Guerrilla Army of the Poor, EGP) against certain landowners in Quiché, the army unleashed a brutal counterinsurgency campaign in Ixil region. The defenseless peasant and indigenous organizations, an easy target for repression, were more badly hurt than the guerrillas. In 1975 the army massacred thirty-seven cooperatives in Ixcán, and began to occupy towns and cities (Nebaj, Chajul, San Juan Carzal, and others) the next year. By early 1977, more than 100 local leaders had been murdered (Davis and Hodson 1983).

More than 100 Kekchi men, women, and children were massacred on May 29, 1978 in Panzos, in the department of Alta Verapaz, as they peacefully protested the loss of their lands. This action, carried out in broad daylight by troops in fatigues with the cooperation of the local landowners, persuaded the indigenous Kekchi and Ixil of the northern border region that no institutional resource could protect their villages against the military and large landowners. A large proportion of the support that the EGP received in Alta Verapaz and parts of Quiché was a defensive response to this massacre.

In January 1980, thirty-nine peasant leaders were killed in an army assault on the Spanish embassy in Guatemala City, where they were protesting the kidnapping of leaders and the confiscation of land. This massacre was further evidence that state power had become an instrument for supporting the landowners, even at the cost of the extinction of the indigenous population. Some of the occupants of the embassy came from Nebaj; after the massacre, the army occupied that Ixil town, killing men, women, and children. Entire Ixil communities decided to join the guerrillas in response.

In July 1981, military troops kidnapped Emeterio Toj Medrano, the leader of the *Comité de Unidad Campesina* (Peasant Unity Committee, CUC). Founded in 1978, CUC was the first indigenous-led labor organization, and the first to connect the indigenous peasants of the highlands with the poor Ladinos working on Pacific-coast farms. In a spectacular raid, the EGP freed Medrano from the army base where he was held, after which indigenous peasants joined the guerrillas—especially the EGP—in unprecedented numbers: as the number of indigenous commanders increased, the greater the influx. The *Organización Revolucionaria del Pueblo en Armas* (Revolutionary Organization of the People in Arms, ORPA), another guerrilla organization, had a similar experience: at the beginning of the 1980s, 90 percent of the rebels in ORPA were indigenous (Handy 1989).

Until the mid-1970s, the bulk of state violence was concentrated in the departments in which capitalist expansion had its greatest impact. After that, however, violence spread across the entire country in response to the sustained growth of social and labor mobilization: teachers' strikes, industrial workers' and miners' strikes, and student protests and demonstrations. In May 1976, the first instance of united action emerged in the form of the *Comité Nacional de Unidad Sindical* (National Labor Unity Committee, CNUS). The *Movimiento Nacional de Pobladores* (National Shantytown Dwellers' Movement) appeared after the 1976 earthquake. After an ebb between the second half of the 1950s and the 1960s, the industrial labor movement entered a modest recovery as well.

Repression escalated brutally during the presidency of Lucas García (1978 to 1982), which adopted a systematic iron-fist policy against the labor movement. In addition to the now-notorious murders at Panzós and the Spanish embassy, sixty people were killed by military troops in Quiché in August 1980. In January and

February 1981, intensified military repression in Chimaltenango claimed the lives of an estimated 1,500 indigenous peasants. An August 1981 military operation in Huehuetenango left 200 peasants dead. A year later, approximately 1,000 more died in a massacre at San Sebastián Lemoa in Quiché, and another 700 died in military operations in Alta Verapaz the following September (Figueroa Ibarra 1991:121–65; Dunkerley 1987: 476–77; Falla 1992). Twenty-seven leaders of the *Central Nacional de Trabajadores* (National Workers' Organization, CNT) were murdered in June 1980, and another seventeen were killed that August: it was the government's and business's method of putting a stop to labor disputes at the Coca-Cola bottling plant (Frundt 1987).

In January of 1979, a paramilitary group assassinated Alberto Fuentes Mohr, leader of the opposition *Partido Socialdemócrata* (PSD). After Fuentes Mohr's assassination, a broad coalition of social organizations and political parties formed the *Frente Democrático Contra la Represión* (FDCR) to demand an end to terror and violence. The system's answer was the assassination of Manuel Colom Argueta, former mayor of Guatemala City and leader of the opposition *Frente Unido de la Revolución* (FUR), in April. The two murders severely shocked both organizations, which were small groups fighting to open a space in the center of Guatemala's convulsive politics through alliances with the *Partido Demócrata Cristiano*.

The guerrilla organizations that had formed in the early 1970s began in October 1980 to coordinate their actions with those that had emerged later, and in February 1982 they formed the *Unidad Revolucionaria Nacional Guatelmuteca* (Guatemalan National Revolutionary Unity, URNG).

Nicaragua

The Somoza regime, installed in the late 1930s by U.S. military intervention, ruled the destinies of Nicaragua for forty-five years. A combination of fraudulent elections, agreements, constitutional measures, corruption and repression enabled the Somoza family to monopolize political power and pass it from father to son. The Somoza dynasty rested on three pillars: the Guardia Nacional, its instrument of coercion and control; a system of political alliances with the *Partido Conservador*; and the assurance of support from the U.S. government.

Dynasty is not merely a metaphor for the Somoza regime. Following the death in 1956 of Anastasio (Tacho) Somoza García, the founder of the regime, the power he had monopolized was divided between his two sons. The eldest, Luis Somoza Debayle, assumed the presidency, while control of the Guardia Nacional went to the younger son, Anastasio Jr. (Tachito). In 1971, Anastasio Jr. assumed the presidency while keeping his position in the Guardia; it is not unreasonable to presume that his son, Anastasio Somoza Portocarrero, would have succeeded his father and grandfather had the Sandinistas not ended the succession in 1979.

The Somozas' alliance with the *Partido Conservador*, and that party's willingness to accept a subordinate role in the system, supplied the regime with a broader base of legitimacy than the typical dictatorship enjoys. This alliance was built, in turn, upon the agreement between the Somozas and the Conservatives on the kind of country Nicaragua ought to become; on their mutual obedience to U.S. leadership; and on the client status of the popular masses, especially those in the countryside, which could be mobilized for voting and confrontation whenever necessary. This system of alliances left opposition groups unable to gain an effective political foothold. Their minority status made them dependent on alliances with the *Partido Conservador* based on an anti-Somoza common denominator (Booth 1982; Vilas 1986; Walter 1993).

The only time the Somoza regime leaned toward the other side of the political spectrum came in the late 1940s. Anastasio Somoza García emerged unscathed from the wave of student and middle-class protest that swept across Central America in that decade and ended the dictatorships of Jorge Ubico in Guatemala, Maximiliano Hernández Martínez in El Salvador and Tiburcio Carías Andino in Honduras. In response to intensive social mobilization demanding political modernization and democratization, the dictatorship took measures that gained some support among the country's fledgling labor organizations and the *Partido Socialista de Nicaragua* (PSN). It established a labor code that was technically progressive, and then a social security system. It was the Conservatives' opposition to these measures, rather than the measures themselves, that enabled the regime to seem for a time to take on a certain progressive coloring—one that did not exclude the repression of worker activism when necessary (Gould 1990:79ff). Once that danger was past, an April 1950 pact with Gen. Emiliano Chamorro, the leader of the *Partido Conservador*, put everything back in its place.[3]

Anastasio Somoza García's excellent relations with the United States government enabled him to take control of the National Guard, the police body created in the 1930s by U.S. occupation troops—a position that served as the launching pad for his long political career. Somoza's ties with the United States became even closer during World War II, when the U.S. armed forces built a Navy base at the Pacific port of Corinto and Air Force bases in Managua and Puerto Cabezas. Somoza confirmed his loyalty to the United States by declaring war on the Axis powers, a move that enabled him to benefit personally from the confiscation of the properties of German and Italian citizens who had settled in Nicaragua.

Somoza authorized the United States to use the Managua airport for flights in support of Guatemalan Col. Castillo Armas's successful 1954 mission to overthrow the government of Jacobo Arbenz. Some of the forces in the 1961 invasion of Cuba trained on Nicaraguan territory, sponsored by the United States. In 1965, the Nicaraguan government helped form the "Inter-American Peace Force" through which the U.S. government "internationalized" its invasion of the Dominican Republic. The Somoza regime was consequently the United States' firmest and most enduring ally in Central America for almost half a century. After the overthrow of dictatorships in Guatemala, El Salvador and Honduras in the 1940s, and the events of 1948 in Costa Rica, the Somoza regime became an important stabilizing factor in a region increasingly riven with tension and conflict between the traditional ruling groups, the emerging middle classes, and the armed forces. This regional instability was aggravated by the Cuban revolution and by the enthusiasm it stirred up in a broad range of political organizations and social groups. Under these circumstances, Washington saw the Somoza regime as a valuable piece in the hemisphere-wide projection of its national security policies within the anticommunist framework of the cold war.

This was no military regime in the classic sense; not the top brass but the Somozas, both father and son, exercised complete control over the Guardia Nacional (Guzmán 1992). At their exclusive personal pleasure, they decided on promotions, honors, and pensions; loyalty to Somoza, not military merit, was the key to promotion. The Somozas' powers extended to skipping ranks in the promotion scale when necessary: Anastasio Somoza Portocarrero, the founder's grandson, began his Guardia career as a colonel. None of these measures provoked any complaints or protests.[4]

After Tacho Somoza was assassinated in 1956, his sons attempted to loosen their formal political control, in the context of an economic bonanza and the new winds of the Alliance for Progress. The Congress named Luis Somoza president, without benefit of any constitutional or legal provision; the move was ratified through an election whose results were conveniently guaranteed. Luis Somoza's "constitutional" term from 1957 to 1963 was followed by a similarly guaranteed vote for René Schick, on the Somozas' own *Partido Liberal Nacional* ticket. The *Partido Conservador* refused to participate in these elections upon the government's refusal to allow an observation group from the Organization of American States. Schick, who served under the strict vigilance of the Somoza family, was the beneficiary of an economic boom that extended the room for negotiation with the traditional groups.

Schick died in 1966 without finishing his term; the elections called to replace him demonstrated that the Somozas were not willing to extend the political opening. The *Partido Conservador*, behind presidential candidate Fernando Agüero, joined the *Partido Liberal Independiente* (PLI) and the *Partido Social Cristiano* (PSC) in a broad opposition coalition. On January 22, 1967, an opposition rally was brutally repressed by the Guardia Nacional, at the cost of between 500 and 600 dead and wounded (Gutiérrez Mayorga 1985; Dunkerley 1987:233). Many of the demonstrators had been trucked in from the countryside, unaware that they were participating in a political activity. Anastasio Somoza Jr. won the elections with an alleged 70 percent of the votes.

When his term ended in 1971, Somoza reached a new agreement with the conservatives, guaranteeing them 40 percent of the seats in Congress. The pact also called for a Constitutional assembly that would authorize a triumvirate consisting of Agüero and two Somocistas, who would govern until new elections were held in 1974. Somoza would remain in charge of the Guardia Nacional.

This agreement, clear evidence of the Conservative Party's acceptance for a minority and subordinate role, dealt a severe blow to the legal opposition. Neither the PLI nor the PSC had the strength to occupy the space left vacant. In the 1974 elections, Somoza declared that he had received almost 90 percent of the votes, and the conservatives occupied their agreed-on share of parliamentary seats under the 1971 pact. Voter abstention was high at 40 percent.

Like the Salvadoran and Guatemalan regimes, the Somozas attempted a timid reform at the insistence of international organizations and U.S. government agencies, on a similarly limited scale. On a visit to Nicaragua in 1952, a delegation from the International Bank for Reconstruction and Development recommended that the country develop its agricultural exports, particularly livestock, and take measures to stimulate the influx of foreign capital (IBRD 1953). The *Instituto de Fomento Nacional* (National Development Institute, INFONAC) was established the same year in response to the IBRD report, with the task of designing and financing investment projects in agriculture, forestry, and infrastructure. The *Instituto Agrario Nicaragüense* (IAN) was founded in 1963 to promote agrarian reform projects by colonizing agricultural frontiers—specifically, the tropical rainforest. It facilitated the creation of an enormous reserve of labor and land for agroexport. Neither of these measures reversed the negative impact of the spread of agroexport on the peasantry; that was not their purpose. On the contrary, these mechanisms to open up agricultural frontiers to livestock expansion for export were designed to benefit the groups closest to the Somoza regime (Taylor 1970; Núñez Soto 1980; Vilas 1989b:65ff).

So complete was the subordination of the ruling economic groups to the Somoza regime that only as late as 1978—when the Sandinista revolutionary challenge began to prove itself to be uncontainable—was the *Movimiento Democrático Nicaragüense* (MDN), which can be considered the first political party of the Nicaraguan bourgeoisie as a class, formed. The situation in business was no different. It was almost thirty years after the cotton boom of the early 1950s that the first cotton growers' association was organized in 1978, followed by the *Unión de Productores Agropecuarios de Nicaragua* (Nicaraguan Agricultural Producers' Union, UPANIC) the next year.

The years 1958 and 1959 saw the failure of a few attempts at anti-Somoza guerrilla warfare by Liberals, Conservatives, and Socialists unhappy with the traditional parties' subordination to the Somoza regime (Blandón 1980; Camacho Navarro 1991). The creation of the *Frente Sandinista de Liberación Nacional* (FSLN) in the early 1960s came in the context of those earlier attempts, in which some of the FSLN's original members had participated. The early expressions of armed struggle, with students playing a decisive role, expressed the discontent of radicalized segments of the middle classes with the somocista system and what they regarded as the complicity of the political parties. The guerrillas' early *foquista* tactics reflected both the influence of a particular interpretation of the Cuban guerrilla experience and lack of contact with the rural and urban workers' movement and the peasantry. But the FSLN expanded its presence in sectors of the peasantry and in poor neighborhoods of the major cities in the 1970s, and it also attracted the sympathy of some younger members of the traditional families. Beginning in the mid-1970s, the FSLN stepped up its activity in areas where rural wage earners were concentrated, promoting land occupations and union organization. The institutional framework of profound social changes brought on by capitalist growth, within a political system that was closed to the needs of those hurt by such changes, ensured receptive audiences for revolutionary arguments regardless of the ebbs and flows of guerrilla action.

When James Earl Carter became president of the United States, Washington's policy toward Latin America shifted: respect for human rights took a much more important place in U.S. relations with Latin American governments. This shift, in turn, led to pressure on the Somoza regime from several of the region's governments—notably Panama, Costa Rica, Mexico, and Venezuela. The FSLN, which split into three tendencies in 1976, expanded its guerrilla activity and began to create mass fronts that recruited broadly from the cities. On that basis, the FSLN began to approach traditional groups that had become increasingly distanced from the Somoza regime. The assassination of conservative leader Pedro Joaquín Chamorro in January 1978 heightened the strain between the conservative elites and the Somoza regime that had started in the aftermath of the Managua earthquake in December 1972. The Somozas' "disloyal competition" in credit and investment had given rise to frictions that now carried segments of the conservative business elite over to the growing opposition. Nevertheless, the failure of the first business strike to get Somoza to resign in 1978 showed that there were limits to the traditional opposition's power to change things.

The popular classes had organizational weaknesses of their own. The peasant movement was small and essentially confined to the department of Matagalpa. The workers' movement, in a society with a small proletariat and with high levels of seasonal unemployment, was weak as well. Some of the more important popular organizations took shape directly as part of the FSLN's revolutionary project in what turned out to be the closing months of the struggle against Somoza: the *Asociación de Trabajadores del Campo* (Rural Workers Association, ATC), the *Comités de Defensa Civil* (Civil Defense Committees, subsequently renamed *Comités de Defensa Sandinista*), the women's association, and others. The first national organization of peasants and medium farmers—aside from the short-lived *Confederación Nacional Campesina* founded by the *Partido Socialista de Nicaragua* in the mid-1960s and easily repressed by the regime—came after the Sandinista victory.

The *Movimiento Pueblo Unido* (United People's Movement, MPU), a broad alliance of social organizations tied to the FSLN and to the small communist party, was created in July 1978. The MPU's agenda included replacing the Guardia Nacional with a modern, professionalized army; confiscating and nationalizing Somoza property; nationalizing natural resources and the companies exploiting them; free labor organization; agrarian reform; and other concerns. In a climate of growing popular mobilization, the FSLN launched an insurrection in several cities in early September 1978. An incipient coup within the Guardia Nacional was aborted later in September. A second business strike the same month was overshadowed by mass action, which was now taking on the character of a Sandinista mobilization rather than a civic demonstration. The bourgeoisie, too weak to negotiate Somoza's departure, renewed its appeal to the U.S. government, which was under pressure at the same time from Somoza himself to keep him at the head of the state.

The rise of the Sandinista struggle, international pressure, and the breakup of the ruling bloc isolated the Somoza regime from society as a whole. Sandinista strategy reinforced this effect by concentrating its attack on Somoza and the Guardia Nacional, thereby cushioning the struggle's class repercussions in pursuit of a call for national democratic consensus among a broad spectrum of actors. This was in contrast with the events of the same years in El Salvador and Guatemala, where the state kept a stronghold in society's traditional groups and the political confrontation took on a clearly classist, or at least social, cast. Nicaragua reached a confrontation point pitting the state against society (Torres Rivas 1980), with society immersed in the conflict and unified as much by the Sandinista struggle as by dictatorial aggression. Not purely a class struggle, the final confrontation was democratic in its meaning, popular in its activism, and national in its reach.

The United States and the repressive apparatus

Beginning in the early 1960s, as a reaction to what it regarded as the threat of the Cuban revolution, the U.S. government developed a policy of military and security support for dictatorial or fraudulent regimes in Guatemala, El Salvador, and Nicaragua. Even before real insurgent threats surfaced, various U.S. government agencies committed themselves to the preservation of those regimes, thereby consolidating the power of the social groups whose interests the dictatorship served or expressed. In a span of a few years, the peaceful evolution envisioned by the Alliance for Progress was transformed into preventive counterrevolution and early militarization of states. Democracy, once thought of as an alternative to communism, came to be seen instead as a potential instrument for its intrusion.

The view in Washington that governments in the region were perilously vulnerable seems to have been the basis for these regimes' preoccupation with security. This conviction followed the bitter experience of Batista's dictatorship in Cuba, which the U.S. government supported to the end. The *ancien regime* in Central America was part of an inter-American system that rested on two pillars: U.S. political and military hegemony in Central American political and military affairs and foreign relations, and (with the partial exception of Costa Rica) the domination of society by traditional elites and oligarchies firmly aligned with the United States. In view of the historical bonds between internal systems of rule and the international order, a challenge to the local ruling class almost inevitably implied a challenge to the United States.

Equipping and training the military and security bodies and creating new intelligence services (all designed to preserve social and political order) were the priority objectives of U.S. aid to the regimes of the region. In 1963, Secretary of Defense Robert McNamara enunciated the doctrine under which the internal security of their states was the fundamental task of the Latin American officers trained in the special academies in the Panama Canal Zone and in the United States. The result was the emergence of what some observers later called the "counterinsurgency state" (Jonas 1991:116–23), but in this case a counterinsurgency state that was born before the enemy it was meant to combat had shown any significant signs of activity.[5]

The Salvadoran government, with U.S. assistance, began to develop its system of military intelligence in 1961. The government modernized the apparatus's equipment and organized a vast network of paramilitary irregulars, serving as auxiliaries to the army, to feed it information and provide the labor for the dirty work of counterinsurgency. This was the role of the *Organización Democrática Nacionalista* (known as ORDEN), whose members were recruited from the military reserve and operated under army orders (McClintock 1985:201ff). By 1974 ORDEN had mobilized between 100,000 and 150,000 men. The *Agencia Nacional de Seguridad de El Salvador* (Salvadoran National Security Agency, ANSESAL) was formed during the same period, under the command of Maj. Roberto D'Aubuisson; one report indicates that in 1983 ANSESAL had one informant for every fifty Salvadorans (McClintock 1985 I:207–08, 219).[6]

The goal of the U.S. Military Assistance Program in Guatemala, during the presidency of Col. Enrique Peralta Azurdia (1963 to 1966), was to help establish and maintain the military strength to guarantee internal security against domestic violence and any Castro-inspired invasions. The assistance consisted of creating special parapolice bodies in charge of kidnapping, disappearances, torture and assassinations. U.S. cooperation with internal security intensified between 1966 and 1974. In 1966 the Centro Regional de Comunicaciones, a structure similar to El Salvador's ANSESAL, was created. This Center (which would later change names several times) was a complex, modern communications system linking all police bodies, local army bases and commands, headquartered in the Presidential House.[7] Between 1950 and 1977, U.S. military assistance to Guatemala amounted to $40.5 million, and more than 3,000 Guatemalan cadets were trained on U.S. bases (Black et al. 1984:20). Nicaragua's *Escuela de Entrenamiento Básico de Infantería* (Infantry Basic Training School, or EEBI), where elite troops were trained, also depended on U.S. trainers and advisers.

U.S. government officials helped establish the *Consejo de Defensa Centroamericano* (Central American Defense Council, CONDECA) in late 1963. Its official aim was the collective security of the region, but in practice its attention was focused on safeguarding the member countries' internal security. Costa Rica was the only country not to join the council. In the 1960s, CONDECA paid some attention to "civic action" programs, which were thought to be effective against the "expansionist plans of communism" (LaFeber 1984:152). "Civic action" attempted to use the army's involvement in community activities to improve the public image of the armed forces. CONDECA fell into crisis after the 1969 war between El Salvador and Honduras, despite efforts by the U.S. Army Southern Command to revive it.

2. Central American reformism

All five Central American governments received recommendations on economic and social reform in the 1960s from foreign agencies and programs such as the Alliance for Progress and USAID and multilateral organizations such as the Inter-American Development Bank. These urgings had little to do with the reigning power relations in the region; they received a warmer welcome from the state agencies and the bureaucracy than from economic elites. These reformist policy recommendations were not generally seen as an integral component of development, but were made primarily as political concessions to the middle classes, to the bureaucracy, or to the army, and therefore as an added external factor in growth strategies. Only in Costa Rica, and for a short time in Honduras to a degree, did they become a constituent part of the state and its relationship to society.

Costa Rica

The armed movement of 1948 led by José Figueres and the *Partido Social Demócrata* (later *Partido de Liberación Nacional*, PLN), brought with it broad economic, social, and political reforms that were to reinforce democratization and mitigate the socially regressive effects of agroexport modernization, which came on the scene not much later. The nationalization of banking allowed credit resources to be enlisted for the policy goals of the groups whose interests the state expressed: a wide stratum of export-linked small and medium rural producers and the professionals associated with them. The *Instituto Costarricense de Electricidad* (ICE), created in 1949, encouraged the development of infrastructure and irrigation programs that improved growing conditions in the countryside. These measures, among others, helped promote investment outside the traditional agroexport sector. A simple tax reform allowed part of the profits that had until then remained in the hands of the coffee-growing oligarchy to be appropriated by the state; the funds went into rural infrastructure programs for electricity, sewage and roads.

Land distribution improved under the government's agrarian transformation policy: the Gini index of land concentration fell by 10 percent between 1950 and 1973, and by 16 percent on coffee lands (Rubén Soto 1982:209–10). Spontaneous colonization of un-cultivated land was the main pressure valve for landless workers until 1961, when a lands and colonization law made it illegal. The *Instituto de Tierras y Colonización* (ITCO) was established the following year to address the agrarian problems stemming from population growth, the exhaustion of the agricultural frontier, the shortage of industrial employment in the cities, and the fear that the example of the Cuban revolution could feed social protest. Despite its limited scope, the agrarian reform reflected a shift in the relationship between the state and the subaltern rural classes. The state's capacity to respond to the demand for land, and its particularized approach to the problem, enabled it to prevent the formation of strong peasant organizations as was the case in Honduras.

Having won a stable measure of political autonomy from the traditional ruling class and capturing a significant portion of coffee-generated wealth for the state, Figueres and the PLN were able to balance the imperative of distributing wealth in order to build mass consensus with the need to stimulate productivity and rationalize the nation's most important economic activities. While the initial economic restructuring programs had to be imposed on a resistant land-owning class, the most powerful elements of that class were further strengthened in the long term by the modernization of the coffee sector.[8] This process stands in marked contrast with other Latin American attempts at expropriating the agricultural surplus, in most of which the surplus was transferred to industrial capital in order to spur the process of import substitution, provoking a political confrontation with land-owning groups and exporters that left little room for agreement or negotiation.

The state's efficacy for reform, therefore, rested on its ability to neutralize the opposition of workers and small farmers through social welfare policies, land distribution, and the institutional legitimization of labor organizations. Workers who sympathized with the communist *Partido Vanguardia Popular* (People's Vanguard Party, PVP) found their organization outlawed, but in return they were offered social security, cooperatives, and unions.

Public employment grew fivefold in the course of twenty-five years, from 16,000 workers in 1949 to almost 87,000 in 1973. The state expanded its role in market regulation, price-setting for products and basic services, and the like (Sojo 1984:55; Mora y Arias 1984). Labor organization advanced further in the public sector than in the private. In 1973, 43.4 percent of public sector employees were organized, compared with only 5.5 percent in the private sector. Nevertheless, Costa Rica's overall rate of unionization, both rural and urban, was the highest in Central America (Barahona Riera 1980:36, 143–44; Sojo 1984:55–56). Rural unions enjoyed some growth as well, thanks to the relatively permissive institutional atmosphere; 20 percent of unionized workers in the early 1970s were in the rural sector.

The state's intervention in the reproduction processes of the subaltern classes—in the form of education, living standards, health care, and social security—generated a network of institutions that became legitimized channels for expressing social tensions and organizing consensus. The country's social profile improved: between 1961 and 1971, the share of income going to the wealthiest 20 percent of the population fell from 60 percent to 50.6 percent, while the GDP grew by 6.5 percent a year. Infant mortality declined from 83.2 per thousand to 43.1 per thousand, and life expectancy rose from 63.3 to 68.3 years. Heavy public spending on social welfare was made possible by, among other things, the low rate of security spending. In 1960, 18 percent of the central government's budget went to public education. That proportion rose to 22 percent in 1970 and 30 percent in 1976, while spending on security remained around 5 percent for the whole period (Céspedes 1979; Denton and Acuña 1984). At the end of the 1970s, defense spending represented less than 3 percent of Costa Rica's total public spending; it was three to four times higher in Guatemala, El Salvador, and Honduras. Costa Rica's spending on education, health and social security, meanwhile, was more than double that of Guatemala, and more than 40 percent higher than in El Salvador and Honduras.

The growth of the cooperative movement and of urban solidarity groups created the conditions for a small but increasing presence of women in training activities, and the growth of the overall labor market reinforced this trend. The political result of the state's reform policies was to channel mobilization into a system of parties and elections—to convert social mobilization into electoral mobilization. It must be noted, however, that this reorientation was not simply a matter of political sleight-of-hand: the masses' integration into the political system was actually accompanied by better living conditions, in marked contrast with the situation on the rest of the isthmus.

In addition to its impact on the budget, the abolition of the army deprived the bourgeois coffee growers and the ruling groups of what is usually, in Latin American politics, their basic tool of power. In its place they were offered policies aimed at accumulation and modernization. The army's disappearance thus endowed the political-reform system and the party regime with greater stability, as Vega Carballo (1989) has pointed out. Political parties did not have to compete with the military, as they did in Honduras, and could therefore control the pace and direction of social change. At the same time, the weakness of the corporative organizations—unions, chambers of commerce—expanded political parties' opportunities to serve as sites for articulating social interests. In sum, reformism endowed the state with a broad-based clientele that expressed its loyalty to the political system, most notably the electoral system, through its acceptance of institutional channels for proclaiming interests.

The proscription of the PVP for more than two decades served to ensure that social pressures would be channeled through the regime's own parties. An effective reformist system thus fused with a broad base of legitimacy, immune to threats from the right, having eliminated the army, and from the left, having proscribed communism. The political regime built a hegemonic bipartisan system for alternating control over the executive branch, with a stable congressional majority for the PLN until the beginning of the 1980s. This enabled the democratic principle of rotation in office to be combined with the political stability derived from control of the legislature.

Honduras

The agrarian reform process in Honduras, within the framework of a mild reformist military regime with a degree of social sensitivity, made it possible to mitigate social tensions in the countryside and to nourish expectations of the state's ability to solve conflicts and meet demands. The inadequacy of the traditional *Partido Nacional* (PN) and *Partido Liberal* (PL) in articulating the energy of the social forces that were proliferating in the wake of capitalist modernization increased the vulnerability of the representative political system and channeled social pressures along corporatist lines.

The democratizing design of the PL in the 1950s clashed with the rigid political system shaped by the traditional groups and the transnational banana companies through the conservative PN and segments of the armed forces. Under these conditions, pressures for democratization in the political realm did not necessarily imply socioeconomic democratization. The emphasis on political democratization did not extend to social relations and access to resources, and conversely, socioeconomic advances were not necessarily antagonistic to politically authoritarian regimes.

The predominance of the corporatist approach limited the political expression of social interests and enabled the state, particularly the army, to exercise a marked autonomy from the competing classes in the name of society as a whole. Due to the structural characteristics of Honduras, the scope and limits of this scheme were particularly evident in the agricultural sector, especially around the land issue.

With the support of multilateral organizations and U.S. government agencies, the Honduran state acquired powerful tools for intervening in economic life. Using agricultural and industrial credit policy, and developing the road and energy infrastructure, the state supported and promoted economic diversification and the country's integration into postwar capitalist modernization. This activity helped shape new business groups in livestock and cotton growing, and later in sugar, with outlooks and interests distinct from those of the traditional groups linked to the banana enclave.[9]

The liberal government of Ramón Villeda Morales passed the first agrarian reform law in 1962, in response to the rural mobilizations and strikes that had rocked parts of the country since 1954. Villeda's government reflected a broad-based alliance among modernizing groups (the incipient industrial bourgeoisie and parts of the urban middle class) and popular sectors, that expressed itself in measures like a labor code, public education, and agrarian reform.

The *Instituto Nacional Agrario* (INA) was created in 1961 to administer state land occupations and to take charge of the agrarian problem. INA expedited the recovery of national and public lands illegally taken over by landowners. Lands were awarded to their occupants, with state financial support for associative production. Soon after INA's creation, several peasant groups created the *Comité Central de Unificación Campesina*, which in August of 1962 was transformed into the *Federación Nacional de Campesinos de Honduras* (FENACH). A month after the formation of FENACH, the *Asociación Nacional de Campesinos de Honduras* (ANACH) was formed, with support from the AFL-CIO and its ally, the *Organización Regional Interamericana de Trabajadores* (ORIT). Government sponsorship rapidly gained it official recognition.

Landowners, alarmed by the agrarian mobilization, found an echo for their concerns in sectors of the army (Posas 1979). A 1963 military coup ushered in a repressive and antipopular military government that put a stop to agrarian reform. In 1969, evictions of Salvadoran peasants and farmers increased, especially in the border regions, with support from INA. Many Salvadorans chose to leave Honduras for fear of reprisals. The military expulsion of Salvadoran peasants, many of whom had lived in Honduras for decades, came in response to calls from landowners who expected to benefit from it. The Salvadorans' presence enabled the landowners to characterize as a conflict between nations what was actually a struggle between two social classes.

After a brief civilian interregnum, Gen. Oswaldo López Arellano led a second military coup in 1970. López's second presidency, in frank contrast with his first, injected new momentum into agrarian reform. The *Federación de Cooperativas de Reforma Agraria de Honduras* (FECORAH), in which the government would exercise a significant role through the INA, was formed in 1973. FECORAH had some 10,000 members by 1982. In November 1979, the *Frente Unido Nacional Campesino de Honduras* (National Peasant United Front, FUNACAMH) was founded in an attempt to unite all the peasant organizations.

Agrarian reform was mainly directed at lands belonging to the state. Some 73 percent of the land involved in the 1973–1974 reforms was public, 19 percent was private, and 8.5 percent belonged to *ejidos*. Military governments redistributed more than 240 thousand hectares between 1973 and 1982, to the benefit of almost 39,500 peasant families. It was, however, an agrarian reform of severely limited scope. More than 125,000 small-farming families—almost 75 percent of the total—were untouched by the program (PREALC 1983a:29). The first decade of agrarian reform covered 8 percent of the land, to the benefit of 13 percent of all rural families (Ruhl 1984).

Nevertheless, no other agrarian reform program until the Sandinista reform in Nicaragua had as broad a reach. Furthermore, the way the reform was carried out, using occupation as the criterion for assigning lands, had a strong impact on peasant organization. The agrarian struggles' main result paid more in encouraging organization than in reassigning lands.

Despite its limited scope, the agrarian distribution fed an intense rural mobilization and the development of a degree of peasant organization unparalleled in Central America. It developed a dynamic relationship with the state; attempts by the latter to control peasant organizations encountered an uneven capacity for response and resistance. By 1982, some 142,000 families belonged to the peasant organizations (Salgado 1992).

Still, it must be pointed out that the Honduran peasant movement was never able to become a force independent of the political parties. The most important organizations kept very close party ties, despite relatively high operational autonomy; even so, they were not able to insert the demand for agrarian reform into the parties' platforms. Moreover, the Honduran peasantry remained divided by its traditional political loyalties—mainly *Liberal* and *Nacional*—throughout the reform process, which weakened the peasant organizations and strengthened the state's ability to manipulate them. The organizations also had difficulty mobilizing broad rural masses in order to extend their base in the reform struggle. They tended rather to concentrate their efforts on the market consolidation of cooperatives and joint enterprises by peasant associations, and on expanding production.

The agrarian struggles and the state's reformist response to them had far-reaching implications in the context of global capitalist modernization. The urban labor movement also grew during the 1960s and 1970s, but was only occasionally able to coordinate with peasant mobilization. The rigidity of the traditional structure generated reformist sympathies among the new segments of the industrial bourgeoisie and widened the space for labor activism. Reformism, to the extent that it was a constituent part of the state, generally favored the more innovative sectors of society, while always staying within the parameters of a capitalist regime. The banana industry's character as both a foreign enclave and the most dynamic sector of the national economy, together with the weakness of the bourgeoisie and the limitations of popular organizing, helped endow the state, and particularly the armed forces, with substantial autonomy from society.

The United States and Central American reformism

Attempts at reform also enjoyed the encouragement and cooperation of the United States government and multilateral organizations. The aforementioned World Bank delegations of the 1950s were joined in the 1960s by USAID missions. At the operative, field level, projects like the Peace Corps and some religious missions helped the population generate new attitudes about their living conditions. In the 1950s, the aim of reformism was to put the Central American states and their economies in shape to join in the world economic growth that followed the end of the war, with a new form of capitalist organization, the transnational company, as its protagonist. The goals of political stability and hemispheric security were added in the 1960s, bringing with them changes in social policy and agrarian issues. But as these policy changes helped activate social tensions, their emphasis on social and economic modernization lost ground to the goal of hemispheric security, which in turn was firmly integrated into the logic of the cold war.

Reform recommendations included modernizing and strengthening all five countries' state apparatus. Very much in accordance with the political and intellectual climate of the times, the state was considered to be called upon to play an active role in stimulating the workings of the market, by supporting the development of new economic groups that could act as local counterparts to foreign investors and by helping to modernize the traditional groups. Banks and state institutions for promoting production emerged in all five countries during this period to channel foreign credit into new business activities and modern technologies. Agricultural schools and research and development centers were founded, either as part of higher education systems or as direct dependencies of the central government.

Guatemala, Honduras, and Nicaragua opened national planning offices in the early and middle 1950s, under the auspices of President Herbert Hoover's "Point IV." El Salvador joined them in 1962, and Costa Rica in 1963, on the recommendation of the Alliance for Progress (Wynia 1972). The creation of these offices was mainly a response to the international agencies' requirements for granting development financing. Their effectiveness was limited and their recommendations were poorly attended by the executive, but they did help improve the governments' capacity for information and analysis. Support for agrarian modernization led to the creation of agencies for agrarian reform in all of the region's countries, as described earlier.

U.S. government involvement also had more direct manifestations. Rosenberg (1987), describing the clout of U.S. government

Table 3.2
Central America: Taxation Coefficient (% of GDP)

	1955	1965	1975	1980
Costa Rica	10.1	11.8	12.7	11.5
El Salvador	10.8	9.9	12.0	11.1
Guatemala	8.5	7.6	9.5	8.6
Honduras	7.3	9.7	12.1	14.0
Nicaragua	10.8	10.2	10.6	10.6[a]

Source: Vilas 1990:123.
[a] 1979.

agencies in designing the economic programs of each Central American country, says, "The U.S. embassy's budget may be the only budget in those countries that is growing." This increased the possibility that it would be the U.S. government that would define these countries' economic and social agenda. The U.S. role was magnified by the weakness of most of the institutions (structures, budgets, programs, personnel) of the host country.

Reformism's fiscal tensions

The political limits of Central American reformism were also reflected in fiscal accounts. The ruling groups' reluctance to pay taxes in proportion to their income and capital held the Central American states to a meager tax base, which led to crisis as the public sector extended its function of promoting economic and social development (Table 3.2).

The growth of public spending was targeted at the consumption and earning demands of middle and upper groups, leaving out the majority of the population. Although lower income groups supply most of the users of hospitals, public schools, literacy campaigns, vaccinations, drinking-water programs and the like, these services clearly remained on a symbolic level for the majority of the population, except in Costa Rica (Table 3.3). By the end of the 1970s, Central American governments' yearly expenditures toward the health of each citizen came to an average of five dollars and change, and less than fifteen dollars on their education. When Costa Rica is excluded from the average, the annual figure sinks to $4.55 on health and $9.22 on education.

Table 3.3

Central America: Per Capita Public Spending on Health and Education (in 1970 Dollars)

	Costa Rica		El Salvador		Guatemala		Honduras		Nicaragua		Central America	
	Health	Education	Health	Education	Health	Education	Health	Education	Health	Education	Health	Education
1970	2.2	20.6	4.3	8.3	3.6	5.8	3.9	8.6	5.9	9.2	3.9	10.5
1975	5.7	26.6	4.7	9.3	3.5	5.6	5.4	9.3	4.4	10.1	7.7	12.2
1979	8.1	35.1	4.2	9.6	4.3	7.0	6.4	10.1	3.3	10.2	5.3	14.4

Source: SIECA 1981 and author's calculations.

Table 3.4

Central America: Budget Deficits, 1970-80

	Deficit[a]			Deficit/spending[b]			Deficit growth[c]	
	1970	1975	1980	1970	1975	1980	1970-75	1975-80
Costa Rica	21	38	339	6.8	8.7	42.4	12.7	54.9
El Salvador	22	42	195	7.2	8.9	32.3	13.5	36.1
Guatemala	56	20	365	12.5	3.4	33.0	-18.8	79.1
Honduras	48	43	199	21.8	12.1	34.3	-2.2	35.8
Nicaragua	24	146	136	11.4	32.1	23.2	42.9	-1.4
Central America	172	288	1233	12.0	13.0	33.0	9.6	40.9

Source: IICA/FLACSO 1991: 111-113.

[a] Millions of 1980 dollars.

[b] Budget deficit as a percentage of central government spending.

[c] Annual rates.

The combination of increasing public spending and a fragile tax structure generated a rapid growth in fiscal deficits (Table 3.4). An adequate tax reform could have prevented this, but that would have meant confrontation with the traditional ruling groups. Those reforms that were attempted (Nicaragua in 1962 and Guatemala during Méndez Montenegro's presidency, for example), were timid and insufficient. The growing gap between ordinary revenues and expenses was covered by foreign debt, which increased—as it did in the rest of the hemisphere as well—thanks to high international liquidity of the 1970s.

Central America's total external public debt more than quadrupled between 1960 and 1970, from $203 million to $879 million; it quadrupled again between 1970 and 1976, to $3,643 million, and grew 2.5 times more between 1976 and 1980, to $8.51 billion (IADB 1965, 1980; IICA/FLACSO 1991). Several factors explain the rapid growth of debt in the 1970s. The foremost was the oil shock, which affected all five countries equally. The rest of the factors are specific to each country. In the second half of the decade, the rise of political violence led to increasing military spending in Nicaragua and El Salvador, eating up growing slices of their new debt. In Costa Rica, the government's decision to maintain spending despite the deceleration of economic growth seems to have exerted upward pressure on the deficit.

Across Central America—except for Costa Rica, where social spending was a priority—public debt was contracted mainly to finance state subsidies to domestic and foreign private enterprise and to middle- and high-income social groups, in the form of lower taxes, cheap imports, and security and defense spending against social protest. Domestic prices that in previous decades had been kept under relative control grew rapidly as a result of rising foreign prices, especially in foodstuffs; the impact was felt mostly in lower-income sectors (IICA/FLACSO 1991:99-100). The agroexport and industrialized sectors' high import ratio weighed heavily on trade balances. Although the Central American power groups cannot be blamed for the oil shock, the mode of development they chose increased their economies' vulnerability to the changes in the world economy.

Table 3.5 traces the rapid shift from the price stability of the 1960s to the relatively high inflation, by the standards of the time, of the

1970s. High levels of debt and the inflationary pressures they unleashed marked the limits of Central American reformism; fiscal tensions made the model's political rigidities ever plainer, and increased both the level of social dissatisfaction and its manifestations.

3. The new church

The social and political transformations Latin America underwent in the 1960s had their effect on the continent's churches, and on the Catholic Church in particular. Pope John XXIII's encyclical *Mater et Magistra*, his successor Paul VI's *Pacem in Terris*, and the Second Vatican Council's *Gaudium et Spes* apostolic constitution introduced wide-ranging changes in pastoral activity and in the Church's approach to social problems. *Gaudium et Spes* declared the independence of political from theological judgments: no Christian could legitimize a political choice through "truths of the faith," a formulation that could not but severely undermine the authority of conservative religious hierarchies. One significant element in the Church's critique of capitalism was a partial return to Patristic doctrine, which stressed the collective origin of worldly goods and revived the Church's traditional condemnation of the profit-based economy. The demarcating of the political and social spheres from the strictly religious effectively softened Church attacks on leftist groups and legitimized the involvement of Church workers in social reform movements against the most naked expressions of capitalism. Doctrinal renewal, restoring boundaries between judgments of faith and theology and political and social doctrine, in turn opened the door to cooperation between Christians and Marxists in political and social fields—a matter of controversy in Europe since the end of World War II.

The renewal of Catholic ministry placed special emphasis on direct contact between the "People of God" and the gospel. Bible reading and commentary spread to an unprecedented degree, with help from literacy campaigns carried out by Church workers. The Vatican's recommendation that mass be celebrated in the language of each country helped narrow the historical gulf between the people and the Church; the traditional sermon often gave way to dialogue between priest and parishioners. The 1968 Latin Ameri-

Table 3.5
Median Annual Inflation Rates, 1960s and 1970s (Consumer Prices)

	1960-72	1972-77
Costa Rica	2.4	13.4
El Salvador	0.5	12.8
Guatemala	0.7	13.8
Honduras	2.6	9.1
Nicaragua	1.8	12.6
Central America	1.4	12.8

Source: SIECA 1981.

can bishops' conference at Medellín adapted the Vatican's new guidelines to the continent and reaffirmed the past few years' collective experience. To the more socially sensitive sectors of the Central American Church, this was a green light for a wider involvement in a ministry of social change.

The growing presence of some Evangelical denominations, especially in Guatemala, also influenced this reorientation in the Catholic Church. Unlike the traditional Catholic ministry, which confronted indigenous communities' own traditional religiosity, the Protestant denominations avoided conflicts with native religious expressions while putting much of their energy into competing with the Catholic Church. This approach facilitated their entrance into village life, or at least let them avoid repeating some of the early confrontations that the Catholics had experienced. Competition with the Protestants does not fully explain the reform-ist tilt of pastoral work, but it may have been one reason why rural Catholic pastoral work adopted the organizational and development styles that would in time help make them a significant, and increasingly radical, social force.

An appraisal of this new Catholic ministry's involvement in the Central American revolutionary crisis should be conducted on two levels. First, it contributed to a general mass awakening, especially among the rural masses. More particularly, it led people to collectively reject living conditions that, as a result of this same pastoral activity, they were beginning to see as iniquitous and unacceptable. The activities of the Christian base communities, which linked community development to social ideas derived from new readings of the gospel, contributed significantly to the breakdown of the rural social order. Secondly, the new ministry helped recruit a significant number of parishioners as well as priests and nuns into the revolutionary struggle.

The Church hierarchy's attitudes toward both levels of activity varied widely, and this influenced the scope and effectiveness of pastoral activity. The hierarchy generally supported the first level, while on the second it wavered, with very few exceptions, between ambivalence and condemnation.

The impact of the new religious message on large segments of the Central American population is impossible to minimize. The Church's traditional conformist and legitimizing role was replaced, in many places, by an approach based on questioning society and spelling out its latent conflicts. The development of new theological concepts (the notion of "structural sin," for example, to denounce the objectively unjust situations created by capitalism); the emphasis of many theologians and clergy that the Christian commitment implies a commitment to revolution; the celebration of the priest Camilo Torres's experience with the Colombian guerrillas and the elevation of his death to a martyrdom: all helped build what became, for large parts of the peasantry and the urban petty bourgeoisie, a bridge that enabled them to reject the state of things and join in collective confrontation with ruling powers. The new ministry broke with the Central American Catholic tradition of submission to established political power—meaning the oligarchy and the military—and in its stead legitimized social protest and insurrection.

The political efficacy of the new ministry depended in large part on its ability to fit into the Church's institutional structure and to gain the protection of the local hierarchy. El Salvador was the clearest case: the support of the archbishop of San Salvador, Msgr. Oscar Arnulfo Romero, for the new generation of priests and lay people working in his diocese—like that of his predecessor, Monsignor Chávez—was central to the new ministry's ability to expand across much of the country and to pose a growing challenge to political power. On the other hand, the need for support from the hierarchy was one of the new ministry's limitations. Opposition from a given diocese's bishop could put a stop to the renewal process in that area, for priests, religious, and lay people who would not comply could be excluded from the Church community. The Church hierarchy's conservatism in Ahuachapán, Santa Ana, and Sonsonate, El Salvador's eastern departments where the 1932 rebellion had its deepest roots, helps explain the absence of evidence of the pastoral renewal in these areas. Similarly, the priests of Guatemala's Quiché diocese lost much of their institutional legitimacy when their own Church hierarchy refused to back them against government repression. Left unprotected, they and their bishop were forced to leave the country.

In other social organizations, such as political parties and trade unions, internal dissension can often give rise to new organizations. While this is not impossible in the Church, a "new church"—even a new parish—is much more difficult to launch than a new party or union. Staying within the organization is therefore much more important for a religious leader than for a labor or party leader. Still, the fact that many of the priests and religious associated with the new ministry were foreigners and members of the "regular clergy"—Spanish Jesuits and Brothers of the Sacred Heart, and American Capuchins, Benedictines, and Maryknolls, among others—helped limit the authority of the bishops that opposed or distrusted them.

The new ministry spread unevenly across the region. Its influence was relatively strong in parts of El Salvador, Guatemala, and Honduras, weaker in Nicaragua, and not very significant in Costa Rica.

Guatemala

Acción Católica (AC) had been present in Guatemala since the late 1940s. At first, AC's fight against indigenous religiosity only deepened the instability that successful Protestant missionaries and some political parties had brought to the villages. Although AC's effects varied from village to village, its clearest result was the weakening of the traditional indigenous religious hierarchy, which it regarded as a negative influence. The democratic governments of Juan José Arévalo and Jacobo Arbenz encountered some tensions with the Catholic hierarchy, but the hierarchy's relations with the government improved after Arbenz was toppled by the 1954 invasion. The number of priests in the country grew quickly, from

195 in 1954 to 242 in 1955, and to 423 in 1965. The number of nuns grew from 96 to 354 between 1950 and 1965 (Sierra Pop 1982; Berryman 1984:183). The increase mainly reflected the arrival of a great number of priests and nuns from abroad: by the late 1960s, only half of Guatemala's priests were Guatemalan. The growing number of priests, with their decreasing dependence on the hierarchy, made way for a progressive decentralization of Church work. In 1968 there were 160 Catholic schools in the country, with about 41,000 students. Slightly more than half of them were in Guatemala City, but the rest were distributed across the highlands, contributing to changes in traditional village life.

Foreign priests, less tied to the Guatemalan hierarchy and culture, promoted communal and local organization alongside the work of *Acción Católica*. This reorientation was partly an effort to put into practice the Second Vatican Council's "preferential option for the poor," but it also reflected the need to compete with Protestant missionaries, who were very active in the highlands. Priests began in the early 1960s to emphasize organizing cooperatives and social improvement programs; the "social training workshops" that they started in 1962 were commonplace across Central America by 1965. They built a widespread network of literacy trainers and radio schools in native languages. The priests' work was reinforced by social workers and by the growing presence of opposition political parties, especially the Christian Democrats, and by the ethnic revivalist work of some United States anthropologists (Carmack 1991:38, 70-71).[10] All of these new features of the rural dynamic contributed to indigenous people's aspirations, consciousness of identity, and confrontational approach to the government.

When sharp conflicts between priests and the authorities began to arise in Quiché in 1978, some priests came into contact with guerrilla organizations, and a few joined them. In July 1980, government and landowner attacks forced the bishop and priests of Quiché to leave the country in fear for their lives, after the senior Church hierarchy in Guatemala City showed little disposition to come to their defense. In the twenty-month period between January 1980 and August 1981, ninety-one priests and sixty-four nuns were forced to flee Guatemala by government repression and the indifference of the Catholic hierarchy; six Catholic radio stations were destroyed, and forty-two religious training centers were closed (Sierra and Siebers 1990).

El Salvador

The process that led to the formation of El Salvador's popular organizations was closely tied to pastoral work, initially in the form of Catholic cooperation with the *Partido Demócrata Cristiano* and Church involvement in organizing cooperatives in the 1950s. Caritas Clubs, offering job training, activities, and evangelism courses for housewives and youths, appeared in 1965; the PDC also offered training courses, with help from the Church and USAID. In the late 1960s the PDC began to organize agricultural workers, especially peasants. Church support was critical to these first efforts: under the restrictions the political system imposed on the opposition parties in the countryside, the priests and nuns themselves had to become activists and organizers. The first "communal unions" appeared in early 1968 and multiplied quickly. By the middle of that year, some twenty of them, representing some 4,000 small farmers (not wage workers) merged to form the *Unión Comunal Salvadoreña* (UCS).

Influenced by the Medellín bishops' conclave and the effects of the war with Honduras, the Salvadoran Catholic hierarchy in 1969 took an unprecedented position in defense of the peasants and issued a modest appeal for agrarian reform. In a pastoral letter, the Salvadoran Bishops' Conference called on landowners to support fairer land distribution; they urged them to sell some of their land to the peasants who worked it and to give up lands lying idle. They also announced that the San Vicente diocese had donated land of its own to a private agrarian reform project. The statement had a major impact on public opinion, to the alarm of the large landholders.

The greatest impact, however, belonged to the Christian base communities that had been organizing since the late 1960s in Suchitoto, San Salvador, Cuscatlán, Chalatenango, and San Vicente. These communities, marked by a strongly prophetic character, were to earn a major presence among the peasants. Their challenge to traditional structures through the new pastoral practices, and their new interpretations of Biblical texts, forged powerful ties between peasant Christian identity and social activism.

The appearance of the *Federación Cristiana de Campesinos Salvadoreños* (FECCAS) in 1969 marked a turning point in this process. FECCAS was founded as a federation of peasant leagues that had begun as affiliates of the *Unión de Obreros Cristianos* (Christian Workers' Union, or UNOC), created in 1960 with the support of the *Central Latinoamericana de Sindicatos Cristianos* (Latin American Organization of Christian Trade Unions, CLASC). After corruption and government intervention led to the dissolution of UNOC, the peasants' leagues were left without representation. In 1974, FECCAS and other organizations created the *Frente de Acción Popular Unificada* (Unified Popular Action Front, FAPU), which they later left to start the *Bloque Popular Revolucionario* (BPR).

The priests' active role in founding social organizations and in bringing them together with the revolutionary groups was not limited to BPR. Christians participated heavily in the mass organizations tied to FARN, at least two of whose founding members were Baptist ministers. ERP was founded by elements of the Communist Youth and former members of the youth wing of the Christian Democratic party.

The Jesuit-run *Universidad Centroamericana* played an important role in radicalizing the younger generations of Christians. It actively backed the thwarted 1976 agrarian reform program, and set up support groups for the efforts at change in the countryside and for the new pastoral methods. The government responded by arresting and deporting several priests known for leading this work.

Monsignor Chávez, Archbishop of San Salvador and head of the country's Catholic Church, had greeted the new forms of ministry and the commitment of priests and nuns with sympathy, but the appointment of Msgr. Oscar Arnulfo Romero to succeed him became a turning point in the Church's involvement in social and political mobilization. Monsignor Romero courageously condemned the ruling groups' primitivism and their transformation of the government and armed forces into instruments for defending privilege and social exploitation. Romero's appointment coincided with an escalation of violence and repression against priests. Between February and May 1977, ten priests had been murdered, another ten had been expelled from the country—some of them after being tortured—and several more had been arrested. Romero took a very active part in the defense of priests and nuns persecuted by the authorities and hurt by the repression, and endorsed Christian participation in the struggle for social change.

In March 1980, Romero was assassinated by a "death squad" as he held mass in a chapel before dozens of communicants. He had been Archbishop for less than three years. Investigations by United Nations-connected organizations years later determined that the operation was carried out on the direct orders of Maj. Roberto D'Aubuisson (Truth Commission 1993:142).

Nicaragua

Christian renewal had a smaller presence in Nicaragua, where the Church hierarchy's support for the Somoza regime remained strong until 1970. The Christian base community movement spread more slowly and unevenly. "Delegates of the Word," led mainly by Capuchin priests, appeared in the 1960s in parts of the north-central region and the agricultural frontier (CIERA 1981; Cáceres et al. 1983:83ff). They linked religious teaching with training in literacy and techniques for improving the peasants' health conditions and farming practices. The movement spread rapidly between 1972 and 1977; an estimated 900 Delegates of the Word were active in the eastern department of Zelaya in 1975 (Samandú and Jansen 1982; Berryman 1984:70).

The *Centro de Educación y Promoción Agraria* (CEPA), founded in 1969, carried out intensive pastoral work by organizing workshops, preaching, and raising consciousness. By mid-1970, many of CEPA's members were helping the FSLN organize poor peasants and wage workers in the countryside; they backed land seizures and helped found the *Asociación de Trabajadores del Campo* (ATC) in the closing months of the struggle against Somoza.

In 1970 a degree of change came to the hierarchy with the appointment of Msgr. Miguel Obando y Bravo as archbishop of Managua and head of the Catholic Church in Nicaragua. Himself the scion of a rural family and a member of the Salesian order, Obando y Bravo distanced himself from the government and accepted the new forms of ministry that were emerging in his diocese. By 1972, base communities were operating in some 50 Managua parishes, and their number increased after the earthquake late that year. Still, Obando behaved cautiously. His aim was above all to preserve the Church's independence from temporal power, whether of the state or that of social and political opposition groups.[11]

The Catholic hierarchy's support for the Somoza regime until the 1970s, and its ambivalent attitude thereafter, limited the scope of the new ministry by depriving it of institutional support. In Guatemala and El Salvador the intersection between revolutionaries and Christians was the result of the radicalization of the ministry; in Nicaragua it was not. A young generation of Christians took up reciprocal initiatives with the FSLN after the Managua earthquake in December 1972, around the Jesuit-run *Universidad Centroamericana* and several base communities in Managua parishes. These experiences gave many young middle-class Christians an opportunity to participate in community action and to discuss their country's problems, from which their class position had until now buffered them. Many became disenchanted with the existing political parties, which they regarded as either ineffectual or complicit with the regime; they began to show an interest in the activities of the FSLN and tried to get in touch with its members. The FSLN greeted these efforts with interest, adopting what was to become a successful strategy of openness to these groups. Within a few years the majority of the Christian student movement leaders were involved, in one way or another, in the Sandinista struggle (Molina 1981; Serra 1985; Carrión 1986). Their experience with the ministry of Father Ernesto Cardenal on the islands of Solentiname, in the south of Lake Nicaragua, helped persuade many youths to join the "Southern front" of the FSLN's *tercerista* tendency (Cardenal 1979).[12]

The evangelical churches, too, began to get involved in social action after the 1972 earthquake, although with slighter political implications. The *Comité Evangélico para la Ayuda al Desarrollo* (CEPAD) actively moved evangelical churches into a greater commitment to the temporal needs of their members, and into transcending the competition and rivalry that separated the numerous (often very small) denominations. With a lower political profile than that of the Catholic communities, CEPAD's social action helped create community development projects—cooperatives, social services, and the like—that helped reinforce social organization.

Overall, Nicaragua shows marked contrasts with Central America's other revolutionary processes. In Nicaragua, some segments of the Christian movement joined an already-existing revolutionary movement, while in Guatemala and El Salvador they were among its founding elements.

Honduras

The main activity of the Honduran Church took the form of an ethical indictment of social conditions. The erratic agrarian reforms of successive military regimes widened the space available for rural ministry, although government tolerance did not mean protection against resistance from landowners or repression by local military chiefs. Delegates of the Word began to appear in the 1960s, and their influence spread during the 1970s. Like their Nicaraguan counterparts, they combined gospel preaching with reflection on living conditions in the countryside, and their identity as natives of the areas in which they worked rendered their message all the more persuasive. Housewives' clubs allowed women to escape the narrow bounds of the household and begin to think about social problems. In 1975 the national *Clubes de Amas de Casa* (Housewives' Clubs, CAC) broke with *Caritas*, the Catholic organization that had given birth to them; some of their members in 1978 helped found the *Federación Hondureña de Mujeres Campesinas* (FEHMUC), which offered training programs for women of the *Unión Nacional Campesina* (UNC). The *Asociación Nacional de Mujeres Campesinas* (ANAMUC), tied to the ANACH, had existed since 1974 but was relatively inactive.

With its combination of propheticism and developmentalism, the new motion in the Church encouraged growing ties with peasant organizations of a social-Christian political bent, particularly the UNC. Christian groups were active in land occupations, contributing to the climate of social agitation. Landowners, threatened by peasant demands for land, held some priests responsible for the growth of rural activism: priests, nuns, and lay people involved in peasant ministry were accused daily of being communists and guerrillas. A group of local landowners and politicians in the cattle-raising Olancho region placed a price on the head of the local bishop and several priests. The clergymen were killed in June

1975, along with several lay workers, in an operation led by a local landowner (Blanco y Valverde 1987).

The greatest contribution of the Honduran Church's new ministry was in peasant organization and community development. Peasant organizations were not the creations of pastoral work, but the strength and effectiveness some of them achieved unquestionably owes much to the social radicalization promoted by the new evangelism, with its legitimization of peasant resistance. "Liberation theology" as such was not widespread, perhaps because of the hierarchy's own involvement in the new pastoral practices—the doctrinal aspects of liberation theology never won the support of the Catholic hierarchy loyal to the Vatican. The new ministry created tensions with the hierarchy, which was torn between its loyalty to Church members persecuted by landowners and the military and its desire to maintain flexible relations with the government.

The new ministry saw its greatest growth between 1972 and 1975, which coincided with the period of greatest activity in agrarian reform. The limitations of this process and the obstacles to the peasant ministry, along with the repression of the popular movement that arose in the early 1980s, led some priests and laity into active involvement with political action and some thwarted attempts to launch guerrilla struggles.[13]

Costa Rica

The low profile of the Costa Rican Church in social affairs contrasts with the reformist activism of the PLN. The Church, allied with the Calderón Guardia government that was overthrown in 1948, was forced to redefine its relations with the new political authorities and the institutional system they put into place. The hierarchy's firm vertical control prohibited direct involvement in the "social question"—which was in any case less pressing than in the countries to the north. After an initial period of disorientation, the Costa Rican Catholic Church actively cooperated with state reforms, helping to design some social policies, train officials, etc., and opting for a role mediated through government agencies rather than direct action (Opazo Bernales 1987). However, the weakness of the grassroots church movement limited the scope of Church involvement and diluted the potential for action autonomous from the state. Some of the evangelical denominations were able to take advantage of this ambiguity in the Catholic Church during the 1980s.

FOUR

A Lost Decade?

It was the intersection of all the factors examined in the preceding chapters that steered the political dynamics of El Salvador, Guatemala, and Nicaragua in the direction of revolution and counterrevolution. After the reforms of the 1970s were thwarted, the groups that initiated or supported them were repressed, and the electoral system proved powerless to change anything, many became convinced that revolution was the only possible course.

Neither in El Salvador nor in Guatemala did revolutionary options gain state power by force of arms. In Guatemala, the armed forces' resistance to the peace process keeps armed confrontation alive as a latent factor even today. In El Salvador, prolonged and difficult negotiations, with help from the United Nations and the international community, afforded conditions enabling the integration of the FMLN into the institutional political system after the conflict ended. Thoughout the 1980s the FSLN tried to transform Nicaragua's economic structure, broaden popular participation, redirect development and win the counterrevolutionary war. The February 1990 elections ended the Sandinista government, and events since then are reversing very important elements of the Sandinistas' social transformations.

The peculiar denouement of the Nicaraguan and Salvadoran revolutionary processes, and perhaps that of Guatemala as well in

Table 4.1
Central America: Recent Behavior of Some Economic Indicators

	1981–1990 (Annual cumulative variation, in %)					
	Costa Rica	El Salvador	Guatemala	Honduras	Nicaragua	Central America
Per capita GDP	-5.0	-15.3	-18.0	-14.2	-40.8	-17.2
Exports, f.o.b.	35.6	-50.4	-19.5	2.7	-14.3	-9.4
Imports, c.i.f.	41.7	29.0	13.9	-3.4	-25.0	10.5
Cumulative trade balance (in millions of US$)	-942	-3,058	-2,918	-1,066	-4,592	-12,576

Source: CEPAL 1990, 1992a.

the near future, raises a number of questions. What did these processes achieve? Who benefited from them? What is their legacy? This chapter explores some answers.

1. Economic crisis

Revolution and counterrevolution emerged in the context of the economic crisis that had ensnared all five republics, regardless of their governments' ideology, since the end of the 1970s. The crisis in the Central American economies long predates the outbreak of the international crisis of 1982. Economic growth had begun to slow in 1977 and 1978, and by 1979 symptoms of stagnation began to appear. In 1980 and 1981, a generalized contraction emerged and imbalances worsened, developments that were reflected in deepening fiscal and current account deficits, growing monetary volume, overvalued exchange rates, and rising domestic prices. Per capita income in Costa Rica, Guatemala, and Honduras in 1983 had retreated to its 1972 value, while in El Salvador and Nicaragua it was back to that of the early 1960s. The region's political instability added to the economic tension, especially in the private sector, and encouraged massive capital flight (Glower 1987; Timossi 1989).

The international crisis of 1982 dovetailed with and reinforced Central America's internal sources of crisis: Central America's per capita GDP shrank twice as fast throughout the 1980s as that of Latin America and the Caribbean as a whole. In the three countries battered by military conflict, it fell even further, with Nicaragua's falling twice as far as that of Central America overall (Table 4.1).

The value of foreign trade remained practically stagnant throughout the decade. In fact, leaving out Costa Rica, which had the most active foreign trade, it actually fell by almost nine percent (Table 4.2). The value of exports shrank as a result of declining physical volume and unfavorable world prices. The value of imports, in contrast, grew everywhere except in Nicaragua. At the end of the 1980s the value of intraregional trade stood at less than half its level at the beginning of the decade, after almost tripling in the 1970s. Intraregional trade fell from 23 percent of Central America's total trade volume to little more than 12 percent. Such trade was almost entirely confined to El Salvador, Guatemala, and Costa Rica, which between them accounted for almost 75 percent

Table 4.2
Central American Foreign Trade
(f.o.b. Exports Plus c.i.f. Imports)

	Value (Millions of US$)			Share (%)		
	1981	1985	1990	1981	1985	1990
Costa Rica	2,093	1,940	3,199	21.0	23.0	31.5
El Salvador	1,696	1,574	1,692	17.4	18.7	16.7
Guatemala	2,831	2,137	2,639	29.1	25.4	26.0
Honduras	1,683	1,669	1,718	17.8	19.8	16.9
Nicaragua	1,431	1,099	902	14.7	13.1	8.9
Central America	9,734	8,419	10,150	100.0	100.0	100.0

Source: See Table 4.1.

of the value of intraregional transactions at the beginning of the 1980s and almost 84 percent in 1990.

The Nicaraguan economy shrank furthest. Nicaragua was hurt not only by the war but also by the loss of financing from multilateral organizations, the economic weight of efforts to shift the production structure, and the costs of reorienting trade under the United States embargo. War was a factor in other countries as well, but no other economy was damaged on the same scale. The treatment El Salvador and Guatemala received from the United States government stood in sharp contrast with the military, economic and financial aggression that Washington unleashed on the Sandinista regime beginning with Ronald Reagan's inauguration in January 1981. The total war expenditure for the regional governments is now estimated at almost 18 billion U.S. dollars, in a country whose GDP at the end of the 1980s amounted to between $1.2 and 1.4 billion (INEC 1989, table 5.2). The cost of the war in El Salvador is estimated at about $6 billion (Karl 1992).

The region's foreign debt more than doubled during this decade, and almost quadrupled for Nicaragua, which absorbed 61 percent of the growth of the overall regional debt and almost half of all debt in 1990 alone (Table 4.3).

The public sector's ability to mobilize resources did not improve compared with previous decades, except in Nicaragua. In that country, however, the extraordinary increase in public spending relative to revenue—to pay for the expanding public sector, invest-

Table 4.3
Central America: Total Foreign Debt (in Millions of Dollars)

Country	1981	1985	1990
Costa Rica	2687	4140	3874
El Salvador	1471	1980	2226
Guatemala	1148[a]	2536[a]	2386[a]
Honduras	1588[a]	3034[a]	3526[a]
Nicaragua	2566	4936	10616
Central America	9460	16626	22628

Source: See Table 4.1.
[a]Total foreign public debt.

ment programs, and the war, and to make up for the falling earnings from nationalized foreign trade—made for rapid growth in the budget deficit (Table 4.4). In Guatemala, attempts by President Vinicio Cerezo's civilian government to introduce moderate tax reform failed in the face of belligerent business opposition and lack of support from the army.

The inflationary pressures that had been building up since the 1970s exploded in the 1980s, particularly in Nicaragua. The war effort, along with the growth of public investment in large production projects, brought on hyperinflation by mid-decade (Table 4.5). In Costa Rica, the inflation of the early part of the decade was brought under control through early adjustment policies. Real wages declined everywhere, but in Nicaragua they experienced a collapse that could not be compensated by the increase registered at the end of the decade—the highest growth in wages in the entire region in a three-to-seven-year period.

In Guatemala, open unemployment in the formal labor market grew from around three percent of the EAP to almost 13 percent during this decade; in El Salvador the figure grew from 16 percent to more than 25 percent, and in Nicaragua from 18 percent to almost 30 percent (IICA/FLACSO 1991:213, 153).

Crisis and macroeconomic adjustment

All five Central American countries resorted to stabilization programs between 1979 and 1982. These efforts, based as they were

Table 4.4
Central America: Tax Revenue and Budget Deficits (as Percentage of GDP)

	Tax revenues			Budget deficit		
	1981-83	1985-87	1988-90	1981-83	1985-87	1988-90
Costa Rica	13.4	14.4	14.4	3.5	2.4	3.7
El Salvador	10.9	11.9	8.4	7.5	3.5	3.6
Guatemala	7.0	7.1	7.8	4.6	1.8	2.8
Honduras	12.3	13.4	13.4	9.8	7.4	6.9
Nicaragua	21.6	26.9	19.5	17.2	19.2	19.9

Source: See Table 4.1.

on the misconception that this was a momentary crisis and would soon be over, were belated and incomplete. The policies' effects bore little resemblance to their intent, but they did have severe social consequences, contributing to a profound recession and even further damaging the already precarious living conditions of large segments of the population.

Faced with a prolonged and deepening crisis, the Central American governments joined almost all of Latin America by mid-decade in introducing structural adjustment programs. The Costa Rican and Honduran versions were backed by agreements with and funding from the World Bank.[1]

The U.S. Agency for International Development, through the system of conditionality, played an important role in the decision to resort to adjustment measures and to homogenize the various governments' economic policies (Timossi 1989:41ff; Sojo 1991; Cuenca 1992; Rosa 1993). In February 1982, for example, after granting Costa Rica's government an initial disbursement from the Economic Support Fund (ESF), USAID conditioned further disbursements on the adoption of legal reforms allowing repatriation of foreign funds and the financing of private enterprise without intervention by the nationalized banking system. In August 1983, the U.S. government held up the delivery of already-approved funds when the Costa Rican legislature proved reluctant to reform its banking law.

The previous June USAID had delayed an already-approved credit line of $20 million (U.S. dollars), while the IMF coincidentally held up $609 million, until the Costa Rican government agreed to reform tax policy in line with the two agencies' wishes.

Table 4.5
Central America: Variation in Prices and Wages (in Percent)

	Prices[a]			Wages[b]		
	1981-83	1985-87	1988-90	1981-83	1985-87	1988-90
Costa Rica	53.3	14.5	18.8	-5.5	1.9	-0.7
El Salvador	13.2	26.4	20.5	-11.6	-8.1	-8.3
Guatemala	5.4	22.6	21.2	8.3	-8.4	-2.5
Honduras	8.9	3.4	12.5	2.6	-3.3	2.2
Nicaragua	26.5	604.3	8836.9	-11.3	-41.8	28.3

Source: See Table 4.1.
[a]Median annual consumer price variation.
[b]Median annual real wage variation deflated by consumer price index.

In March 1984, USAID conditioned the delivery of US$140 million from the ESF on blocking a law to help cooperatives purchase several public companies that were being privatized.

Similar pressures were brought to bear on Honduras. In 1989, USAID froze delivery of $70 million until that country's government signed an agreement with the IMF—pending since 1984—that steeply devalued the lempira, increased tax revenues, drastically cut government spending and public employment, and broadly deregulated economic activity.

These programs had uneven results. Even where they were successful, their success often reflected different factors or mechanisms than those intended, or involved higher costs than initially estimated. Their main impact was on the growth of nontraditional exports to markets outside the region. Between 1983 and 1989, nontraditional exports from Costa Rica grew from 39 percent of total exports to 52 percent, and the proportion shipped to countries outside Central America grew from 15 percent to 43 percent. Guatemala's total nontraditional exports jumped from 21 percent to 41 percent, with those shipped outside the isthmus growing from 9 percent to 21 percent. In El Salvador extraregional shipments grew from 6 percent to 15 percent, and in Honduras from 20 percent to 28 percent. Costa Rica's nontraditional exports consist primarily of agricultural products: pineapples, melons, tropical plants, fresh flowers, fish and shrimp, and garment assembly. Guatemala's chief items are garment assembly, handicrafts, fresh flowers, vegetables, and fresh, frozen, and canned fruit—all, with the possible exception of handicrafts, products with a very low aggregate value (Timossi 1993; Arancibia 1993).

Whatever successes these policies scored, on the other hand, owe more to exchange rate devaluations, specific preferential stimuli, and special terms for foreign financing than to the removal of tariff protection and the structural reforms urged by the adjustment programs (Walker 1991; Caballeros 1993). The success of Costa Rica, unmatched by any of its neighbors on the isthmus, is closely linked to the extraordinary increase in economic aid the country received in this period, especially from the United States. Vunderink (1990–1991) goes so far as to assert that it was only these high levels of aid that prevented the collapse of the Costa Rican economy. Costa Rica became the second-largest per capita recipient of U.S. foreign aid (after Israel) once it accepted the conditions of the international financial agencies and USAID. Although the nonorthodox elements in the Costa Rican adjustment programs are not to be ignored—there was certainly an "anti-orthodox bias" in the country's institutional structure that stressed the need to build social consensus (Fürst 1989)—it is reasonable to conclude that the economy's immediate recovery owed more to a massive influx of funds on relatively generous terms than to the diversification and redirection of exports.

The adjustment programs did permit budget deficit reductions and a certain amount of control over inflationary pressures linked to trade imbalances. But the overwhelming focus on structural adjustment put regional integration, with all its potential for ending the crisis and reviving development, on the back burner. Rebuilding an integration strategy was envisioned as merely one part of a strategy built around adjustment—or even, because of its emphasis on national and regional markets, as one of the factors to blame for the crisis.

In El Salvador, war and the political interest of the United States in militarily defeating the FMLN, moderated the pressure toward adjustment policies, on the understanding that their social effects would strengthen support for the revolutionaries and weaken the "internal front" led by the Christian Democratic government, and later by the rightist ARENA government.

The Sandinista government, excluded from the mutilateral financial organizations—and of course from USAID programs—

also tried its hand at macroeconomic adjustment policies in 1988 and 1989. Despite the absence of foreign financial support, there was a degree of success in controlling the principal macroeconomic variables. The enormous social cost of that control, however, together with the corrosive effects of the war, helped mobilize the anti-Sandinista vote in the February 1990 elections (Taylor et al. 1989; Vilas 1991a).

2. The dirty war

The United States was unable to avoid the revolutionary explosion of social and political tensions, but it did manage, through direct, open, and broad involvement, to contain the insurgent process in El Salvador and to brake the Sandinista regime's revolutionary changes in Nicaragua. The central aim of United States policy toward Central America during the administrations of Ronald Reagan (1981 to 1989) and George Bush (1989 to 1993) consisted of stopping a revolutionary advance that, in the eyes of both presidents, had no other aim than to create "another Cuba," or even "another Vietnam," in the region. The strategy for achieving the counterrevolutionary goal was called "low-intensity warfare" and consisted of a small direct commitment of combat troops combined with a large mobilization of logistical and financial resources. This strategy fitted well with previous experience in training Central America's armed forces and security bodies, and it also satisfied United States public opinion's rejection of any broad role for U.S. troops.

United States military aid to Central America grew from $10 million in 1980 to $283.2 million in 1984, targeted at three countries: El Salvador (69 percent), Honduras (27 percent), and Costa Rica (4 percent). Guatemalan military governments' human rights violations, which had drawn U.S. government condemnation during James E. Carter's presidency, precluded such assistance until 1985, when Christian Democrat Vinicio Cerezo took office. Nicaragua was excluded for the obvious political reasons. In the second half of the decade, U.S. military aid totaled $852 million, two-thirds of which went to El Salvador (IICA/FLACSO 1991:207). Besides the funds, equipment, and supplies, 500 to 800 Central American officers were trained at bases and military schools in the United

States every year. In Honduras, the construction of military bases and the presence of a significant number of U.S. troops, as well as the U.S. military mission's control of Honduran military policy, swiftly turned that country into the main platform for Washington's counterrevolutionary strategy in the region. The U.S. embassy in Tegucigalpa acquired a prominence in the country's affairs that it did not relinquish until very recently.

The pace of parapolice and paramilitary training, begun in the previous decade, picked up in the 1980s. Guatemala's newly-created "peasant self-defense patrols," modeled on forces organized by the United States in its war against Vietnam, swelled the number of paramilitary troops from around 3,000 in 1980 to more than 900,000 in 1985; the patrols are still active today in spite of massive protests from civil society. These bodies have occasioned great suffering for the civilian population, and forced it to take sides in the conflict. Formally made up of volunteers, the peasant self-defense patrols functioned as control mechanisms over the indigenous population, which was suspected of collaborating with the insurgency, and as an instrument for settling personal or business scores that had nothing to do with politics. The patrols have been blamed for a long and cruel list of human rights violations—kidnappings, murders, rapes, and tortures (Paul and Demarest 1991; Handy 1992; Jay et al. 1993). In El Salvador, paramilitary troops grew from 5,000 to 8,300 in the same period, and in Honduras from 3,000 to 4,500.

The Nicaraguan counterrevolutionaries by 1985 numbered about 15,000 troops, armed, trained, and financed by agencies of the U.S. government (Aguilera 1989:81). In the category of "humanitarian aid" alone, the U.S. government had given the "Nicaraguan resistance" the equivalent of $27.1 million by mid-1989 (U.S. General Accounting Office 1990:14). The Nicaraguan "contra" camps in southern Honduras caused much trouble for the neighboring peasant populations, threatening personal safety and disrupting people's productive activities and daily lives (Boyer 1993).

President Bill Clinton's decision to open the United States government's archives made it possible to test the veracity of several accusations that U.S. agencies and senior officials in Alfredo Cristiani's ARENA government were directly or indirectly involved in either executing or covering up serious human rights violations against civilians.[2] It was established that 75 percent of the Salvadoran Army officers implicated by the United Nations Truth Commission in eight massacres of civilians were graduates of the School of the Americas in Fort Benning, Georgia. Among these are nineteen of the twenty-seven involved in the killing of six Jesuit priests at the end of 1989 (including Maj. Roberto D'Aubuisson, one of the founders of El Salvador's "death squads.") Four of the five senior Honduran Army officers charged in 1987 by Americas Watch with organizing the death squad known as "Batallón 316" were also trained at this school (Truth Commission 1993; Waller 1993). Batallón 316, created and initially led by Gen. Luis Alonso Discua—now commander in chief of the Honduran Armed Forces—is responsible for the documented disappearances of at least 184 persons for political reasons during the 1980s.[3]

The sadism of the repressive military and paramilitary forces exceeds the reach of the most perverse imagination. Tens of thousands of Central Americans were subjected to savage torture and a hideous death. Ricardo Falla's chronicle of the massacres at Ixcán (Falla 1992), and the report of the Truth Commission for El Salvador (1993) supply truly hair-raising evidence of the lengths to which Central America's ruling classes and their armies, and the government of the United States, were willing to go to smother a people's desire for justice.

The claim by El Salvador and the United States that both sides committed human rights violations in equal measure was thoroughly discredited by the United Nations Truth Commission's investigation, which laid almost 97 percent of the violations to government forces (Table 4.6). In the specific category of homicide, those forces were found responsible for an even higher proportion.

Table 4.7 offers an idea of the collective brutality of the terror: only in one year did acts of terror yield an average of fewer than ten victims each; overall, such acts would result in an average of approximately thirty victims each.

The public justification for U.S. involvement was the claim that it was a response to Cuban-Soviet meddling: in Washington's view, the Central American revolutions were a product of communist intervention, channeled through the Sandinista regime.[4] The

Table 4.6
El Salvador: Shares of Responsibility for Human Rights Violations
1980-1991

Force responsible	Cases	
	Number	%
Armed forces	11,977	49.4
Security forces	5,276	21.8
Paramilitary bodies	4,273	17.7
Death squads	1,844	7.6
FMLN	858	3.5
Total	24,227	100.0

Source: Truth Commission 1993. Includes information from direct and indirect sources.
Note: Cases include homicide, disappearance, kidnapping, torture, rape, and beating.

Sandinista People's Army did, in fact, receive significant logistical support from the Soviet Union, Cuba, the German Democratic Republic and the People's Democratic Republic of Korea, and the Sandinista government never concealed its sympathy for the Salvadoran and Guatemalan revolutionary processes. Nevertheless, no evidence ever backed U.S. arguments about Sandinista involvement in those processes (Schoultz 1987; LeoGrande 1986; Blasier 1986).

The political strategy that complemented military strategy consisted of replacing military regimes in Honduras, El Salvador, and Guatemala with elected governments and promoting certain social reforms. These aspects of counterrevolutionary strategy were meant mainly to improve the international image of U.S. intervention, and to gain the support of Central America's middle sectors. From the beginning of the 1970s, the Central American revolution had enjoyed a favorable climate of opinion in the world community, which saw in it a response to intolerable living conditions derived from underdevelopment, poverty, and political oppression. By appearing to support elections, the United States joined, in its own fashion, the worldwide pressure for democratization in the region, and could still stress the military character of the Sandinista government. Simultaneously, the electoral system offered large segments of the middle classes in El Salvador, Guatemala, and Honduras renewed access to political influence.

Table 4.7
El Salvador: Extent of Collective Human Rights Violations
1980-1990

Year	No. of incidents	Est. no. of victims per incident
1980	138	19
1981	65	64
1982	62	45
1983	32	42
1984	16	21
1985	3	9
1986	7	22
1987	4	13
1988	2	33
1989	11	22
1990	2	20

Source: Truth Commission 1993.

Washington's strategy adapted itself to existing conditions in each of the five republics. In Nicaragua it promoted the counter-revolutionary military forces, sought to destabilize the Sandinista government, and sponsored Costa Rica's anti-Sandinista diplomacy. In El Salvador it combined counterinsurgency with limited reforms, and pressed to replace the military regime with a civilian government. In Guatemala it urged military governments to call elections, and it used Honduras to headquarter the Nicaraguan counterrevolutionaries.

This counterinsurgency strategy also included appealing to the drug trade. Drugs are said to have played an important role in U.S. foreign policy since the beginning of the twentieth century (Scott and Marshall 1991), and that role expanded enormously during the 1980s. The Kerry Report, from the U.S. Senate International Relations Committee's Subcommittee on Terrorism, Narcotics, and International Operations (U.S. Senate Committee ... 1989), substantiates the direct involvement of U.S. government agencies, armed forces officers from several Central American countries, and the Nicaraguan contras in drug trafficking operations during both of Ronald Reagan's presidential terms as part of Washington's regional counterrevolutionary strategy.[5] Relying principally on the Honduran armed forces, U.S. diplomacy reinforced its ties to international drug traffic networks and drew them into support for the anti-Sandinista combatants operating from Honduran and Costa Rican territory.

3. A preliminary summation

Did revolution triumph or fail in Central America? There is no simple answer. Which effects and results were caused by the action of revolutionary forces and which by other factors is difficult to discern; Central America's scenario, like any other, was driven by complex reciprocal causation among agents and conditions, actions and reactions. Any summation of the results of revolutionary mobilizations must take this reciprocity into account. The presence of a revolutionary option was important not only for its own sake, but also for the reactions and counterstrategies it evoked from the groups that were the beneficiaries of the established order.

The human cost

The war in El Salvador is estimated to have left some 75,000 persons dead; in Nicaragua the figure is estimated at 58,000. Three decades of violence in Guatemala have left more than 150,000 dead, about 50,000 of them in the period from 1980 to 1985 (Karl 1992; INEC 1989; COPPAL 1992). The war wounded are difficult to count; the best guess in El Salvador alone is some 20,000, counting both sides' combatants and civilians (Rivas y Mejía 1993). The impact of violence on Central America's children is also difficult to gauge: it would be necessary to measure both the direct effects of the acts of war—bombings, ambushes, deaths of relatives and other children, wounds, and amputations—and the forced resettlements, the internalization of fear, and the rationalization of violent conduct, among other things (Moreno Martín 1991).[6]

Violence and terror focused primarily on the civilian population; the aim was to separate the guerrilla organizations from their base and deprive them of their rearguard and logistical support. The massacres at the Sumpul River in May 1980, El Mozote in December 1981, and Finca San Francisco in July 1982 stand today as testimony to the strategy of mass execution of defenseless children, women, elderly people, and refugees by military troops: illustrations of a policy of annihilation.

Hundreds of thousands of people were torn from the places they lived in, a large portion of them seeking refuge in other countries. Between 11 and 13 percent of Central America's population—some 1.8 million people—were refugees or displaced by the end of the 1980s (IICA/FLACSO 1991:204; Sarti 1991; ONG 1991). El Salvador, Guatemala, and Nicaragua became net population exporters, and Costa Rica and Honduras net importers. Most of the Guatemalans who make up an estimated 43 percent of the population of Belize arrived there during the 1980s.

Life in the refugee camps and resettlement areas was precarious, to say the least: material want, threats of repression, abuses by the authorities. Lack of interest from their own governments and the persistence of unsafe circumstances—most notoriously in the case of Guatemala—made returning home difficult at best, and many of the displaced became dependent on international aid.

The mobilization of "new subjects"

The rise of revolution was the result of an intensive social and political mobilization by a wide array of actors—particularly groups that until then had lacked an identity of their own, or had existed as subordinate parts of other collective actors: women, indigenous people, shantytown inhabitants, religious groups. This process represented the mobilization on a vast scale of a civil society that had always been distinguished for its fragmentation and apparent passivity. This flowering of Central American society attained a traumatic, convulsive worldwide resonance from the emergence of testimonial writing, popular poetry, and a new literary narrative.[7] This new cultural effervescence, stoked by the climate of insurrection, in turn fanned the flames of revolution.

The relationship between these new expressions of social discontent and the revolutionary organizations ran the gamut from subordination, through various degrees of autonomy and coordination, to outright hostility. In Nicaragua, the new labor and social organizations tended to follow the lead of the FSLN and the state, while the ethnic groups of the Atlantic Coast rapidly took up a violent antagonism to it. In Guatemala and El Salvador, on the other hand, the social organizations seem to have had a greater relative autonomy from the political-military organizations, especially in the second half of the decade.

With uneven efficacy, this varied spectrum of actors and organizations broadened the agenda for social change and democratization from a predominantly class perspective to a more pluralistic one that explicitly included the issues of gender, ethnicity, and culture. The struggle to endow these demands with legitimacy within the revolutionary project was not a simple one, and the fact that the cycle of insurrectional mobilization has closed in the 1990s does not mean that that struggle is over. Even though the activation of the "new subjects" was closely tied to the revolutionary offensive, those subjects did not retreat with revolution's ebb. Their socioeconomic, cultural, and political demands are part of the current agenda for democratization and social change in Central America, independently of the fortunes of the revolutionary projects that were their original launching pad.

Religious groups

The involvement of the Guatemalan and Salvadoran Catholic Church hierarchies in their countries' peace negotiations and in defending human rights has enabled Christian base communities there to keep up a degree of activity despite the repression they have suffered. The shift has been especially notable in Guatemala, where the Catholic hierarchy had been severely antagonistic to the new ministry in the 1970s and the early 1980s. The new ministry undeniably has a lower profile today, however, than it did in previous decades.

The Nicaraguan Catholic hierarchy's confrontation with the Sandinista government, its public sympathy for Washington's anti-Sandinista policies, and its backing for the post-Sandinista government elected in 1990 have placed Nicaragua's "popular church" in a difficult situation. Many base communities relinquished some of their autonomy by accepting a subordinate role to the Sandinista government, leaving them vulnerable today both to the FSLN's ambiguous behavior toward the government and to confrontation from the Church hierarchy. The combined effect has been a marked reduction in the base communities' activity, their scope, and their membership (Aragón y Löschke 1991).

The Protestant groups are a different case. In Guatemala, the counterinsurgency policy of the early 1980s was articulated to the activities of some evangelical denominations (Samandú 1991; Stoll 1991). El Salvador's ARENA government encouraged evangelical activity among poor populations in San Salvador and those fleeing rural violence (Montes 1988). Stoll (1990) suggests that the development of evangelical denominations in Nicaragua during the 1980s was part of the Central Intelligence Agency's anti-Sandinista strategy—an idea the Sandinistas themselves took up for a few years.

Neither repression of base communities, government sponsorship nor CIA manipulation is sufficient, however, to explain the rapid growth of the evangelical churches in Central America. By the mid-1980s, a third of Guatemala's population was estimated to belong to some evangelical denomination, and considerably more in some areas.[8] Furthermore, evangelical churches grew throughout the region, not only in the countries in conflict. Pentecostal churches grew at a dizzying pace in Costa Rica: from 215 in 1974 to 738 in 1982, and 1,088 in 1985 (Valverde 1987). Linking the growth of these denominations to Washington's counterinsurgency policy clearly fails to explain this case.[9]

The evangelical groups not only served counterinsurgent regimes and U.S. government agencies, enjoying corollary official protection and encouragement; they also offered a kind of spiritualist religiosity that advocated individual conversion, passivity, individualism, and an ethic of personal abstention, in sharp contrast with the appeals of liberation theology and the base communities to active commitment—sometimes radical, always collective. If the radicalized social-Christian groups mobilized their faithful against "structural sin"—that is, social injustice, the root cause of evil among humans—evangelism moved sin back to its traditional location within each individual, absolving society and its rulers. Evangelism also confered greater personal safety on religious practices in that it eliminated or restricted the projections of such practices that raised questions regarding social order.

Migration, motivated directly or indirectly by counterinsurgency war and the climate of political repression, fractured the traditional organizational ties that bound the populations of the villages and urban outskirts. For many migrants and displaced people, this brought emotional strain and a powerful sense of loss. The Protestant denominations, with their propheticism and their lofty displays of repentance and conversion, tried to compensate for this uprooted feeling with alternative forms of belonging and spiritual integration into the new social environment.

In Nicaragua, the evangelical churches presented themselves as an alternative to an overly politicized Catholic Church—pro-Sandinista among the base communities and anti-Sandinista in the hierarchy. At certain times their close ties to their denominations' U.S. headquarters drew aggressive ideological attacks from the Sandinistas, who saw them as imperialist beachheads. Toward the end of the 1980s, however, the Sandinista government changed its mind and began to approach the evangelical churches through CEPAD, perhaps in an effort to compensate for its conflict with the Catholic hierarchy, with an eye to the upcoming elections.[10]

Spread of evangelism heavily impacted upon the communities' internal differentiation. The evangelical paradigm of the good Christian overlapped with the capitalist paradigm of the good worker: one who does not drink, gamble, betray one's employer, or cheat on one's wife or husband; one who works hard and saves money. This match influenced the living conditions of the faithful, as the newly converted often quickly became their companies' most trusted workers. It is not surprising, therefore, that many of them attributed improvements in their economic lot to their conversion (Goldin 1992; Sexton 1978).

The relationship between religiosity and economic differentiation is more complex than that, however. Annis (1987) found in Guatemala a greater propensity to convert to evangelical faiths among individuals with looser ties to their communities, where Catholicism was the official form of religiosity. For some, poverty made it impossible to continue to honor commitments based on traditional rituals, and the tangible expressions of community solidarity eroded as a result. Many were forced to seek work away from the family plot and often far from the community. Other individuals, those with some economic success, no longer needed the solidarity of the village; they were entering into entrepreneurial activities and exploring commercial, labor, or other kinds of connections outside the community. Consequently, the propensity to change religious identity was conditioned by the degree and solidity of attachment to one's community.

The conversion to evangelistic faiths, in turn, tended to generate even greater socioeconomic differentiation. In several highland communities, it was found, families that remained Catholic and those that converted to evangelical faiths both remained active in the weaving trade, but with a fundamental difference: those who remained Catholic continued to work as weavers, while those who converted showed an increasing involvement in marketing weavings outside the village.

The Protestant offensive also bore fruit among the middle sectors and in the ruling classes, even among their most traditional families. Casaus Arzú (1992a) found numerous members of Guatemala's most prominent families to have converted, particularly to the Church of the Word (*Iglesia del Verbo*), whose best-known leaders are former presidents Gen. Efraín Ríos Montt and Jorge Serrano Elías. The *Fraternidad de Hombres de Negocios Cristianos del Evangelio Completo* (Christian Businessmen's Whole Gospel Fraternity) operated in El Salvador on a strategy of expanding its role in public affairs by converting political and business leaders and socially influential people (Recio Adrados 1992). Evangelical activity does not exclude partisan politics: two evangelically-defined political parties, the *Movimiento de Solidaridad Nacional* and the *Partido de Unidad*, took part in the March 1994 elections.

Women

Women's movements also rode the ebbs and flows of each country's political situation. Their advance was based to a large degree on the changes in the labor market. The female EAP grew more than its male counterpart throughout Central America during the 1980s, especially in the cities. The growth of the informal sector accounted for the bulk of this growth (Pérez Sáinz and Menjívar 1991; Pérez Sáinz and Castellanos 1991). Women's presence in the EAP reached its highest levels in El Salvador and Nicaragua. However, the sharpening economic crisis and the demobilization of the army and security forces in Nicaragua after the war pushed female employment downward. As women were displaced from jobs by recession and by men returning to civilian life, the underutilization of the female labor force (open unemployment plus underemployment) began to exceed that of the male work force (García and Gomáriz 1989 I:37-38; Fernández Poncela 1992a).

Women played a significant role in revolutionary organizations and their support networks. Women made up an estimated one-fourth of FMLN troops by the mid-1980s, and an even larger proportion in some of the Front's member organizations (García and Gomáriz 1989 I:196–97). Women took up significant support functions in the Sandinista insurrection, but had a limited role in guerrilla activity (Vilas 1986, ch. 3).

The gender issue took shape in close and frequently subordinate relationship with the revolutionary challenge to the political and economic system. Women's growing involvement in political, political-military, neighborhood, and labor groups, rather than theoretical discussion, gave rise to a specific women's agenda. Beginning from what might be termed a "revolutionary feminist" (García and Gomáriz 1989 II:213) argument that only in the framework of revolutionary struggles and class confrontations can the issue of women's gender subordination be resolved, women developed approaches involving ever-greater autonomy— approaches that post-war conditions would later reinforce.

The persistence of systematic human rights violations in Guatemala kept the issue of political disappearances and related forms of repression at the frorefront; such groups as the *Grupo de Ayuda Mutua* (Mutual Aid Group, GAM) and the *Comisión Nacional de Viudas de Guatemala* (National Commission of Guatemalan Widows, CONAVIGUA) have earned well-deserved recognition in this context. In El Salvador, women in the refugee camps and in the resettlement and repatriation movements took up intensive action against repression.

Gender subordination and the myriad expressions of sexism still occupy a secondary political space that is mainly inhabited by urban and professional women. Nevertheless, the overwhelming presence of women in organizations against repression and in defense of human rights has helped build a general consciousness of gender. Participating in mobilizations, confronting government and the armed forces, and negotiating with other social organizations helped equip women with the self-confidence to break with the traditional stereotypes of *woman* = *home* = *submission*. Women shed their fear, learned to move in the "public" world, took up roles traditionally reserved for men, became politicized, and began to connect their own experiences and their understanding of political violence—disappearance, torture, murder—with personal violence against women: rape, battering, denigration, marginalization (Rodríguez 1990; Schirmer 1993).

The Nicaraguan women's movement is undergoing multiple divisions and dispersion against a backdrop of loosening ties with women of the popular sectors. The Sandinista electoral defeat accelerated and deepened disagreements within the FSLN-linked *Asociación de Mujeres Nicaragüenses* "Luisa Amanda Espinosa" (Luisa Amanda Espinosa Association of Nicaraguan Women, AMNLAE), made room for the rise of a number of small organizations and centers independent of the FSLN, and encouraged friendlier approaches to urban, professional, and middle-sector women than had previously been possible. The end of the war, the deepening economic crisis, and some of the new government's policies laid the groundwork for reversing the feminization of the labor force, especially the rural labor force, that had spread during the second half of the 1980s. Women of the popular classes were forced back into their traditional domestic environment (Olivera et al. 1990; Fernández Poncela 1992a). Even considering the women's movement's bitter disappointments and minute advances, however, there is no doubt that the issue of gender discrimination is now irrevocably on the social agenda in its own right, in clear contrast with the situation a decade ago.

Indigenous women did not stand aside from these changes. Shifts in indigenous women's perception of themselves and their role in society were the inevitable result of both internal and international migrations; growing exposure to urban phenomena; changing labor relations and labor markets; the growth of evangelical churches; and the search for new work opportunities (Carrillo 1991; Fuentes 1991; Pérez Sáinz et al. 1992). In all, these changes are associated with a degree of loosening in women's ties to communities and villages, where male social and political domination remain strong.

Workers, peasants, and agrarian reform

The presence of these new protagonists of social discontent does not diminish the importance of the "traditional" actors—peasants and urban and rural wage earners. Guatemalan and Salvadoran trade union activity made important improvements in the 1970s, until institutional deterioration and repression closed off their mobilizing space. As union demands were met with repression, and workers' movements were increasingly locked into a predominantly political-military struggle, the tension between labor struggles and political struggles was resolved in favor of the latter (CINAS 1985; Figueroa Ibarra 1991:128ff). The political took on a marked priority over the strictly labor-related in Nicaragua for different reasons. The Sandinistas' cross-class "national unity" strategy, and later the economic crisis, reinforced the tendency to turn the labor movement into an apprartus of the revolutionary state, more active in carrying out global policy than in promoting its members' immediate interests (Vilas 1989a, ch. 4).

The mobilization of the peasants and rural semiproletarians was one of the most visible aspects of the 1980s. Rural organizing laid the groundwork for revolutionary activism, which in turn promoted agrarian protest. In Nicaragua and El Salvador, two different types of agrarian reform, with dissimilar motivations, brought profound changes in the direct producer's access to land.

Land reform in El Salvador came at first as an element of the reformist military coup and later as part of the Christian Democratic strategy of preventive change aimed at reducing the guerrillas' rural support. Agrarian reform cooperatives received more than a third of the land that changed hands. This agrarian reform is generally thought to have benefited more than a third of the agrarian EAP (Baumeister 1991a, b; Ellacuría 1987). The FMLN, for its part, encouraged the seizure of lands in the areas it occupied, which amounted to 30 percent of the country. Finally, the activization of the land market involved large portions of the total available land; 59 percent of the land that changed hands belonged to farms smaller than 100 manzanas (Goitía 1991: 167–93). After the large landholders succeeded in blocking agrarian reform, land from large farms was sold in increasing amounts to middle-sized proprietors at bargain prices, due to guerrilla threats to landowners, the general instability, and specific state policies. The Sandinista agrarian reform, in contrast, covered almost half of Nicaragua's agricultural land area, to the benefit of two-thirds of the country's peasant families; land belonging to large landowners shrank by 80 percent. By 1988 the land reform sector held almost 49 percent of arable land. State agrarian reform enterprises held less than a fourth of this; almost three-quarters belonged to various kinds of cooperatives, and something under 5 percent belonged to indigenous communities on the Atlantic Coast. The fall in land prices that accompanied the revolution—sparked at first by the agrarian reform itself and later accelerated by the economic collapse—meant anyone bold enough to invest a relatively small amount of money could become a small or middle-sized farmer.[11]

The upshot of all of this was, by the end of the 1980s, an agrarian profile very different from the one that prevailed at the beginning of the decade. Changes in land tenure patterns, in the levels of rural organization, and in wage-earners' and farmers' power to enforce their demands dealt a blow to the traditional principle of landowner authority, challenged the large landowners' right to dispossess peasants, and forced the political system to accept the legitimacy of rural protest.

After the Sandinistas' electoral defeat, the land question—defending or reversing land redistribution, giving lands to former *contras*, and privatizing or returning agrarian reform lands—moved to the center of Nicaragua's political and social tensions. The Chapultepec Peace Accord that the Salvadoran government and the FMLN signed on January 16, 1992 refers explicitly to the lands in the hands of peasants in the "conflict zones"—i.e. lands under revolutionary control—and sets guidelines for resolving agrarian issues, which have been a source of tension in recent years.

The success of these expressions of social protest, by making plain the advantages of working together and applying joint pressure, fed people's sense of their own political power and their confidence in popular organizing. Moreover, it pointed up both the importance of linking people's specific demands to far-reaching political designs, and the need to keep within them the specificity and autonomy of their particular demands.

Now that the cycle of armed struggle, mobilization, and repression has given way to one of rebuilding political systems, social and labor organizations are in a position to strengthen their bar-

Table 4.8
Central America: Estimated Extent of Poverty, 1980 and 1990

	Costa Rica		El Salvador		Guatemala		Honduras		Nicaragua		Central America	
	1980	1990	1980	1990	1980	1990	1980	1990	1980	1990	1980	1990
Population in millions												
Total	2.2	2.9	4.7	6.5	7.4	9.2	3.7	5.1	2.7	3.9	20.8	27.6
Urban	1.0	1.6	2.1	2.9	2.5	3.9	1.6	2.2	1.5	1.6	8.4	12.2
Rural	1.2	1.3	2.6	3.6	4.8	5.3	2.5	2.9	1.3	2.3	12.4	15.4
Population in poverty (in millions)												
Total	0.5	0.6	3.3	4.9	4.6	6.9	2.5	3.9	1.7	2.9	12.6	19.2
Urban	0.1	0.2	1.2	1.8	1.4	2.4	0.5	1.6	0.7	0.9	4.0	6.9
Rural	0.4	0.4	2.0	3.1	3.2	4.5	2.0	2.3	1.0	2.0	8.6	12.3
Population in poverty (by percentage)												
Total	25	20	68	71	63	75	68	76	62	75	61	69.5
Urban	14	11	58	61	58	62	44	73	46	60	48	56.5
Rural	34	31	76	85	66	85	80	79	80	85	69	79.9
Distribution of poor by country (%)												
Total	3.9	3.1	26.2	25.5	36.5	35.9	19.8	20.3	13.5	15.2	100.0	100.0
Urban	2.5	2.9	30.0	26.1	35.0	34.8	12.5	23.2	20.0	13.0	100.0	100.0
Rural	4.6	3.2	23.2	25.2	37.2	36.6	23.2	18.7	11.8	16.3	100.0	100.0

Source: CEPAL 1992b.

gaining power and political autonomy and to negotiate approaches to national development with the political system's traditional actors—parties, unions, bureaucracies—that reflect their own viewpoints. Any appraisal of the outcome of these decades of revolution, counterrevolution, repression, and crisis, should pay attention to these factors—consciousness, power, and identity—and not just to specific material gains only.

Poverty

Crisis and war came together to produce an explosion of poverty. The ranks of the poor grew by 52 percent across the region, excepting only Costa Rica (Table 4.8). Poverty increased in the three countries where armed conflict took place, yet there was no relevant difference between them and Honduras, where no war was waged. Although overall poverty figures are much the same for Nicaragua, El Salvador, and Guatemala, poverty in Nicaragua and El Salvador grew more in the countryside than in the cities, and Guatemala displayed the opposite tendency. The distribution of poverty across the region did not change significantly between 1980 and 1990, except that Nicaragua's share of the region's total poor population grew. In contrast, Nicaragua's share of the isthmus's urban poverty came down more than that of any of the other four countries, indicating that deterioration of living conditions was most pronounced in the countryside.[12]

Poverty in Central America has tended to become urban. Although the proportion of poor people is still larger in the countryside than in the cities, 60 percent of the increase in poverty over the decade took place in the cities. The ranks of the urban poor grew by almost 73 percent over the decade, compared with a 43 percent rise in poverty in the countryside. Migrations and the displacement of populations fleeing war zones, repression, and worsening living and working conditions in vast swaths of the countryside are principally behind this trend. Seeking refuge in the cities, growing numbers of people put increasing pressure on social services and the labor market and intensified the problems of shantytown growth.[13]

Social differentiation

Central America's social structure underwent marked changes during the 1980s. The peasantry grew in economic and political weight, while indigenous communities were exposed to profound changes in divergent directions. The presence of urban and rural wage-workers in the EAP shrank, as did the scope and effectiveness of their labor organizations. The urban informal sector strengthened its economic and demographic position, especially in its most traditional forms, and mass migration of Central Americans to the United States generated a large flow of foreign exchange remittances. Central America's bourgeoisie, too, began to experience an important process of internal economic and political differentiations, in a context of profound social polarization.

a. Consolidation of the peasantry

Changes in the condition of peasants were especially significant in Nicaragua and El Salvador, as a result of the aforementioned improvements in access to land. Nicaragua's agrarian reform gave land access to some 138,000 peasant families, something over two-thirds of the total (CIERA 1989 IX:41). Associative modes of production appeared or were strengthened. Almost 30 percent of the land covered by the Sandinista agrarian reform was assigned to various forms of cooperative organizations (Serra 1990, table 7). Nicaragua's permissive institutional climate encouraged small and middle-sized producers to organize themselves. The *Unión Nacional de Agricultores y Ganaderos* (National Farmers and Ranchers' Union, UNAG) became the most active social organization in Nicaragua, a country that until well into the 1970s had been marked by its extremely low level of peasant organization. UNAG retained a large degree of operational autonomy from the Sandinista regime, in spite of its open support for the FSLN. That enabled the union to hold onto much of its bargaining power after the 1990 change in government, and even to take up the demands of peasants who had earlier joined or supported the counterrevolutionary forces.

From 1990 on, privatization and the return of properties distributed during the agrarian reform injected powerful tensions into Nicaragua's peasantry. It is estimated that almost 70 percent of the properties privatized or returned by the Violeta Barrios de Chamorro government were among the lands redistributed under the Sandinista reform (Vilas 1992b). This political reorientation, combined with an emphasis on market relations, restricted credit, the elimination of subsidies, a currency exchange policy subsidizing imports, and the former owners' revanchism, has posed complex challenges to the peasantry, creating tensions in its organizations and fueling social instability.

El Salvador's agrarian reform cooperatives received 37 percent of the land area in question. Improved access to land resources had political effects here as well, in the form of a strong presence for the Christian Democratic Party among broad sectors of the rural population in the first half of the decade.

The strengthening of the peasantry in Nicaragua and El Salvador contrasts starkly with the reversal of agrarian reform and peasant organizing in Honduras. The Honduran governments of the 1980s at first put the brakes on agrarian redistribution, then toward the end of the decade threw it into reverse, threatening repression to quiet social protests. The consequent profound crisis in the reform sector has been aggravated by macroeconomic policy, shrinking credit, and pressure from landowners and armed forces officers interested in entering the agroexport business (Díaz Arravillaga 1992; Murillo 1992). Families still landless or without sufficient land number some 370,000 (Salgado 1992). Honduran government policy throughout the 1980s encouraged dismantling associative agrarian reform enterprises and privatizing services to producers (Melmed-Sanjak 1992). Since Honduras's political stability owes much to the availability of an ample supply of national and communal lands for the use of land-hungry peasants, and to the limited mercantilization of the peasant economy (Ruhl 1984; Brockett 1988; Rubén 1992; supra ch. 2), the spread of agrarian privatization and mercantilization can be expected to help create unstable social conditions in the future.

The outlook for the Costa Rican peasantry is no better. Structural adjustment policies struck hard at the living and production conditions of the small farmers who produce for the domestic market, who are not in a position to switch to nontraditional agricultural exports. Weakly organized before the 1980s, Costa Rica's peasants have been unable to change the main contours of economic policy, or to play a significant role in the debate over structural adjustment. Recent Costa Rican governments have made firm commitments to the international financial agencies; the peasant organizations' own diverging aims, weak coordination, and tenuous links to the labor movement and other social organizations have made them increasingly vulnerable to these policies. (Vunderink 1990–1991; Edelman 1993).

The Guatemalan government's economic and land policy and its counterinsurgency strategy both wrought havoc among the country's Mayan rural producers. Toward the end of the 1980s, the Catholic hierarchy shifted its position on the social movement and began to support dialogue with the insurgent forces, which made room for some revival of peasant protest. A March 1988 pastoral letter from the Guatemalan Bishops' Conference, "The Clamor for Land," offered a modest argument for some sort of agrarian change to give small farmers more access to land and better growing conditions. While the document had no practical impact, it reflected the church's relative distancing from the Christian Democratic government and from the armed forces' counterinsurgency strategy.

To speak of "peasants" in Guatemala, more than in any other Central American country, a conceptual distinction must be made. Guatemalan peasants are in reality Mayan small producers, themselves a sector riven with myriad differentiations. Whether to speak of peasants or indigenous people, therefore, is not an academic question, for the very features that signal the fragility of the Guatemalan peasantry—its fragmentation into local communities, its lack of national-level organizations—can also be taken to indicate the vitality of the Mayan population's ethnic identity. The consolidation of village organization and their cultural and territorial lines of demarcation with other ethnic groups are indicators of a strong ethnic identity; at the same time, they reflect the obstacles to building class-based organization.

Recent capitalist growth and counterinsurgency strategy have dealt severe blows to Guatemala's small farmers, regardless of how we categorize them: they suffered both as indigenous people and as peasants. But any discussion of their future depends greatly on how they are identified—above all, how they themselves unfold the process of building their own identity.

b. Indigenous communities

The growing importance of ethnic identities is one legacy of the 1980s. Ethnicity, as an issue in itself and as an identifying and organizing factor for broad sectors of Central America's population, has become part of the region's political agenda, even though the current governments and the forces on which they rest obviously have little enthusiasm for the topic. Confrontation with the state, repression impelled by racism, and the refugee camp experience have all reinforced cultural differentiation, giving Indian peoples and other subordinated ethnic groups a new outlook on autonomous collective action. Experiences from revolutionary war waged by *mestizo-* or *ladino*-led organizations also exerted influence on this; in order to escape counterinsurgency offensives, organizations often retreated from the areas where they had built up support, leaving the villages at the mercy of the enemy. Many indigenous groups still hold this against the guerrillas.

Mobilization around ethnic issues aroused brutal reactions from the state. More than one million Guatemalan indigenous people are estimated to have fallen victim to the counterinsurgency operations of the military governments between 1980 and 1986, and to the less brutal repression that went on thereafter. More than 400 indigenous villages were destroyed, their populations massacred or forced to flee, as part of an explicit policy of ethnicide. Uprooting, economic crisis, forced urbanization, and the collapse of local economies have brought profound changes in the ethnic identity of those concerned—changes that have been compared in magnitude with those that followed the Spanish conquest in the sixteenth century.

The creation of "model villages" or "development villages," adapted from the U.S. experience in Vietnam, was a way of tightening military control over the population in areas of guerrilla activity and isolating the guerrillas from a population that supported them. By restricting people's access to their fields, it damaged local economies and broke up markets for products and labor, eroding the material basis for ethnicity. "Civilian self-defense patrols," formally voluntary but in fact recruited by force and threat, and under military command, later mobilized more than 900,000 persons, the great majority of them indigenous. The patrols functioned as paramilitary bodies for repression and surveillance, pitting Mayans against Mayans.

The confrontation that quickly developed between the ethnic groups of the Nicaraguan Atlantic Coast and the Sandinista regime led to a period of violent confrontation (Vilas 1989ba). Some of the groups concerned were forcibly resettled, while others fled to Honduras and Costa Rica. A shift in the Sandinistas' approach enabled dialogue to resume in 1985, and the conflict began to subside, leading to the formal granting of autonomy to the region and the creation of institutions of self-government. Revolution, war, and crisis have sparked or speeded definite changes in several dimensions of the coastal populations' ethnic identities. Traditional leadership has been increasingly challenged; internal political differentiation has accelerated; new attitudes have appeared toward the symbolic components of identity (Matamoros 1992; Vilas 1992a:167ff; García 1993). The 1990 government change prompted a reversal in every aspect of this process, due to the ethnocentrism of the new authorities, splits in the ethnic movement, and the impact of structural adjustment policies and privatization. Bilingual-bicultural education programs, starved for resources and unable to gain the interest of the new authorities, are now in crisis.[14]

The indigenous movement in El Salvador, where officially there is no indigenous question, is in a lethargic state.[15] Despite a similar official position in Honduras, recent years have witnessed some indigenous mobilizations take back ancestral lands and confront landholders and *ladino* peasants.

c. The labor movement

As the working class and the labor movement were reshaped throughout the 1980s, political repression, the regional crisis, population displacements, and wage policies put a regressive stamp on the process. In Guatemala and El Salvador, intense legal and extralegal repression, combined with government economic policy, weighed heavily on the trade union movement through the first half of the decade. Not only were labor organizations proscribed, the right to strike revoked, and public demonstrations of collective protest prohibited, but union leaders and organizers were kidnapped, disappeared, imprisoned, and murdered. Some of the Salvadoran and Guatemalan labor organizations' acknowledged links with revolutionary organizations made them especially easy targets for repression.

The retreat of El Salvador's labor and mass movements between 1980 and 1983 began to turn around when José Napoleón Duarte was elected president in 1984. The first attempts at unity emerged between 1983 and 1985, and culminated in February 1986 with the creation of the *Unión Nacional de Trabajadores Salvadoreños* (National Union of Salvadoran Workers, UNTS). The 1985 election of Vinicio Cerezo in Guatemala brought relative improvement in the institutional climate and helped make room for union activity. A presidential decree in December 1986 proclaimed government employees' right to organize in unions. By 1988, however, only 5 percent of all workers had union representation. The labor movement has developed a degree of coordination with a wide range of popular organizations in recent years.

One government response to labor organizing was parallel progovernment unions, created with the support of U.S. government agencies or trade unions. In Guatemala, Gen. Efraín Ríos Montt's government sponsored the *Confederación de Unidad Sindical de Guatemala* (Guatemalan Labor Unity Confederation, CUSG). In El Salvador, the United States' AFL-CIO helped President Duarte's government build the *Unión Nacional de Obreros y Campesinos* (National Workers' and Peasants' Union, UNOC) in March 1986, in response to the creation a month earlier of the combative UNTS (Spalding 1992–1993; Castañeda Sandoval 1993).

The governments of Costa Rica and Honduras, where labor movements did not propose radical confrontation, supported *solidarista* initiatives (analogous to labor-management partnership schemes in the north) backed by U.S. agencies. Trade union *solidarismo* advocates conciliation of class interests, opposes organizing based on class interests, and stresses the importance of training, individual initative, and pragmatism for improving workers' living conditions; it encourages the formation of small credit associations to foster consumption. Some aspects of the *solidarista* doctrine coincide with those of the evangelical denominations, particularly their criticism of unionism and their recommendation that workers stay out of unions (Fernández 1991; Valverde 1987).

The new institutional climate did not mean an end to repression against the trade union movement, as events demonstrate from the mass murder of the UNTS leadership in El Salvador in October 1989 to the deteriorating political climate in Guatemala during the presidential term of Jorge Serrano Elías and afterwards. In any case, the labor movement that survived the years of savage repression entered the new period with its negotiating power diminished, its membership rolls shrunken, and its outlook defensive. The task of rebuilding the workers' movement has continued to face significant obstacles, among them the growth of unemployment in the formal sector and the transfer of labor force to the informal sector, where no unions exist; the economic policies of the second half of the decade, and the contraction of public spending.

The revolutionary victory in Nicaragua and the economic recovery that quickly followed favored the growth of salaried employment, improved working conditions, an increase in union membership, more unions and collective labor contracts, and a broad revival of class struggle (Vilas 1989a, ch. 4). The outbreak of counterrevolutionary war in 1983–1984 and the economic decline from 1984–1985 on, led the labor movement—then under clear Sandinista hegemony—to concentrate on building support for state policies, to the detriment of mobilizing for specific labor demands. Abdicating the struggle for labor demands in turn reduced the Sandinista unions' foothold in the working class. Their subordination to the government kept them from defending workers' interests even when the Sandinista government began in 1988 to apply a macroeconomic adjustment strategy that further damaged workers' living conditions, drastically reducing real wages, raising open unemployment levels, tightening the basic food supply, etc.[16] The revival of Sandinista unions after the February 1990 elections, and their new quest for autonomy from the FSLN, contrasts markedly with the pre-1990 picture.

d. The urban informal sector

Several factors encouraged the growth of the urban informal sector (UIS) during the 1980s. Structural trends made it difficult for the formal sector to absorb labor supply; rural populations were displaced to the cities; economic and financial policies took their toll. A third of Central America's metropolitan workers were in the UIS in 1982, and the proportion rose to 40 percent by 1988–1989 (Pérez Sainz and Menjívar 1991). This growth suggests that a large informal sector is a structural feature of Central America's economies, and not merely a conjunctural phenomenon. The recent growth in the UIS took place particularly in the sector's most traditional expressions, such as self-employment, which accounted for between half and two-thirds of the UIS at decade's end. The inclination of some international finance organizations to approach informal self-employment as "microentrepreneurs" is inadequate, in view of the obvious precariousness of a great many of these "enterprises": street vendors, ambulatory peddlers, people marketing the surplus of what they have grown for their own consumption, and other such pursuits.

Changes in the business class

Revolutionary conflict framed a process of internal differentiation within the ruling classes as well. As their economic bases shifted, younger modernizing generations came of age, and elements from the armed forces and the drug trade joined their ranks, the physiognomy of Central America's ruling classes has changed. At the same time, these changes have weakened the influence of the traditional arrangement of kinship networks that reciprocally sustained and maintained the Central American elites. The cycle of revolution and counterrevolution that shook the region, along with the penetration of the parvenus, have made El Salvador's "fourteen families" little more than a historical reference, in the same way that they have deflated the aristocratic flourish of Nicaragua's "Calle Atravesada" set and broken open the exclusive circle of the Guatemalan oligarchy.

The image of the isthmus's ruling groups as a semifeudal landowning oligarchy had already been partially dispelled by accelerating growth and economic change before the 1970s (Tapia 1989, 1993). That decade's spurt of growth in industrial production, agroindustrial markets, and technological innovation brought further differentiation within the property-owning classes. A new generation of entrepreneurs, including many educated at universities in the United States and Europe, emerged with its own ideas on how to manage the region's economies, its business, and its political affairs.

These modern businessmen's direct involvement in politics contrasts with the traditional management mode of Central American economic elites, who had delegated day-to-day control of politics and the state to the armed forces since the 1930s.[17] This new generation of leaders advocated economic efficiency and broad openness to the exterior, combined with a form of political modernization designed at once to eradicate patronage and other traditional varieties of corruption and to block the aspirations of the left.

Once placed in a position to defend the interests of their class, the new businessmen began to differ with some aspects of U.S. counterinsurgency strategy. In El Salvador, for example, they opposed the agrarian reforms and nationalizations of the civilian-military juntas and the Duarte government, and mounted effective protest movements against it. In Guatemala, they successfully blocked the reform program of Vinicio Cerezo, Duarte's fellow Christian Democratic president.

As part of its deep involvement in strategies to head off revolution in El Salvador, USAID in 1982 sponsored the creation of the *Fundación Salvadoreña de Desarrollo* (Salvadoran Development Foundation, FUSADES) and began to channel copious funds through it. USAID-financed FUSADES projects between 1984 and 1992 had an estimated value of close to $196 million (Rosa 1992, tables 3–4).

FUSADES served as a nucleus for businessmen willing to cooperate with the Reagan Administration's strategy for Central America. Strongly criticizing the previous decade's import-substitution development scheme, FUSADES devoted much of its attention to formulating proposals to revive the Salvadoran economy by promoting new agroexport lines and applying adjustment policies to eliminate global imbalances. It also criticized the civic-military counterinsurgency strategies favored by the Christian Democrats, and even argued against the U.S. strategy of low-intensity conflict. FUSADES argued that low-intensity conflict, far from curtailing FMLN military activity, fueled corruption in the state and the armed forces with its ceaseless flow of funds, most of which were not spent on the war.

In Guatemala, USAID backed the 1985 creation of the *Cámara Empresarial* (Business Chamber), an organization for policy analysis and recommendations. Cámara Empresarial stressed the need to modernize agroexport by exploiting the comparative advantage afforded by the country's supply of cheap, abundant labor (Escoto and Marroquín 1992). Using funds from the Reagan Administration's "Caribbean Basin Initiative," USAID helped create Costa Rica's *Coalición e Iniciativas para el Desarrollo* (Coalition and Initiatives for Development, CINDE). USAID channeled resources through this organization to promote diversified agroexport and foreign trade investment. CINDE has also begun to pressure for government policies to privatize public corporations and further stimulate export-led deregulation (Güendal and Rivera 1987).

Due to a number of factors, modernization of Nicaragua's business groups developed at a much slower pace. First, the Somoza dictatorship confined the lion's share of the benefits of economic growth and modernization to its own members and affiliates. Such "disloyal competition" to the detriment of other business, land, and incipient industrial interests estranged those groups from the dictatorship, although their objections were different from those of the Sandinistas. Moreover, the class was as divided on the Sandinistas as it had been on the Somoza regime. Those businessmen who consented to deal with the government had to cut their ties to the business groups, which as a result came more and more thoroughly under the control of the most hardline anti-Sandinista sectors. The latter enjoyed extraordinary international promotion as the U.S. government systematically presented them as the authentic, not to say the sole, expression of Nicaraguan private enterprise. Thirdly, with the deterioration of U.S.-Nicaraguan diplomatic relations, USAID, which played a key role in creating the institutions for expressing the new business trends in other countries, was deprived of its opportunity to do the same for Nicaragua.

Business in fatigues

Central America's armed forces emerged from the conflict as an important center of economic power. The growing business interests of high-ranking officers in Guatemala, Honduras, and El Salvador had been a feature of the internal differentiation within the ruling economic groups since at least the 1970s. Taking advantage of government policies of peasant eviction, privileged access to information, and the manipulation of public credit and development project financing, senior Guatemalan and Honduran officers became big businessmen, landowners, and investors. The Guatemalan army's major position as a partner in banks, pension funds, airlines, real estate projects, and so on, amplified the senior officers' personal role in business.[18] El Salvador's *Instituto de Previsión Social de las Fuerzas Armadas* (Armed Forces Social Security Insitute) channeled vast funds into real estate and commercial investments, with help from U.S. military aid and a swelling defense budget.

Instead of taking the place of traditional forms of patronage and corruption, these new accumulation mechanisms were overlaid on them. The abundant influx of war and development funds from U.S. government agencies throughout the decade only increased the size of the pile (Millman 1990; Ross 1992). The Nicaraguan army, for its part, is apparently joining this entrepreneurial trend in the context of the privatization of state assets under the Chamorro government.[19]

Another factor behind this rapid conversion of many Central American military officers into important economic forces is Central America's place in international drug-trafficking network. The militarization of U.S.-Central America relations, the covert nature of many counterinsurgency operations, and U.S. support for the Nicaraguan counterrevolutionaries were all favorable conditions for the growth of the drug trade. The U.S. government relied on drug networks to channel support to Nicaraguan counterrevolutionary troops, and these networks expanded as a result: the same military transports that ferried arms and provisions to the "Nicaraguan Resistance" also transported drugs. Drug-trafficking money and financial aid to the contras often flowed through the same channels.[20] The U.S. government clearly was not above any method of overthrowing the Nicaraguan government—an outcome that in the end was delivered by Nicaraguan citizens, not by support to drug dealers.

Dependence on foreign subsidies

By the end of the 1980s, more than 1.3 million Nicaraguans, Guatemalans, and Salvadorans had migrated, legally or illegally, to the United States. The displacement of Central America's population gave rise to a flow of remittances that, in the aggregate, exceeded the region's revenues from its main export markets. At the microeconomic level, remittances from abroad helped the families that stayed behind to survive—a survival strategy that enjoyed the obvious acquiescence of the U.S. authorities. El Salvador received $3,367 billion in family remittances between 1980 and 1989, Guatemala $1,705 billion, and Nicaragua $294 million. In 1989 alone, 575,200 Salvadoran emigrants sent home $759.4 million from the United States, while 500,000 Guatemalans remitted $248.1 million and 255,000 Nicaraguans sent $59.8 million. For El Salvador, remittances are equivalent to 15 percent of the GDP or 96.7 percent of export revenues; for Guatemala, respectively, 2.9 percent and 16.4 percent; and for Nicaragua, 2.4 percent and 17.4 percent (Cepal 1991).

The remittance phenomenon is a function of the growing dependence on international financial assistance of the Central American societies most exposed to political and military conflict. The Salvadoran case illustrates the Central American societies' extreme dependence on foreign funds in order to operate. During the 1980s this country received close to $7.3 billion in U.S. aid and remittances from its citizens in the United States, plus almost $315 million in official development aid from Europe, Canada, and Japan, and in direct foreign investment (Vuskovic Céspedes 1991). The sum of this foreign revenue exceeded the value generated by Salvadoran exports during the same period, which amounted to slightly more than $7.5 billion.

Nicaragua received 42 percent of the development aid sent to Central America in the 1980s, an average of $667 million a year, not including military aid (Vuskovic Céspedes 1991). The United States afforded Guatemala $574.9 million in economic and military aid between 1980 and 1988. El Salvador received $3,919 billion, an average of $357 million a year, in development and military aid from the United States alone between 1980 and 1990 (Cuenca 1992:27-30). Costa Rica and Honduras, both of which figured prominently in Washington's counterinsurgency regional strategy, also depended heavily on foreign assistance. Costa Rica received $1.2 billion in economic and defense assistance, and Honduras $1,446 billion (Benítez Manaut 1989b).

The Kissinger Commission estimated in 1984 that Central America would need $24 billion in multilateral assistance by 1990 in order to increase its GDP by 6 percent and bring its population back to its 1979 standard of living. On the eve of the January 1992 signing of the peace agreement with the FMLN, president Alfredo Cristiani estimated that the country would require an influx of $2 billion from the international community if the Salvadoran economy was to recover. The Nicaraguan vice-president, for his part, said that since his government took office, the White House had supplied his country with the equivalent of $2 million a day.[21]

These figures give an idea of the extent of foreign involvement in the Central American conflict and in the institutional processes that followed; the picture that emerges is clearly one of countries that subsist on subsidies from abroad. Whatever else they do, the figures once again bring up the complex—and, to some, unwelcome—question of these countries' viability as individual nation-states. Throughout the 1980s, USAID took a frontline role in designing and financing the economic policies of the Costa Rican and Salvadoran governments (Sojo 1991; Cuenca 1992; Rosa 1993); after the February 1990 change in government, it began to play a similar role in Nicaragua (Saldomando 1992).

4. Elections and institutional democratization

The United States' backing for electoral democratization in the region was part of a counterinsurgency strategy that sought to delegitimize the revolutionary appeal and deprive it of social support. In this sense, the Guatemalan and Salvadoran elections of the 1980s can properly be viewed as one chapter in an overall counterrevoutionary strategy (as in Jonas 1988, for example). As one senior Guatemalan army officer put it, elections made politics "the continuation of war by other means."[22] Observers were lavish with terms to discredit the regimes that emerged from these elections: "democracies under guard" (Vilas 1990); "national security democracies" (Timossi 1993); "low-intensity democracies" (Torres Rivas 1993). All stressed the fact that such elections invariably took place under the vigilance of the armed forces—which remained immune to civilian institutions—and of U.S. counterinsurgency policy. The "façade democracies" of the 1960s and 1970s (Solórzano Martínez 1983) gave way to these ambiguous creatures of the 1980s.

Washington's strategy succeeded because it recognized in some fashion the conviction of a relatively broad sector of the population that dictatorship and electoral fraud had closed off any other route than revolution. Support for revolution among a wide stripe of Central America's population was based on its call for political democratization, rather than its promise of radical social change. The Kissinger Report saw this clearly, even if at bottom the report did no more than give a conceptual expression to what was already going on in El Salvador.[23]

Christian Democratic parties carried out this strategy in El Salvador and in Guatemala. In both cases, these parties offered a modestly reformist perspective, a mass presence, and proven anticommunism. They were without a doubt the closest thing to an ideal ally the United States could hope for. In Honduras, where Christian Democrats' electoral clout was minimal, this role was played by the most rightward fractions of the Liberal party.

The strategy succeeded not only because elections were held and won by U.S.-backed candidates, but also because the revolutionary organizations were thrown off balance. Due to both ideological tradition and recent historical evidence, these groups assumed that the proper form of bourgeois rule in their countries was dictatorship, fraud and open repression: what other conclusion was possible from political history? The rupture with inertia and tradition took them by surprise.

The revolutionaries, for their part, can claim some credit for the advent of honest vote-counting: it took a revolutionary challenge to bring it about. The FSLN takes this argument especially seriously, with some justification: the February 25, 1990 elections mark the first time in Nicaragua's history that ballots changed a government. It is also true, however, that this is not the kind of democracy the revolutionaries intended to create two decades ago. Their ideal then was a kind of democracy that, while not excluding elections, could not be reduced to them. It involved changes in the socioeconomic structure itself: above all, better access for workers to basic

resources: food, education, health, jobs, land. The structural transformation of society was regarded as the essential condition for
building a political system in which the economically powerful
could not impose their will on the economically weak—in which,
in fact, there might not even be any economically powerful (see
FSLN 1980; CDR 1980).

Things did not turn out that way. Revolution, as a strategy for
taking political power and profoundly changing society, did not
come about except in Nicaragua, where it was unable to consolidate itself. Where the goal of profound social transformation has
not altogether disappeared from the platforms of the organizations
that first raised the banner of revolution, it has been relegated to a
later time, after an institutional democracy with very moderate
social features has been consolidated (FMLN 1990).[24] But society
did change, and the political system did open up; it is more
competitive and far less violent than it was two decades ago, even
though in both respects there remains a long way to go.

The process of rebuilding Central America's political systems
around elections displays a few recurring features. First, all of the
elections carried out in the 1980s were won by political tendencies
friendly to the right or the center-right, with the sole exception of
the 1984 Nicaraguan elections. With the defeat of the Sandinistas
in the 1990 elections, citizens' ballots have shaped a region with
governments uniformly sympathetic to the United States. This may
change in the 1990s, however: in the November 1993 general
election in Honduras, the opposition Liberal party, behind a candidate linked to the defense of human rights, critical of the neoliberal economic policies of Leonardo Callejas's Nacional party
government and explicitly interested in subordinating military to
civilian power, won a resounding presidential and legislative victory.

Elections, while useful for neutralizing political conflict and to
define who is going to manage society through the state, have the
additional effect of highlighting the weakness of political parties
as mediating agents and as locations for the representation of mass
interests. Organizational fragility is a problem most of all for
parties on the left of the political spectrum, which have been
persecuted, repressed, and forced to work underground. Even
those that did not propose revolution were barred from participat-

ing in elections. The murder of quite moderate leftist leaders was common political coin until very recently; paramilitary groups and death squads remain active today in Guatemala and El Salvador. According to FMLN sources, thirty-six of its members and leaders have been murdered since the peace agreements were signed in February 1992.[25] The new institutional scene poses new challenges to the political parties that stand for social change and broad-based democratization.

Right-wing parties show signs of weakness as well. These are mainly clientelistic groups with fragile structures that have functioned above all as agencies for mobilizing the vote among captive populations—laborers, poor peasants, urban subproletarians. Revolutionary mobilization largely did away with such submission, and today any party that desires to attract votes must put forward concrete proposals. In all, the modernization of the Central American right progressed much further in the business world than in the sphere of party politics, which helps explain the younger business leaders' increasingly direct involvement in electoral politics. Traditional Central American politicians aspired to becoming millionaires; today it is the other way around.

There is much evidence of a disjuncture between the inertia of the political system and the dynamism of civil society. Most notable, perhaps, are the relatively high abstention levels in Salvadoran and Guatemalan elections (Table 4.9). The representative system as it functions in those countries does not appear to attract a large or even a growing portion of the potential electorate. Without much specific information—the underdevelopment of representative democracy has a corollary in the primitive state of electoral sociology—we can only suggest a few preliminary hypotheses to account for this.

Reformist parties, as is well known, faced serious obstacles to institutional activity during the time covered in Table 4.9. To publicly express sympathy for Christian Democrats—notwithstanding U.S. support—for social democrats, or for any party that proposed any social change became extremely dangerous in some of the region's countries. Moreover, persistent vote fraud canceled the effect of what little institutional politics was tolerated, and helped weaken collective faith in the power of the vote.

Some of the socioeconomic factors described above may also be

Table 4.9
Central America: Voting Abstention in Recent Elections
(Percent of Registered Voters)

	1980	1981	1982	1984	1985	1986	1988	1989	1990	1991
Costa Rica			21.4[a]			18.2[a]			18.2[a]	
El Salvador			24.8[b]	20.7[a]	38.5[c]		30.3[c]	45.3[a]		48.1[c]
Guatemala			54.2[a]		30.8[a]				43.6[a]	54.8[a]
Honduras	18.6[b]	22.1[a]			15.1[a]			20.6[a]		
Nicaragua				24.6[d]					13.8[d]	

Sources: Torres-Rivas 1991 and author's calculations.
[a] Presidential election.
[b] Constitutional Assembly elections.
[c] Legislative elections.
[d] Presidential, legislative, and municipal elections.

at work. The growth of the UIS, for example, means more than growing informal unemployment and an expanding informal economy. Informality includes a vast array of social practices of a political nature: authority structures, social hierarchies, measures of prestige, and cultural norms take shape that have little in common with the formal dimension of society, however intimately they may articulate to it. The relatively high abstention in recent voting in Guatemala and El Salvador may express not so much repudiation or indifference to politics as disaffection from the kind of politics, of discourse, of appeal, that dominates "official" institutional politics. Official politics addresses neither the expectations nor the demands of the growing slice of the population that is impelled to live, not just work or shop or sell, outside the practices and institutions of formal society.

The growth of mass poverty, aggravated by the biases in government economic and social policies, have accentuated the absence, loss, or relaxation of institutional reference points for participating in the political system. Political systems are based on a system of reciprocities; legitimacy, even if it consists of nothing more than passive acquiescence, is the result of a complex matrix of implicit day-to-day transactions by virtue of which the governed judge that they receive a fair reward for their consent: access to resources, safety, symbolic compensation (a feeling of belonging, of dignity, etc.). The question is worth asking: What real feeling of belonging to the political system—in other words, what feeling of citizenship—can more than 19 million Central Americans living below the poverty line have?

Sociocultural factors may also be important. In societies with a strong indigenous component, institutional politics is still an affair for *mestizos* or *ladinos*; in countries that still have a large rural population, it remains largely a matter for city dwellers. It is reasonable to suppose, therefore, that this politics of mestizos, ladinos, and urbanites bears little appeal for those who do not belong to those groups. What real sense of citizenship—as defined by constitutions and state policies—can there be for the approximately 12 million Central Americans forced to express themselves politically in a language not their own, through institutions that have little to do with their cultural patterns and authority structures?

Demilitarization

Ten years of revolutionary and counterrevolutionary war fed a vast process of militarization that today has proved difficult to reverse. In a region that had already been traditionally vulnerable to the phenomenon, the Central American military apparatuses' role in defending established order and their close ties with the U.S. government made fertile ground for the political supremacy of the armed forces.

Paradoxically, the militarization of the conflict gathered momentum just as regional efforts to put politics back in the center of the regional agenda began to appear. Militarization and demilitarization became the two faces of the Central American drama. From Contadora in 1983 to Esquipulas II in 1987, the region's governments consistently attempted to defuse armed conflicts— the counterrevolutionary war in Nicaragua, the revolutionary wars in El Salvador and Guatemala—and to reach peaceful solutions. The broad-based domestic support for these initiatives extended to business groups that saw an end to war as the condition for reviving their economies and rebuilding regional markets. The Central American governments also enjoyed the support of Mexico, Panama, and Venezuela at first, and later that of a broad group of Latin American countries; finally joined by the United Nations and almost the entire international community, with the United States virtually the sole holdout.[26]

Washington, which had managed to maneuver the Contadora process into failure, was unable to head off an agreement at Esquipulas. The "Procedure for Establishing Firm and Lasting Peace in Central America," signed August 7, 1987 by all five Central American presidents, called for national reconciliation based on political dialogue and broad amnesties. It proposed an end to hostilities and committed the signers to pluralistic and participatory democratization with respect for human rights, social justice, national self-determination without foreign interference, and free elections. It ruled out aid from outside the region to irregular forces (the Nicaraguan contras) or insurrectional movements (the FMLN and the URNG) and prohibited the use of any state's territory for aggression against another. The document also established a procedure for verification and international followup.

George Bush's accession to the presidency of the United States brought a relative retreat from the crude dogmatism that had guided Ronald Reagan's Central America policy. With the outbreak of crisis in the Soviet Union, meanwhile, Soviet diplomats eager to reconcile with Washington pushed to reduce both countries' roles in the Central American conflict and support the region's motion toward peace. The call to elections in Nicaragua, and then the opposition victory there, further shifted Washington's outlook and the United States finally joined in the peace effort.

Demilitarization in the strict sense—the postwar rearrangement of the armed forces—has made significant progress in Nicaragua and El Salvador. In Nicaragua both the Sandinista People's Army and the contras have been progressively disarmed and demobilized. In El Salvador, the process of purging and shrinking the armed forces has lagged well behind the demobilization of the FMLN, but all the strata of officers that conducted the counterinsurgency war have been forced into retirement and the army has been reduced in size by 50 percent overall. In Guatemala and Honduras, the prospect of demilitarization has not even been formally raised. Both economic factors and ideology and politics account for the reluctance to address the issue. Honduran President Carlos Roberto Reina's attempt to abolish the compulsory military draft was strongly opposed by the army, which eventually forced the government to step back.

Demilitarization will affect the interests of those who benefited from the swollen military budgets of the last decade and the management of U.S. aid. Many officers earned enormous wealth from trafficking in materiel and other contraband, administering payrolls and related business pursuits, and they can be counted on to resist effective subordination to civilian power or anything else that will interfere with these activities.

Given the vast scale of the Central American armed forces' involvement in the political lives of their countries, demilitarization means much more than simply reducing the size of armies, or bringing military budgets under control. It implies rethinking the relationship between the armed forces and the state and civil society: developing a new concept of the function of the military in societies moving towards democratization after the demise of the cold war system.

For all the difficulty and the resistance there has been, it must be recognized that Nicaragua and El Salvador have moved further down this road than have Guatemala or Honduras, even though the impunity that has traditionally shrouded the activities of the armed forces and the security forces in all of these countries is a matter still to be resolved.

FIVE

Revolution, Reform, Democracy

The contours of the revolutionary situations that emerged in Central America were the end results of economic, political, and cultural factors that took shape over the course of decades. In countries under repressive or exclusionary political regimes, economic change and the tensions it produced led major sectors of the population to take up alternative forms of collective action.

The Guatemalan counterrevolution of 1954 preceded capitalist modernization, and modernization, when it came, carried the marks of a repressive state. In El Salvador, socioeconomic change went on under a continuous oligarchic and military state until 1979. The emerging middle groups never developed a political formula to institutionally incorporate the workers movement or the peasantry. The return of thousands of small farmers from Honduras after the 1969 war aggravated pressure on the land and made plain the political system's incapacity to process popular demands without conflict. In Nicaragua, the Somoza dictatorship designed capitalist modernization to its own benefit, antagonizing at the same time—though unequally—the popular classes and those factions of the bourgeoisie that were excluded from control of the state. The traditional parties held a monopoly on legal political activity, which was limited to occasional rigged elections. In all three cases, political mechanisms that might have permitted the sectors injured by the economic and social transformations to express their demands were absent or useless, creating space for revolutionary appeals. The changes and ruptures in all three countries' rural areas paralleled and reinforced changes in the urban world.

The state in Guatemala and El Salvador fulfilled an eminently instrumental role for the ruling bloc, enabling it to maintain a high degree of cohesion despite internal tensions. This permitted effective resistance to revolutionary attacks while at the same time stamping all the political actors with an explicit class character: the workers, the peasants, the poor and dispossessed on the one hand; the traditional ruling and modernizing sectors, the rich and powerful on the other, with the authoritarian state as their political formula. In Nicaragua, in contrast, the family dictatorship of the Somozas gave the state a marked autonomy from the dominant classes. The Somoza regime's exclusionary nature and its increasing isolation, along with structural conditions and FSLN strategy, laid the groundwork for the ruling bloc to split along democratic and antidictatorial lines, and for elements of the traditional classes to join the revolutionary alliance.

The appearance of organizations seeking access to political power by the armed route does not necessarily or immediately pose a threat to the political regime or the ruling classes, although it does challenge the aspiration of every modern state to a direct or indirect monopoly on armed power. Only when those organizations recruit significant numbers of the population, organize them, mobilize them, and neutralize the regime's repressive capacity do they become an actual threat. Viewed from this perspective, the significance of foreign support for revolutionary organizations—a central argument for U.S. government agencies and the Central American right—becomes secondary. The Cuban government was undoubtedly sympathetic to revolutionary organizations trying to topple governments that supported Washington's anti-Cuban policies; it is even known to have constituted a rearguard for many of them.[1] Nevertheless, to attribute the mobilizing capacity and the broad popular presence of these organizations to whatever support they may have received from outside exaggerates the relationship. On the contrary, access to Cuban support seems to have depended on the organizations' own track record at earning popular support for their struggles.

Trapped as they were by the growth of agroexport capitalism, without significant prospects for work in the cities, without a way to express their demands in the political system, frustrated by the thwarted hopes of reformism, victimized by largely indiscriminate preventive repression, and equipped with a religious discourse that justified rebellion, it is not hard to understand why broad sectors of the popular classes in Nicaragua, Guatemala, and El Salvador would accept, in one form or another, the revolutionary organizations' ideas. Some took them up as an ideological choice; others came along simply for lack of an alternative. Some joined with a view to what they could gain from it, and still others found in it a last line of defense against losing everything.

The political relations among classes in Honduras and Costa Rica were not free of conflicts. Many of the demands of the workers' movement, and especially the peasantry, stood in conflict with the advance of capitalist agroexport and industrial modernization, and the political regimes' capacity to process their demands was limited insofar as capitalist modernization was now part of the very nature of the regime. But the political conditions existed in both countries to articulate these demands as part of the regime's functioning, rather than as a challenge to it.

The slow pace of economic modernization in Honduras and the reformist strategy of the state enhanced the legitimacy of the political system and narrowed the space for revolutionary alternatives. The strength of the foreign enclave, along with the regional fragmentation and economic fragility of the ruling class, reinforced the autonomy of the state and especially of the army, which for two decades became the arbiter of social tensions, accepted by all actors as the legitimate center for processing their contradictions. There certainly were objective reasons for this; the easy availability of land made it possible for Honduras' timid agrarian reform to be less conflictive than the 1976 reform effort in El Salvador. But the people/land relationship in Nicaragua was not very different. There, the regime relied on repression against the recently born peasant organizations demanding land. Somoza's colonization programs covered a small portion of all farmers, and served essentially as an instrument for putting marginal lands into production;

the land was later taken away from the farmers involved and given back to government-connected landowners. The Honduran military looked rather for compromise solutions, and they became an element of social cohesion in a period of change and tension.

Agrarian reform—both in the sense of offering access to land and strengthening peasant organizations—was the central element that distinguished the Honduran case. The expulsion of Salvadoran peasants as a result of the 1969 war increased the land available for distribution without risking collision with landowning interests, and at the same time raised hopes among the peasants. The massive and dynamic nature of Honduras's peasant organizations has no parallel in Latin America except in Bolivia. It stands in contrast with the weakness of the urban labor movement and party system which limited the outreach of rural mobilization. Lacking significant urban allies, the Honduran peasant movement pressed the system to open up and let it in, rather than to replace the system. The military regimes' responses to the demands of the peasant sector were relatively benign, and Honduras's material conditions made it possible to partially satisfy those demands without creating significant tensions with the landowners; these factors help explain the apparent contradiction of a society marked by the region's most widespread, crushing poverty and backwardness, while absent of significant revolutionary mobilizations.

The political system's legitimacy is notorious in Costa Rica, where political modernization preceded economic modernization. New state institutions and roles in social security, the legal recognition of social organizations, the subaltern classes' ability to express their social and political demands through the institutional system, the elimination of the armed forces, and a decent electoral system, all helped cushion peasants and workers from the most disruptive aspects of economic modernization. Notwithstanding the impact of the recent economic crisis on the popular classes, and the progressive hardening of the state's position on "social issues," the Costa Rican political system's unique ability to process the most urgent popular demands is undeniable. Although violence and repression were not absent from either Costa Rica or Honduras, they were mainly the instruments of private groups or local officials, rather than a political resource of the state as a national institution.

The preventive counterinsurgent states in Guatemala, El Salvador, and Nicaragua were maintained, with the open and decisive support of the U.S. government, as a reaction against the victory of the Cuban revolution. Repression, political fraud, proscription, and coups d'état constitute the institutional framework of capitalist modernization in these three countries. Timid attempts at reform in El Salvador and Guatemala in the 1970s were quickly liquidated by military coups, the preventive cancellation of elections by force, or nullification of the results when they favored the emerging forces.

The rigidity of the political system in these countries certainly affected the workers and peasants. But it also damaged the urban middle sectors, including elements of the bourgeoisie that were marginalized by specific state policies for the benefit of the groups that directly controlled the state (the "disloyal competition" of the Somoza dictatorship or of the Guatemalan military governments). The political restrictions aroused an especially intense resentment among urban middle groups—the petty-bourgeoisie of technicians and professionals with more education than jobs; public employees; students; journalists, and others—and among the small industrial and service proletariat, with which they often overlapped. Proscription of modernizing political parties, repression of labor organizations, and electoral fraud deprived these groups of channels for articulating and advancing their interests, or diminished the effectiveness of those channels where they did exist. Their radicalization, therefore, was an answer to the blockage of institutional opportunities. Deprived of the option of participating in institutions, they turned to mobilizing the popular masses, merging their own demands with agrarian and popular discontent. The demand for democratization fused with the demand for social justice.

The closing of the institutional system in El Salvador, Guatemala, and Nicaragua left those harmed by capitalist modernization without legal means to articulate their own demands, complaints, and claims. Electoral frauds played an important part in moving large fractions of the centrist parties toward radical opposition. On the one hand, closing off institutional opportunities for expression created fertile ground for revolutionary strategies to take root among many of the impoverished and marginalized sectors. On the other, the regimes' hostility to all initiatives for reform and political participation, and later their very heavy and generalized repression, made room for political alternatives—whether revolutionary or reformist—that were fundamentally identified by the demand for democracy. This particular configuration of the political system forced most of the revolutionary organizations—or allowed them, depending on the observer's perspective—to adopt political formulas focusing on the democratic question, and encouraged the formulation of national multiclass appeals, with each organization attaining greater or lesser influence and efficacy in the process. By the same token, the degree to which the established political powers were tied to the White House would influence how much space there was, among the revolutionary alternatives, for a politics based on anti-imperialism or national liberation.

The Costa Rican and Honduran cases again stand in stark contrast with the preventive building of counterinsurgent states. In Costa Rica, the events of 1948 laid the foundations for a constitutional, democratic, and reformist political system. The elimination of the army prior to capitalist modernization meant that the traditional ruling classes were left without their principal political tool. Violent responses to popular mobilizations did exist, but most were carried out directly by landowners, and the state proved generally receptive to the claims of those harmed by them. The labor movement, endowed with a degree of institutional legitimacy, grew modestly. In the early 1970s, 11 percent of the country's labor force was unionized, compared with only 2 percent in Nicaragua and 5 percent in El Salvador. Costa Rica's superior performance with regard to social indicators has much to do with the greater openness of its political institutions to the demands of popular organizations, and with the social reformism that its principal political forces adopted as their explicit ideology. Within limits—most of them aimed at the *Partido Vanguardia Popular*—the legal political game offered a certain variety of options. The social security system was effective, if mainly in urban areas.

Costa Rica had politically and socially consolidated domestic control of its traditional agroexport sector before the crisis of 1929, without significant threats from the left or from below. The state resorted to regulatory policy to meet the crisis, sacrificing the immediate interests of the agroexport bourgeoisie and acting as a kind of "collective capitalist." The scope of state intervention, which in the rest of the region and across Latin America was defined as a class question—with the middle class and the emerging industrial bourgeoisie favoring broader intervention and the traditional groups opposed to it—took shape in Costa Rica as an issue internal to the traditional groups and their system of rule, and came to be viewed as a normal function of the state. When the middle sectors, the workers' movement, and small farmers advanced their own social reform proposals in the midst of the mobilizations and disorders that followed World War II, they met an already-developed state apparatus with the technical capacity—and the political capacity as well, once the post-1948 regime was in place—to channel and give an institutional expression to a good part of the emerging groups' demands.

In sum, the capitalist state in El Salvador, Guatemala, and Nicaragua functioned as an apparatus for explicit and systematic popular repression, beginning with the massacre of *la Matanza* of 1932 in El Salvador, the 1954 counterrevolution in Guatemala, and the repression of General Sandino's guerrillas in the 1930s in Nicaragua. The legitimacy of the state was internal to the ruling classes—and in the case of Nicaragua, not even to the whole ruling class. In Costa Rica, in contrast, the state emerged from the compromises upon which the 1948 revolution was negotiated, with space for the pressures and demands of the subaltern classes and groups. In Honduras, military reformism built the state into a sort of arbiter, sensitive to some of the demands of the popular movement, especially of the peasants.

Another aspect that distinguishes the revolutionary forces in El Salvador and Guatemala from those in Nicaragua—besides their more explicitly class character, as described earlier—is the distinctive role of mass movements. The key development in El Salvador and Guatemala in the 1960s was the rise of social struggles—labor, shantytowns, peasants, students, indigenous people. This mass movement would later serve as a base for the revolutionary organizations, through alliances and negotiations, and for front-building—and therefore as grounds for recognizing differences, and even contradictions, in perspective and approach. The Guatemalan and Salvadoran guerrilla organizations attempted to impose their perspectives and strategies on the social organizations and the mass fronts, in some cases more successfully than others, and results for the revolutionary mobilization overall were mixed. A matrix of tensions and negotiations developed that was unknown in Nicaragua. The labor and popular movement against the Somoza family's dictatorial state, on the contrary, showed a marked weakness. This helps explain the mass organizations' heavy dependence on, and limited autonomy from, the state after 1979. The FSLN itself created the Sandinista social organizations— labor, peasant, and women's groups—as part of its insurrectional strategy, in contrast with El Salvador, where some of the revolutionary groups emerged out of already-existing social organizations.

Class and people in the Central American revolution

The type of agroindustrial capitalism that developed in Central America shaped a social structure in which the class character of the actors were less than fully formed during the period of revolutionary gestation; their social contours took shape articulated to other criteria of differentiation, mainly by region and ethnicity. In turn, the confrontation with political systems protected by U.S. government agencies made democracy and national sovereignty as important as social identity in attracting certain groups to the revolutionary cause. Of course, different groups and social classes understand democratization and national sovereignty in different ways.

The collapse of peasant economies, the rise of migration, and the limited job-creating capacity of industrialization helped create a vast rural and urban semiproletariat. Seasonal work in the countryside and the small size of the urban industrial working class reduced the social differentiation between underemployment, small shopkeeping, and self-employment. The experience of partial or seasonal wage work became much more common across this whole period than any "pure" peasant or proletarian experience. The urban environment tended to amplify these features of a popular economy, molding the poor and dispossessed of the city and country into a plebeian mass moving fluidly between a strategy of cautious, incremental, negotiated defense and mobilizations and confrontations with government agencies. These are impoverished sectors that, if they have not yet lost all, have not much left to defend.

El Salvador's department of Chalatenango, which became the scene of intense guerrilla warfare, is a case in point. In the late 1960s, most of Chalatenango's labor force was untrained and worked seasonally in the coffee, cotton, and sugarcane farms in the country's central and southern departments, or migrated to San Salvador and Honduras. The relatively few large landowners concentrated on land-extensive livestock raising, the poverty of the soil having ruled out almost any agroexport development. Little infrastructure was available, and there were almost no local markets. Social services were very limited; a very high proportion of the inhabitants lived in extreme poverty, especially in the countryside, where 73 percent of the department's population lived. Chalatenango had the country's lowest population density, along with some of its highest levels of land tenure concentration: 10 percent of the farms occupied 75 percent of the land, while the other 90 percent held the rest of the land in plots of ten manzanas or less. An estimated 40 percent of the work force was unemployed in 1975, due to the low job-generating capacity of the main economic activity (Pearce 1986:46ff). Chalatenango was by no means one of the dynamic poles of capitalist modernization or a concentration point for the rural proletariat. It was, rather, a reservoir of semi-proletarianized labor force that migrated seasonally into the growth centers of agroexport capitalism.

Similarly, Guatemala's most impoverished departments—Quiché, Huehuetenango, San Marcos, and other areas that in previous decades had supplied seasonal migrants to the capitalist estates on the southern coast—were among the most intense scenes of guerrilla warfare. Meanwhile, departments that did not experience these population shifts or the resulting instability, such as Totonicapána, were relatively free of guerrilla activity and counterinsurgency operations (Paige 1983; Smith 1991).

In both cases, the traditional foundations of life erode but do not altogether disappear, and can therefore be defended, while other alternatives remain unstable. It was this combination, more than the displacement of traditional crops by agroexport, or the replacement of a plot of land with a wage, that (together with the other factors described in this chapter) moved broad segments of some

Central American countries' rural and urban populations to respond to the appeal to revolution. In agrarian societies experiencing the blows of agroindustrial capitalism, this situation is particularly conducive to revolutionary situations.

More than the growth of an industrial or agroindustrial working class per se, what encourages revolutionary activity is the emergence of a wage labor force still closely tied to community life. Exposure to capitalism, combined with the preservation of a sort of rearguard in the villages allows the survival of traditional loyalties and networks to reinforce these workers' discontent.

The urban scene was no different. The social profile of the Sandinista insurrection is clearly dominated by segments that have not yet been proletarianized—and perhaps never entirely will be—but are increasingly pushed toward the fringes of the market by the expansion of industrial and commercial capitalism: seasonal wage earners, *gentes de oficio* (tradespeople), small merchants and peddlers. Together they formed a sort of urban and semiurban *pobresia* (underclass), in the sense that many of those living in poor neighborhoods also join their families in the legions of seasonal workers for the various harvests (Vilas 1986, 1988). These factors helped endow the Central American revolutions with a character more popular than proletarian, although in this particular there were differences between Nicaragua, on one hand, and Guatemala and El Salvador on the other.

This rural semiproletariat and its counterpart in the urban *pobresia* are the most politically volatile sectors in agrarian societies subjected to rapid capitalist transformation (Dierckxsens 1981; de Janvry 1981). The erosion of their social foundations and the resulting climate of insecurity are especially stark in these segments of the social structure. Their previous forms and channels for social expression disappear long before a clear alternative arises. They lose access to the land but do not cease to be peasants; they are proletarianized but do not have stable wage-earning jobs; the family begins to split up, and people wander the country. They have no place under the sun.

Structural factors are not sufficient, however, to determine the direction and content of the political choices of these population sectors. The evidence suggests, on the contrary, that Central America's semiproletariat has helped support a diverse array of political options, all of them marked by collective violent action. It is prominent in the social bases of El Salvador's revolutionary organizations and paramilitary counterrevolutionary organizations such as ORDEN; in Guatemala, both the guerrilla organizations and the government "self-defense patrols"; in Nicaragua, the activists of the FSLN and the recruits of Somoza's Guardia Nacional, and later the contras.[2]

The political crisis of the Central American oligarchies was a result of attacks from a broad spectrum of social forces: the emerging impoverished middle sectors, some segments of the incipient industrial bourgeoisie, and the popular classes. Unlike the bourgeois revolutions in Europe, in which the bourgeoisie led the assault on the traditional order with the support of a broad mass mobilization without organized political expressions of its own, the main challenge to the traditional order in Central America came from organizations that in one way or another expressed the radicalized dissatisfaction of the masses, even if such organizations were led by elements from the middle classes. The oligarchic crisis and the bourgeois crisis, as Torres Rivas has shown, accumulated one to the other (Torres Rivas 1982:39–69).

The autonomy that the rural and urban working masses enjoyed, or aspired to, sparked the middle class's fears of being overwhelmed; that threat along with the anticapitalist and socialist implications of workers' movements' pronouncements undermined the middle class's anti-oligarchic stand. The radicalization of the dissident groups in the Salvadoran PDC had no parallel in Guatemala or in Nicaragua. The effect of the accumulating crisis, in consequence, was ambiguous. On the one hand, it forced the oligarchies to accept certain changes in the traditional order; with the weakness of the emerging middle sectors balanced by the mobilization of the popular masses, the traditional elites had no choice but to accept some of the changes the middle groups demanded. On the other hand, it forced the organizations representing the working masses to moderate their class demands so as not to scare off the middle groups, which were motivated more by demands for political democratization than by the contradictions with the economic structure.

The convergence of middle sectors with the popular masses was possible because of their shared rejection of the oligarchic order;

the convergence of the middle groups and the traditional elites was based on their shared defense of the capitalist order. Naturally, the organizations that represented the middle groups and those that represented the popular classes conceived of the scope of the transformation of the oligarchic order differently. In the same way, the oligarchy and the middle sectors diverged on what kind of capitalism should be defended from the revolutionary assault. Although these differences are theoretical, they were advanced in practical terms, with concrete impacts on the strategies and policies of the state. What was at stake in Central American revolution and counterrevolution, therefore, was a conflict over how much of capitalism was in question and how much of capitalism had to be defended to the death, rather than a total rejection or a total defense of capitalism.

Whither Central America?

Fifteen years of armed confrontation did not deliver political victory for popular demands for economic change and social justice. But the orgy of repression, with its generous foreign funding, did not succeed in silencing them, or keeping them at last from finding legitimate expression in a more open political system. People have lost their fear and have gained organizing experience. However much or however little they won, they won it through their direct participation. The very change in the discourse of the ruling groups expresses a recognition of profound transformations in social consciousness. Socialism did not replace capitalism, and it is U.S. hegemony, not *patria libre*, that has been consolidated. But the revolutionary assault on the oligarchic order, by action or reaction, led to the redefinition of political regimes and of social relations, and finally the U.S. government was forced to put aside its long-standing alliances and join in efforts to reach peace. Revolutionaries were unable to eliminate illiteracy or poverty, gender discrimination or ethnic oppression, unemployment or agrarian dispossession, but they did away with resignation to them. Central Americans know today that something else is possible, and the power of collective action has not gone unnoticed. The consolidation of U.S. hegemony, meanwhile, is a hemispheric phenomenon that owes much more to the disappearance of the Soviet Union than to the Central American revolutions' own failures.

The Central American societies emerge from this traumatic period of their history having undergone a wide array of changes. Many of these were not on the revolutionary agenda, and some are of a different sort altogether. But neither could they have occurred without a revolutionary challenge to the system of power. The Central American revolutionary movements failed to change the existing systems at the roots, but they were nevertheless a vital factor in the political and social reforms of recent years, and those that will certainly follow. Paradoxically, the very social and political reform that revolutionaries scorned for twenty-five years has been the most consistent product of their struggle. Perhaps, to romantics, this outcome may seem inconsequential in the face of the magnitude of the popular exertion, with its tremendous costs. To this author, however, the outcome of these terrible decades of revolution, counterrevolution, and war, is but further evidence of the primitivism and the rapacity that still grip some of Central America's ruling elites, which can accept reform only when it is imposed on them by a revolutionary storm.

The recognition of the people's dignity and the evidence of its efficacy may be the most significant fruit of these traumatic decades, and the one that stands out most sharply against the background of the old Central American history, cut to the measure of the elites. It is thanks to this efficacy that today one can publicly raise the flag of political participation and social change in a framework of spreading legitimacy. Still, the prospects for democratizing the political system are as dim as ever if Central Americans do not democratize society itself, and close the profound economic and cultural fault lines that cross it. A great many Central Americans remain plainly dissatisfied with the predominant living conditions. To very large parts of the population, the prospects for democratization are still tied to the prospects for social reform, and to a close relationship between political citizenship and social citizenship. The change of scenery following the close of the revolutionary era means only that social conflict will be processed by different means than in the recent past; but the conflict itself is still open.

Peace involves, at a minimum, a consensual change in the arena and the methods for processing social conflicts and political projects. But conflict remains: the end of the era of armed struggle has neither mended the rifts nor resolved the contradictions that engendered them. If peace is to mean something more than the hypocritical administration of an iniquitous order in which the victors and the vanquished live together muttering their reciprocal frustration, political and social organizations must hold to their commitment to people's aspirations and demands for a more dignified life, if by different methods.

Three great challenges rise before Central America today: effective democratization, sustained development, and social justice. This agenda is not a new one; it was the failure to meet these very challenges—because of the resistance of the ruling groups and the U.S. government, the failure of reform, and structural rigidity—that opened the door to the revolutionary era that today appears to be over. For how long? The answer depends largely on Central America's capacity to confront these basic questions.

The spread of elections as a mechanism for political competition throughout the 1980s inspired triumphalist announcements of the return of democracy to Central America. Leaving aside the candor or cynicism behind such a discourse, what does the "return" of democracy mean? Is it a return to the formal and fraudulent practices of the past, which helped spark the revolutionary crisis, or an advance toward fuller and more effective political participation? The fashion in which the regional conflict was settled allows both conceptions to coexist in the agenda of democratization. But if by the return of democracy we mean fuller and more effective political participation, the worst thing that could happen would be to retreat to the political styles of the past.

Clean, transparent, and competitive elections can certainly help rule this out, but more than that is required. Democratization demands a broad-based process of institution-building that includes honest and independent courts, effective safeguards for constitutional guarantees and human rights, and real subordination of the armed forces and security forces to civilian authority. The last, in particular, means putting an end to the system of training and values that implicitly or explicitly placed the armed forces and the security forces on an ethical and institutional plane above the citizenry as a whole, and led to the acceptance of police arrogance, brutality by the security forces, and unpunished attacks on the civilian population. Democratization therefore means eliminating the idea that *security* refers to the state, and replacing it with a concept based on safety for the citizen.

Advancing democratization in Central America requires strengthening the political party system, in several ways. The first and most obvious is democratizing the parties themselves, which remain captive to clientelism and *caudillo* practices. Internal elections, debate, and criticism are not yet highly developed in most of Central America's parties. Secondly, the parties' capacity to articulate the demands and perspectives emerging from the newly-mobilized sectors—peasants, women, Indian communities, the urban poor—is in question, and this has brought the parties to the verge of a crisis of representation. Who will express the demands of these sectors, which do not appear to feel represented by the kind of electoral politics that is practiced in the region today? If these parties—old, new, or renewed—do not do it, electoral politics will become once again a sophisticated game for minority groups: a democracy for the elites, now expanded to take in the urban middle groups. Third, electoral democracy requires an attempt to organize and consolidate parliamentary action. A strong presidentialist tradition, combined with party-based clientelism and the absence of permanent organizational structures, has stood in the way of building a legislative branch effectively independent of the executive. More generally, the perverse all-or-nothing dynamic that still characterizes Central American politics makes the executive/legislative relationship a particularly difficult one. Central American parliaments vacillate between inactivity and subordination to the executive.

Effective democratization in Central America also depends on developing mechanisms for social integration. The word "integration" horrifies anthropologists when applied to multi-ethnic societies, because it implies squeezing multiple identities and cultures into the mold of the dominant ethnic group, by force if necessary. That, obviously, is not the issue. Integration can serve to subdue and negate cultural diversity—in which case it has nothing to do with democratization—or it can so strengthen this diversity that the homeland, or the country, or whatever it is to be called, can function for all, or at least give all a feeling of belonging and togetherness. Education, health services, social security, employment, and social organization are channels and resources conventionally used to integrate people into the social and political system, to give citizenship a social dimension. This was patently one of the major sources of the Central American political systems' past weakness, as well as one explanation for the much-noted political stability of Costa Rica. To advance democratization, political democracy must be constructed as social democracy, in its broadest and most powerful sense.

A democratization process so conceived must rest on a development strategy. Otherwise, where would the resources come from to finance people's integration into institutions and political and social processes? Not every development strategy, however, is compatible with effective democratization. Central America's own development experience has certainly not proved to be.

All of the available evidence suggests that the predominant economic strategies are of very limited use in promoting democratization. In the first place, their emphasis on deregulation, openings to foreign markets, and agroexport promotion offer, as the essence of modernity, the same old mode of development against whose effects peasants, workers, and middle sectors rebelled more than twenty years ago, sparking a revolutionary cycle that is coming to a difficult close only now. Secondly, neoliberal development recipes invariably amplify the marginalizing effects of the market. Finally, these recipes in themselves carry clearly authoritarian implications: opposition to unions and other labor rights, expansion of unremunerated work time (especially for women), and erosion of basic social services, among other things.

The incipient Central American democracies call for a development strategy that can address the people's needs and concerns. This does not mean closing off access to foreign markets, but it does call for a strategy that makes majority needs its central concern and takes them as a starting point for a more balanced growth scheme. As long as the enormous disparities that divide Central American societies today are not reduced, democratic consolidation will remain at risk, and the threat of renewed violence will remain latent even if development does advance.

Authoritarianism does not merely reside in Central America's institutions and political practices, although they do reinforce it. It is built into the very structure of society. The region's prospects for stable democratization depend on the capacity of these societies to transform their structures and their social criteria for assigning benefits and losses, or at least to accept the legitimacy of debate over the need for such reforms in the framework of a competitive political system. Nevertheless, many of these reforms face the irreconcilable opposition of ruling classes traditionally not very concerned about the procedures and values of democracy. If, on the contrary, the current structural features are reproduced, and things do not improve, the dissatisfaction of broad sectors of the population with their living conditions and with the political system itself will deepen even further. Democracy, to be credible, must prove that it is better than dictatorship, and that proof consists of the citizens' ability to lay out their problems with the guarantee of being heard and eventually satisfied.

It is Central America's ruling elites that will give democratization its trial by fire. It was, after all, their economics of pillage and their politics of authoritarianism—the plundering of natural resources, the impoverishment of the masses, electoral fraud, militarism, and systematic human rights violations—that gave rise to the revolutionary crisis of the late 1970s. Are these elites prepared today to accept the possibility of an electoral defeat? Recent events in El Salvador—the ARENA government's foot-dragging on the "Truth Commission" recommendations, the resurfacing of death squads and the murder of popular leaders, the amnesty for those guilty of murders and other human rights violations—suggest that ruling groups there have not learned much. The revanchism of Nicaragua's privileged elites daily threatens to reopen the floodgates of violent confrontation. At the same time, the events of May and June 1993 when Guatemalan social organizations faced down institutional collapse and a military coup, or Nicaraguan peasants' and workers' resistance to seeing their gains reversed, are evidence of an advance in consciousness, organization, and mobilization among the popular majority.

Posing the problem of democratization and social change in Central America in sequential terms—i.e., democratization first, then social change—would once again jeopardize the prospects for both necessary transformations. Underlying this approach are a strictly formal concept of democratization alongside a purely economistic take on social change—and possibly an intention to postpone both indefinitely. The sequential approach was common to many of the actors on both sides of the recent conflict, and it contributed greatly to the frustration of revolutionary change and effective democratization. The challenge of democratization in Central America is to combine the institutionalization of ongoing conflict resolution with the effective transformation of socioeconomic structures and of cultural rigidities. A process of such magnitude cannot be expected to bear fruit in the short term. The impatience of external observers can be as damaging to this process as those who resist change from within by doing nothing.

During the recent conflict, several factors divided those actors who, in one way or another, supported change in the traditional political and social order: the ideological rigidity and the verticalism of the revolutionaries, the reformists' political and social inadequacy, the skill of U.S. diplomacy. Now that the cycle of revolution, counterrevolution, and war has closed, even as many of the substantive factors that helped set it off remain, it is possible—and perhaps necessary—to redefine the relationship between revolutionaries and reformists in advancing democratization and social change.

Finally, it must be recognized that in Central America, as in the rest of Latin America, not everyone is interested in political democratization or in social progress. Until a very few decades ago, the traditional Central American elites got along very well without democracy, and the democratic discourse they practice today appears to come primarily from fear of a return of the recent past, from the perceived need for social control, or from the usefulness of locating themselves within the predominant discourse of the international community. Even in this limited perspective, though, democratization involves a political project of integration that clashes with the still-dominant marginalizing logic of economic structures and of still-dominant social and cultural relations.

Even more important, to the extent that it implies majority rule, democracy requires acceptance of the majority's power. The effective promotion of democracy, as long as the traditional power centers and their foreign partners persist in defending a way of life and of social organization that is intolerable to the majority of the people and an anachronism by any measure, could very well intensify the region's political and social tensions.

After four decades, Central America's cotton cycle has come to an end. New changes in the international market have sounded the death knell for the "white gold" that ruled the region from the beginning of the 1950s. The dethroned king leaves a trail of exhausted soil, lost forests, and sand and dust where there once was food and birds and streams. This cycle ends together with the cycle of revolutions, whose outcome is more mixed, leaving both realized hopes and bitter frustrations; and as with the eruptions of volcanoes and the convulsions of earthquakes, who can say, after all, that it is over forever?

Notes

Chapter One
Revolutions: Economics, Consciousness, Politics

1. The information in Table 1.4 is generic, since the truly relevant calculations would be those that compare rural population with land area suitable for agricultural use. Ruhl (1984) performs these calculations in a comparative study of Honduras and El Salvador.

2. Sujo Wilson (1991) and Hale (1992) offer examples of this reproduction of custom and of its contemporary mobilizing power on Nicaragua's Atlantic coast.

3. Scott (1976, 1985, 1990) discussed the aspect of resistance without rupture of these practices of the subordinated actors in agrarian societies; see also Pelzer-White (1986). His approach is one-dimensional, in that emphasis on elements of resistance does not allow him to realize what these practices imply about adaptation to the system, and what they contribute to its reproduction. His emphasis on the "moral economy" also obscures the existence of an economic rationality among the peasantry. See, in this light, Popkin (1973), Cummings (1981), Roeder (1984), and more recently Gutmann (1993).

4. The role of the community and the household economy as a rearguard for revolutionary activity has also been noted in studies of the Bolshevik revolution: Bonnel (1983); Fitzpatrick (1984); and the suggestive discussion in Katznelson (1979).

5. As Wickham-Crowley (1992:23) argues.

6. On the concept of "rival sovereignty," see Tilly (1978:189ff).

Chapter Two
The Modernization of Central American Capitalism

1. By the end of the 1970s, these represented 40 percent of cotton inputs and 63 percent of sugar inputs in El Salvador. In Guatemala, 91 percent of inputs for cotton growing were imported by the mid-1960s, although that proportion later declined to 78 percent; in Nicaragua imports were about 50 percent of inputs (cf. Arias Peñate 1988:33; Baumeister et al. 1983; Thielen 1991; figures on Guatemala compiled by *Dirección General de Estadística*).

2. By the mid-1970s only a fourth of the microfarms in Honduras were worked by their owners, compared with 40 percent of one- to two-hectare farms, and 50 percent of those with two to three hectares (Durand 1989). El Salvador by the end of that decade had a similar situation: only 37 percent of microfarms, and two-thirds of the farms with between one and ten hectares, were worked by their owners (Arias Peñate 1980).

3. In Honduras in the mid-1970s, monetary income earned off the farm represented 52 percent of total income on farms of less than two hectares, 41 percent on farms of two to three hectares, 37 percent on farms of three to five hectares, and 26 to 27 percent on all farms of fewer than seven hectares. In El Salvador during the same period, between 30 and 50 percent of the income of landless peasants and those who held less than one hectare came from wages (PREALC 1983a; Durand 1989).

4. In Nicaragua, for example, it represented more than 38 percent of the work force in the countryside by the late 1970s (Vilas 1986, ch. 2).

5. Alonso and Slutzky (1971) is the first serious study of the socioeconomic causes of the war between El Salvador and Honduras that questions both governments' demographic arguments. Carefully analyzing both economies and their political regimes, the authors point to the *latifundista* structure of high land concentration in El Salvador, which expelled impoverished peasants to Honduras, and the expansion of Honduran large landholders at the expense of Salvadoran migrants. Durham (1979) later extended this approach, confirming Slutzky and Alonso's hypothesis.

6. By the beginning of the 1970s, the households in the top 20 percent captured 61 percent of family income in Peru; in Brazil, 66.6 percent; in Mexico, 57.7 percent; in Argentina, 50.3 percent. The bottom 20 percent, in contrast, received only 1.0 percent of total income in Peru, 2 percent in Brazil, 2.9 percent in Mexico, and 4.4 percent in Argentina (World Bank 1988:272–73).

7. For example, the active role of numerous Guatemalan lawyers in the eviction of peasant lands for their own benefit after the overthrow of the Arbenz government (Adams 1970:497ff), and the role of cooperatives of professionals in the appropriation of lands in the Peten during the Mendez Montenegro government (Solorzano Martinez 1984:18).

8. Hintermeister (1982) finds several basic indicators such as life expectancy at birth, mortality rates, and others, to be considerably less deficient in the agroexport areas than in the highland departments. These data reduce the

relevance of the unilateral relationship that Williams (1986) traces between the impact of agroexport development and social instability.

9. This situation leads some authors to speak of a "junker" variety of
agrarian capitalist development in Central America; Baumeister (1983)
offers a theoretical discussion of this approach.

10. Euraque (1991a), however, convincingly challenges the assertion of Stone
(1990:138–40) that the weight of the banana enclave rendered the oligarchy an entirely absent force in Honduran history.

Chapter Three
Political Regimes, the State, and Social Mobilization

1. According to LaFeber (1984:244), intervention by the *Consejo de Defensa
Centroamericano* (Central American Defense Council or CONDECA), at
the urging of the United States, was decisive in defeating the military
coup.

2. UNC General Secretary José Rodolfo Viera was appointed director of the
Instituto Superior de Transformación Agraria in 1980, in charge of im-
plementing the civilian-military regime's agrarian reform program. He
was murdered by an extreme-right paramilitary squad in January 1981.

3. The agreement, dubbed "the Pact of the Generals," began with a denun-
ciation of the "communist threat" that hung over Nicaragua. It conceded
minority representation in the legislature to the *Partido Conservador*, which
would be expanded by a new pact in 1971.

4. Millett (1979) is the best study of the Guardia Nacional.

5. According to LaFeber (1984:176), the then-U.S. ambassador to El Salvador
complained to the State Department that there were more U.S. Air Force
officers assigned to the embassy's military mission in 1963 and 1964 than
there were pilots in the entire Salvadoran Air Force. Moreno and Lardas
(1979) discuss the Cuban role in the revolutionary movements of Central
and South America in the 1960s and 1970s.

6. See Nairn (1984) on the U.S. military's role in founding the death squads;
see also Chapter 4 of the present work. Major D'Aubuisson was the
founder of the ARENA party and its president for many years.

7. According to Torres Rivas (1986), the election that year of Julio César
Méndez Montenegro, a civilian presidential candidate, forced the urgent
transfer of the center to the Defense Ministry, where its name was changed
to *Servicio de Seguridad Nacional*.

8. This interpretation contrasts with Stone (1975), who argues that the
reforms damaged the economic position of the large coffee growers.
Winson (1989) demonstrates that this group, along with rural entrepreneurs growing other crops, were more successful in appropriating state
funds directed to rural revitalization than were the rapidly growing
number of small and marginal producers.

9. On this issue, see the excellent study in Euraque (1990); see also Murga
Frasinetti (1985).

10. The growth of the population identifying itself as indigenous (20 percent

between 1973 and 1980) is one reflection of this revivalism (Lovell 1988; Adams 1991). Since no demographic explanation is available to account for this growth, it is valid to hypothesize that it is a result of peasant mobilization, by virtue of which many indigenous people who did not previously consider themselves indigenous (out of fear, assimilation, or other factors) now began to do so.

11. Kirk (1992) paints a picture of Obando y Bravo as a resolute opponent to Somoza that goes further than the prelate's own account; see Obando y Bravo (1990). Faroohar (1989) and Dodson and Nuzzi (1990) offer more balanced appraisals.

12. The Sandinistas' opposition would later portray the radicalization of these youths as a case of FSLN manipulation and deceit, exploiting boys' and girls' good intentions and social sensitivity to spurious ends. Chow (1992:127ff) presents the matter as a Sandinista conspiracy; see also Kirk (1992:74).

13. Carney (1987, especially pts. 4 and 5) offers a vivid testimony of the new social ministry and its achievements and limitations. Carney, a U.S. priest established in Honduras, was himself radicalized by his pastoral experience in the countryside. After leaving the country for his personal safety, he returned in 1983 as a member of an armed group of the *Partido Revolucionario de los Trabajadores Centroamericanos* led by José María Reyes Mata, a survivor of Che Guevara's Bolivian guerrilla army. He was captured by government troops in early September 1983 along with Reyes Mata and others, and the details of their deaths are still unknown. His book was published posthumously.

Chapter Four
A Lost Decade?

1. Costa Rica signed the agreement in 1985, and Honduras signed one in 1988 and another in 1990. Costa Rica also accepted the principle of cross-conditionality among the World Bank, the IMF, and USAID, and entered GATT in 1989.

2. *La Jornada* (Mexico City), 12 June 1993, 13 June 1993, 4 November 1993, 29 November 1993, 14 December 1993, and 16 December 1993; *Excelsior*, 10 November 1993.

3. *Excelsior*, 30 December 1993; *La Jornada*, 8 January 1994. Soldiers from Argentina were also trained at the Fort Benning facility: see Cardoso (1987); Sklar (1988).

4. U.S. Department of State/Department of Defense (1984a, 1984b); González et al. (1984); McCormick et al. (1988); del Aguila (1985).

5. Scott (1991) and Scott and Marshall (1991) offer the most complete analyses of this aspect of the U.S. policy on Central America, and point out various limitations and omissions in the Kerry report. See also Benítez Manaut (1988).

6. COPPAL (1992) counts some 200,000 orphans and 100,000 widows in Guatemala alone.

7. See, for example, Beverley and Zimmerman (1990).
8. Goldin (1992) finds 48 percent of the inhabitants of Quezaltenango department to be Protestants.
9. It is not unreasonable to suppose that the undue emphasis on a U.S. government role in the growth of the evangelical churches owes much to the cultural influence of Catholicism. In historical perspective, one may ask if the difference between the way evangelism has penetrated Central America today and the way Catholicism came to America in the sixteenth century is really so great.
10. It should be noted that the Protestant denominations of longer standing in Nicaragua—the Moravians, the Episcopalians, and others—strove to distinguish themselves from the more recent arrivals, linked mainly with U.S. Pentecostalism.
11. In some areas, according to Spalding (1991), by 1984 the price of land fell to 10 percent of its value before the revolution.
12. While the impact of the counterrevolutionary war is not to be discounted, the growth of rural poverty in Nicaragua is a reminder of the difficulties agrarian reform faced in handling this problem in the short run.
13. Between 1981 and 1983, army counterinsurgency operations forced about 500,000 people to migrate to San Salvador from the countryside. People seeking refuge from war in Nicaragua more than doubled the populations of the Atlantic Coast cities of Puerto Cabezas and Bluefields.
14. Some populations may even be in danger of disappearing altogether, according to Otis (1993).
15. Diskin (1993) recounts an anecdote that is a cruelly revealing sign of the marginality of Indians in El Salvador. When Adrián Esquino Liso, leader of the *Asociación Nacional de Indígenas Salvadoreños* (ANIS), met Roberto D'Abuisson, leader of the rightist ARENA, he told D'Abuisson: "For us Indians, October 12 [the day in 1492 when Spaniards first arrived in the Western Hemisphere] is a day of disgrace." He explained that he and his fellow Indians are "real communists," to which D'Aubuisson replied, "Adrián is a folkloric fellow." Diskin observes, "the reputed leader of the death squads, to whom 'communist' is the gravest, most damning epithet, cannot take seriously something he is told by a 'folkloric' Indian."
16. By the end of 1988, real wages stood at 7 percent of their 1980 level (Taylor et al. 1989).
17. All of El Salvador's presidents from 1932 to 1980 were army officers, and all of its ministers of agriculture and the economy until the early 1970s were representatives of the coffee bourgeoisie (Gordon 1990). In Guatemala, the economics minister of every successive government after the 1963 coup was directly designated by the *Comité Coordinador de Asociaciones Agrícolas, Comerciales, Industriales y Financieras* (Coordinating Committee of Agricultural, Commercial, Industrial, and Financial Associations, CACIF) (Black 1984:49).
18. According to Dunkerley (1987:461ff), by 1983, 60 percent of the land in Alta Verapaz was owned by military officers; four army officers who had served in the military governments of Kjell Laugerud and Romeo Lucas

García owned 285,000 hectares in the Northern Transverse Strip, in El Petén department. On the army's corporate involvements, see Painter 1987:47-51.

19. According to news reports, about fifty officers of the Sandinista People's Army are currently enrolled in a special business administration course at the Jesuit-run *Universidad Centroamericana* in Managua to take up management duties in a projected *Instituto de Previsión Militar*, a holding company designed to generate economic and financial resources to sustain the armed forces' penurious budget (Reyes Alba 1993). On Sandinista Army enterprises in the context of the institutional future of army-civilian government relations, see Guzmán (1992).

20. Scott and Marshall (1991) and Scott (1991). See also Dickey 1985; Marshall et al. (1987); Sklar (1988); República de Costa Rica (1989a, 1989b); Aguilera Peralta (1991).

21. *Excélsior* (Mexico City) 17 April 1992, p.2.

22. Gen. Héctor Gramajo, Guatemala's defense minister under President Vinicio Cerezo (Timossi 1993:23).

23. See *Report of the National Bipartisan Commission on Central America* (1984).

24. See Béjar (1991) for a discussion of the recent doctrinal reorientation in the FMLN, and Vilas (1991b) on the corresponding process in the FSLN.

25. *La Jornada,* 11 January 1994.

26. Documentation of this process is compiled in Córdova Macías and Benítez Manaut (1989).

Chapter Five
Revolution, Reform, Democracy

1. Cuba was not alone: the governments of Costa Rica and Panama gave significant political and material support to the Sandinista struggle against the Somoza dictatorship.

2. See, respectively, Samaniego (1980); Paul and Demarest (1991); Vilas (1988); Bendaña (1991). Cabarrús (1983:183–84) finds some differences: while more than half of the those organized by FECCAS are semi-proletarianized (52 percent), their presence in ORDEN is smaller (31 percent). This seems to be a recurring phenomenon, and not at all unique to Central America. Some studies on the Cristero rebellion in Mexico in the 1920s point out the similarity between the two warring parties' (Cristeros and Agraristas) social bases: Bartra (1985, ch. 4); Meyer (1987, vol II:5ff).

Bibliography

Adams, Richard. 1970. *Crucifixion by Power*. Austin: University of Texas Press.
————. 1991. "Strategies of Ethnic Survival in Central America." In Greg Urban and Joel Sherzer, eds., *Nation-States and Indians in Latin America*, pp. 181-206. Austin: Texas University Press.

Aguilera, Gabriel. 1989. *El fusil y el olivo. La cuestión militar en Centroamérica*. San José, Costa Rica: DEI.
————. 1991. "La conexión blanca: Narcotráfico y relaciones internacionales de Estados Unidos con Centroamérica." In Alejandro Gálvez Cansino, ed., *Drogas, sociedades adictas y economías subterráneas*, pp. 149-166. Mexico: Ediciones El Caballito.

Alavi, Hamza. 1973. "Peasant Classes and Primordial Loyalties." *Journal of Peasant Studies* 1, no. 1.

Alonso, Esther and Daniel Slutsky. 1971. "La estructura agraria de El Salvador y Honduras: Sus consecuencias sociales y el conflicto actual," in Carias, Slutsky et al. 1971: 241-297.

Amaro Victoria, Nelson. 1970. "Mass and Class in the Cuban Revolution." In Irving L. Horowitz, ed., *Masses in Latin America*, pp. 547-576. New York: Oxford University Press.

Anderson, Perry. 1984. "Modernity and Revolution." *New Left Review* 144 (March/April): 96-113.

Annino, Antonio. 1984. *Dall'Insurrezione al regime. Politiche di massa e strategie istituzionali a Cuba, 1953-1965*. Milano: Franco Angeli Editore.

Annis, Sheldon. 1987. *God and Production in a Guatemalan Town*. Austin: University of Texas Press.

Aragon, Rafael and Eberhard Löshke. 1991. *La iglesia de los pobres en Nicaragua. Historia y perspectivas*. Managua: no publishing house named.

Arancibia Cordova, Juan. 1993. "El ajuste estructural en Centroamérica," in Vilas 1993: 33-50.

Arias Peñate, Salvador. 1980. "Las perspectivas del desarrollo agropecuario en relación con la tenencia de la tierra." *Estudios Centroamericanos* 379 (Mayo): 459-472.

————. 1988. *Los subsistemas de agroexportación en El Salvador.* San Salvador: UCA.

Barahona Riera, Francisco. 1980. *Reforma agraria y poder político: el caso de Costa Rica.* San José: Editorial Universidad de Costa Rica.

Barraclough, Solon. 1982. *A Preliminary Analysis of the Nicaraguan Food System.* Geneva: UNRISD.

Bartra, Armando. 1985. *Los herederos de Zapata.* Mexico: Ediciones ERA.

Baumeister, Eduardo. 1983. "Conceptualización teórica y los análisis sobre el desarrollo del capitalismo en el campo y la formación de su estructura de clases," *Estudios Sociales Centroamericanos* 36 (September-December): 139-164.

————. 1985. "The Structure of Nicaraguan Agriculture and the Sandinista Agrarian Reform," in Harris and Vilas 1985: 10-35.

————. 1991. "La agricultura centroamericana en los ochentas." *Polémica* 14-15 (May-December): 53-79.

———— et al. 1983. *El subsistema del algodón en Nicaragua.* Managua: Cuadernos de CRIES.

Bejar, Rafael Guido. 1991. "La crisis del socialismo en El Salvador." In Arturo Anguiano (coord.), *El socialismo en el umbral del Siglo XXI*, pp. 324-336. Mexico: Universidad Autónoma Metropolitana.

Benitez Manaut, Raúl. 1988. "Narcotráfico y terrorismo en las relaciones interamericanas." *Polémica* 5 (2ª época) (May-August): 2-20.

————. 1989a. *La teoría militar y la guerra civil en El Salvador.* San Salvador: Universidad Centroamericana.

————. 1989b. "La guerra en Centroamérica: Dinámica del proceso de militarización y tendencias." *Síntesis* 7 (January-April): 130-157.

Berryman, Philip. 1984. *The Religious Roots of Rebellion.* Maryknoll, NY: Orbis Books.

Beverley, John and Marc Zimmerman. 1990. *Literature and Politics in the Central American Revolutions.* Austin: University of Texas Press.

Inter-American Development Bank (IADB). 1965. *Economic and Social Progress in Latin America.* Washington, DC: IADB.

————. 1987. *Demographic Trends and Urbanization in Central American and Panama.* Washington, DC: IADB.

————. 1990. *Economic and Social Progress in Latin America.* Washington, DC: IADB.

Blackman, Morris J. et al., eds. 1986. *Confronting Revolution: Security Through Diplomacy in Central America.* New York: Pantheon Books.

Black, George et al. 1984. *Garrison Guatemala.* New York: Monthly Review Press.

Blanco, Gustavo and Jaime Valvuerde. 1987. *Honduras: Iglesia y cambio social.* San José: DEI/CSUCA.

Blandon, Jesús M. 1980. *Entre Sandino y Fonseca Amador*. Managua, self-published.

Blasier, Cole. 1986. "The Soviet Union," in Blackman et al. 1986: 256-270.

Bonaechea, Ramón and Marta San Martin. 1970. *The Cuban Insurrection, 1950-1959*. New Brunswick, NJ: Transaction Books.

Bonnell, Victoria. 1983. *Roots of Rebellion: Worker's Politics and Organizations in St. Petersburg and Moscow, 1900-1914*. Berkeley: University of California Press.

Booth, John. 1982. *The End and the Beginning: The Nicaraguan Revolution*. Boulder: Westview Press.

———. 1991. "Socioeconomic and Political Roots of National Revolts in Central America." *Latin American Research Review* 26, no. 1, pp.33-73.

Boyer, Jefferson C. 1993. "Democratización y militarización en Honduras: Consecuencias de la guerra de la 'contra,'" in Vilas 1993: 217-245.

Brockett, Charles D. 1988. *Land, Power and Poverty*. Boston: Allen & Unwin.

Bulmer-Thomas, Victor. 1987. *The Political Economy of Central America since 1920*. Cambridge: Cambridge University Press.

Caballeros, Rómulo. 1993. "Centroamérica: El recuento de una década perdida." In Casuas Arzu and Castillo Quintana (coords.) 1993: 37-71.

Cabarrus, Carlos. 1983. *Génesis de una revolución*. Mexico: CIESAS.

Cabezas, Omar. 1982. *La montaña es algo más que una inmensa estepa verde*. Managua: Editorial Nueva Nicaragua.

Caceres, Jorge et al. 1983. *Iglesia, Política y Profecía*. San José: EDUCA.

Camacho Navarro, Enrique. 1991. *Los usos de Sandino*. México: UNAM.

Carcanholo, Reinaldo. 1981. *Desarrollo del capitalismo en Costa Rica*. San José: EDUCA.

Cardenal, Ernesto. 1979. *El evangelio en Solentiname*. 2 vols., San José: DEI.

Cardoso, Oscar R. 1987. "El último secreto del Proceso: Apéndice sobre la experiencia argentina." Appendix to Charles Dickey, *Con los contras*. Buenos Aires: Sudamericana/Planeta.

Carias, Marco Virgilio, Daniel Slutsky et al. 1971. *La guerra inútil. Análisis socioeconómico del conflicto entre Honduras y El Salvador*. San José: EDUCA.

Carmack, Robert M., ed. 1991. *Guatemala: Cosecha de violencias*. San José: FLACSO.

Carney, J. Guadalupe. 1987. *To Be a Revolutionary: An Autobiography*. San Francisco: Harper & Row.

Carriere, Jean. 1990. "The Political Economy of Land Degradation in Costa Rica." *New Political Science* 18/19 (Fall/Winter): 147-163.

Carrillo, Ana Lorena. 1991. "Indias y ladinas. Los æsperos caminos de las mujeres en Guatemala." *Nueva Sociedad* 111 (January-February): 109-118.

Carrion, Luis. 1986. *Los cristianos y la revolución sandinista*. Managua, no publishing house named.

Casaus Arzu, Marta Elena. 1992a. *Guatemala: Linaje y racismo*. San José: FLACSO.

———. 1992b. "La metamorfosis de las oligarquías centroamericanas." *Revista Mexicana de Sociología* 3/92 (July-September): 69-114.

Casuas Arzu, M. and Rolando Castillo Quintana (coords.). 1993. *Centroamérica: Balance de la década de los 80. Una perspectiva regional*. Madrid: CEDEAL.

Castañeda Sandoval, Gilberto. 1993. "Panorama después de la tempestad: El movimiento sindical y popular guatemalteco en la década de los ochenta," in Vilas 1993: 275-295.

Coordinadora Democrática Revolucionaria (CDR). 1980. *Programa del Gobierno Democrático Revolucionario.* San Salvador, no publisher named.

Economic Commission For Latin America and the Caribbean (CEPAL). 1982. *Notas sobre la evolución del desarrollo social del istmo centroamericano hasta 1980.* México: CEPAL.

———. 1983. *La crisis en Centroamérica: Orígenes, alcances y consecuencias.* Documento E/CEPAL/G.1261, September.

———. 1986. "Central America: Bases for a Reactivation and Development Policy." *CEPAL Review* 28 (April): 11-48.

———. LC/MEX/L.134, July 4.

———. 1990. *Evolución de la economía centroamericana,*

———. 1989. LC/MEX/L.145, November 13.

———. 1991. *Remesas y economía familiar en El Salvador, Guatemala y Nicaragua.* LC/MEX/R.294 (SEM.43/2) May 27.

———. 1992a. *Centroamérica: Evolución económica durante 1991.* LC/MEXL.193, June 29.

———. 1992b. *Bases para la transformación productiva y generación de ingresos de la población pobre de los países del Istmo Centroamericano.* LC/MEX/G3/Rev.2, January 6.

CEPAL/FAO/OIT/OEA/IICA/SIECA/OCT. 1972. *Tenencia de la tierra y desarrollo rural en Centroamérica.* San José: EDUCA.

Cerroni, Umberto. 1972. *La libertad de los modernos.* Barcelona: Martínez Roca.

Cespedes, Victor Hugo. 1979. *Evolución de la distribución del ingreso en Costa Rica.* San José: Universidad de Costa Rica.

Chow, Napoleón. 1992. *Teología de la liberación en crisis: Religión, poesía y revolución en Nicaragua.* Managua: Banco Central de Nicaragua.

Comité Interamericano De Desarrollo Agrícola/Escuela Facultativa De Ciencias Económicas De Occidente (CIDA/EFCE). 1971. *Tenencia de la tierra y desarrollo socioeconómico del desarrollo agrícola en Guatemala.* Guatemala: Editorial Universitaria.

Centro de Investigaciones y Estudios de la Reforma Agraria (CIERA). 1981. *La Mosquitia en la revolución.* Managua: CIERA.

———. 1984. *...Y por eso defendemos la frontera. Historia agraria de las Segovias occidentales.* Managua: CIERA/MIDINRA.

———. 1989. *La reforma agraria en Nicaragua, 1979-1989.* Managua: CIERA.

Centro de Investigacion y Accion Social (CINAS). 1985. *El movimiento sindical salvadoreño, 1979-1984.* México: CINAS, Cuaderno de Trabajo N° 5.

Colindres, Eduardo. 1977. *Fundamentos económicos de la burguesía salvadoreña.* San Salvador: UCA.

Truth Commission. 1993. *De la locura a la esperanza. La guerra de 12 años en El Salvador.* Report of the Truth Commission for El Salvador. San Salvador/New York: United Nations, March 15.

Comisión Permanente de Partidos Políticos de América Latina (COPPPAL). 1992. *El proceso de pacificación en Guatemala* México: COPPPAL, 19 de noviembre, mimeograph.

Cordova Macias, Ricardo y Raúl Benitez Manaut (compilers). 1989. *La paz en Centroamérica: Expediente de documentos fundamentales 1979-1989*. México: CIIH/UNAM.

Cordova, Arnaldo. 1979. *La ideología de la revolución mexicana*. Mexico: Ediciones ERA.

Cruz Diaz, Rigoberto. 1982, *Chicharrones, la sierra chiquita*. Santiago, Cuba: Editorial Oriente.

Consejo Superior Universitario Centroamericano (CSUCA). 1978a. *Estructura demográfica y migraciones internas en Centroamérica*. San José: EDUCA.

———. 1978b. *Estructura agraria, dinámica de población y desarrollo capitalista en Centroamérica*. San José: EDUCA.

Cuenca, Breny. 1992. *El poder intangible. La AID y el estado salvadoreño en los años ochenta*. San Salvador: CRIES/PREIS.

Cummings, Bruce. 1981. "Interest and Ideology in the Study of Agrarian Politics." *Politics and Society* 10, no. 4: 467-495.

Davis, Shelton H. and Julie Hodson. 1983. *Witnesses to Political Violence in Guatemala: The Suppression of a Rural Development Movement*. Boston: Oxfam America.

Del Aguila, Juan M. 1985. "Central American Vulnerability to Soviet/Cuban Penetration." *Journal of InterAmerican Studies and World Affairs* 27, no. 2 (Summer): 77-97.

De Janvry, Alain. 1981. *The Agrarian Question and Reformism in Latin America*. Baltimore: The Johns Hopkins University Press.

Denton, Carlos and Olga María Acuña. 1984. *Población, fecundidad y desarrollo en Costa Rica, 1950-1970*. Heredia: IDESPO.

Deutsch, Karl. 1961. "Social Mobilization and Political Development." *American Political Science Review* (September) 3: 493-514.

Diaz Arravillaga, Efraín. 1992. "Un breve análisis del ajuste en el sector reformado." In Pino and Thorpe (comps.). 1992: 113-118.

Dickey, Christopher. 1985. *With the Contras*. New York: Simon and Schuster.

Dierckxsens, Wim. 1981. *Política y población*. San José: EDUCA, 1981.

———. 1990. *Mercado de trabajo y política económica en América Central*. San José: DEI.

Diskin, Martin. 1993. "Campesinos e indios: Nuevos sujetos históricos en Centroamérica." In Vilas 1993: 65-83.

Dodson, Michael and Laura Nuzzi O'Shaughnessy. 1990. *Nicaragua's Other Revolution: Religious Faith and Political Struggle*. Chapel Hill: University of North Carolina Press.

Dunkerley, James. 1988. *Power in the Isthmus. A Contemporary History of Central America*. London: Verso.

Dunn, John. 1972. *Modern Revolutions*. Cambridge: Cambridge University Press.

Durand, Guy. 1989. "Política y reforma agraria en Honduras. Crisis de un sistema alimentario." In Lundhall and Pelupessy 1989: 55-71.

Durham, William H. 1979. *Scarcity and Survival in Central America*. Stanford: Stanford University Press.

Eckstein, Susan. 1985. "Revolutions and the Restructuring of National Economies." *Comparative Politics* 17, no. 4 (July): 473-494.

Edelman, Marc. 1993. "Costa Rica: La cultura política de la protesta campesina contra el ajuste estructural." In Vilas 1993: 85-121.

Enriquez, Laura J. 1991. *Harvesting Change: Labor and Agrarian Reform in Nicaragua, 1979-1990*. Chapel Hill: The University of North Carolina Press.

Enriquez, Laura and Rose J. Spalding. 1989. "Sistemas bancarios y cambio revolucionario: La política de crédito agrícola en Nicaragua." In Spalding 1989: 133-157.

Escoto, Jorge and Manfredo Marroquin. 1992. *La AID en Guatemala*. Managua: CRIES/AVANCSO.

Euraque, Darío A. 1990. *Merchants and Industrialists in Northern Honduras: The Making of a National Bourgeoisie in Peripheral Capitalism, 1870s-1972*. Ph.D. diss., University of Wisconsin.

————. 1991a. "La 'reforma liberal' en Honduras y la hipótesis de la 'oligarquía ausente' 1870-1930." *Revista de Historia* 23 (January-June): 7-56.

————. 1991b. "Notas sobre formación de clases y poder político en Honduras, 1870s-1932." *Historia Crítica* 1, no. 6 (November): 59-79.

Faber, Daniel. 1992. "Imperialism, Revolution and the Ecological Crisis of Central America." *Latin American Perspectives* 72 (Winter): 17-44.

Falcoff, Mark. 1989. "Communism in Central America and the Caribbean." In Howard Wiarda and Mark Falcoff, eds., *The Communist Challenge in the Caribbean and Central America*, pp. 13-50. Washington, DC: American Enterprise Institute for Public Policy Research, 1989.

Falla, Ricardo. 1978. *Quiché rebelde*. Guatemala: Editorial Universitaria.

————. 1992. *Masacres de la selva. Ixcán, Guatemala (1975-1982)*. Guatemala: Editorial Universitaria.

Faroohar, Manzar. 1989. *The Catholic Church and Social Change in Nicaragua*. Albany: State University of New York Press.

Feder, Ernst. 1971. *Violencia y despojo del campesino: Latifundismo y explotación capitalista en América Latina*. Mexico: Siglo XXI.

Fernandez, Héctor. 1991. *Solidarismo y sindicalismo en Honduras*. Tegucigalpa: FUTH.

Fernandez Poncela, Anna. 1992a. "Cercada por la violencia: La mujer nicaragüense y la crisis social." *Fem* 112 (June): 30-32.

————. 1992b "Frustración y desencanto dejó el FSLN." *UnomásUno* (Mexico), 10 May, p. 14.

Figueroa Ibarra, Carlos. 1980. *El proletariado rural en el agro guatemalteco*. Guatemala: Editorial Universitaria.

————. 1991. *El recurso del miedo*. San José: EDUCA.

Fitzpatrick, Sheila. 1984. "The Russian Revolution and Social Mobility: A Re-Examination of the Question of Social Support for the Soviet Regime in the 1920s and 1930s." *Politics & Society* 13, no. 2: 119-141.

Flora, Jan and Edelberto Torres Rivas, eds. 1989. *Sociology of "Developing Societies": Central America*. New York: Monthly Review Press.

Frente Farabundo Martí para la Liberación Nacional (FMLN). 1990. *Proclama del FMLN a la Nación. La Revolución Democrática*. El Salvador, 24 September, mimeograph.

Friedman, Jonathan. 1992. "The Past in the Future: History and the Politics of Identity." *American Anthropologist* 94, no. 4 (December): 837-860.

Frundt, Henry. 1987. *Refreshing Pauses: Coca-Cola and Human Rights in Guatemala*. New York: Praeger.

Frente Sandinista de Liberación Nacional (FSLN). 1980. "Comunicado oficial de la Dirección Nacional del FSLN sobre el proceso electoral." *Barricada*, 24 August.

Fuentes, Claudia Dary. 1991. *Mujeres tradicionales y nuevos cultivos*. Guatemala: FLACSO.

Furst, Edgar. 1989. "Costa Rica 1982-1987: ¿Una aplicación heterodoxa 'sui generis" de políticas de ajuste estructural?" In Lundhall and Pelupessy 1989: 179-204.

Gallardo, María E. and J.E. Lopez. 1986. *Centroamérica: La crisis en cifras*. San José: IICA/FLACSO.

García, Ana Isabel and Enrique Gomáriz. 1989. *Mujeres Centroamericanas*. San José: CSUCA/FLACSO/Universidad para la Paz.

García, Claudia. 1993. "El impacto de un proceso revolucionario en la religiosidad indígena: Los mískitos y la revolución sandinista." In Vilas 1993: 187-202.

Geertz, Clifford. 1973. *The Interpretation of Cultures*. New York: Basic Books.

Germani, Gino. 1962. *Política y sociedad en una época de transición*. Buenos Aires: Paidós.

Glower, Carlos. 1987. "La fuga de capitales en Centroamérica." *Estudios Sociales Centroamericanos* 45 (September-December).

Goldin, Liliana R. 1992. "Work and Ideology in the Maya Highlands of Guatemala: Economic Beliefs in the Context of Occupational Change." *Economic Development and Cultural Change* 41, no. 1 (October): 103-123.

Gonzalez, Edward et al. 1984. *U.S. Policy for Central America: A Briefing*. Santa Mónica: RAND Corporation.

Gordon, Sara. 1990. "Guatemala y El Salvador: Dos regímenes de exclusión." *Polémica* 10 (January-April): 12-23.

Gould, Jeffrey. 1990. *To Lead As Equals: Rural Protest and Political Consciousness in Chinandega, Nicaragua, 1912-1979*. Chapel Hill: University of North Carolina Press.

Güendal, Ludwig and Roy Rivera. 1987. "El desarrollo de la política social en Costa Rica: Crisis y perspectivas." *Polémica* 2 (2ª época) (May-August): 51-64.

Guerra-Borges, Alfredo. 1988. *Desarrollo e integración en Centroamérica: del pasado a las perspectivas*. México: CRIES/UNAM.

Gugler, Josef. 1982. "The Urban Character of Contemporary Revolutions." *Studies in Comparative International Development* 17 (Summer): 60-73.

Gutierrez Mayorga, Gustavo. 1985. "Historia del movimiento obrero de Nicaragua (1900-1977)." In Pablo Gonzalez Casanova (dir.), *Historia del movimiento obrero en América Latina*, Vol. 2, pp. 196-252. Mexico: Siglo XXI.

Gutmann, Mathew C. 1993. "Rituals of Resistance: A Critique of the Theory of Everyday Forms of Resistance." *Latin American Perspectives* 77 (Spring): 74-92.

Guzman, Luis Humberto. 1992. *Políticos en uniforme: Un balance del poder del EPS*. Managua: Instituto Nicaragüense de Estudios Socio-Políticos.

Hale, Charles R. 1992. "Wan Tasbaya Dukiara. Nociones contenciosas de los derechos sobre la Tierra en la historia mískita." *Wani* 12 (June): 1-12.

Hall, Carolyn. 1984. *Costa Rica. Una interpretación geográfica con perspectiva histórica.* San José: Editorial Costa Rica.

Handy, Jim. 1989. "Insurgency and Counter-Insurgency in Guatemala." In Flora and Torres Rivas 1989: 112-139.

————. 1992. "Guatemala: A Tenacious Despotism." *NACLA Report on the Americas* 26, no. 3 (December): 31-37.

Harding, Neil. 1984. "Socialism, Society and the Organic Labor State." In Neil Harding, ed., *The State in Socialist Societies,* pp.1-50. Albany: State University of New York Press.

Harris, Richard and Carlos M. Vilas, eds. 1985. *Nicaragua: A Revolution Under Siege.* London: Zed Books.

Hintermeister, Alberto. 1982. *Modernización de la agricultura y pobreza rural en Guatemala.* Santiago de Chile: OIT/PREALC, April, mimeograph.

Hobsbawm, Eric J. 1973. "Peasants and Politics." *Journal of Peasant Studies* 1, no. 1.

————. 1986. "Revolution." In Roy Porter and M. Teich, eds., *Revolution in History,* pp. 5-46. Cambridge: Cambridge University Press.

International Bank for Reconstruction and Development (IBRD). 1951. *The Economic Development of Guatemala.* Washington, DC: IBRD.

————. 1953. *The Economic Development of Nicaragua.* Baltimore: The Johns Hopkins University Press.

Instituto Interamericano de Cooperación para la Agricultura/Facultad Latinoamericana de Ciencias Sociales (IICA/FLACSO). 1991. *Centroamérica en cifras.* San José: IICA/FLACSO.

Instituto Nacional de Estadística y Censos (INEC). 1989. *Nicaragua: Diez años en cifras.* Managua: INEC.

Jay, Alice et al. 1993. *Persecution by Proxy: The Civil Patrols in Guatemala.* New York: The Robert F. Kennedy Memorial Center for Human Rights.

Jonas, Susan. 1988. "Elecciones de transición: Casos de Guatemala y Nicaragua." *Polémica* 6 (September-December): 3-15.

————. 1991. *The Battle for Guatemala.* Boulder: Westview Press.

Katznelson, Ira. 1979. "Community, Capitalist Development and the Emergence of Class." *Politics & Society* 9, no. 2: 203-237.

Karl, Terry Lynn. 1992. "El Salvador's Negotiated Revolution." *Foreign Affairs* 71, no. 2 (Spring): 147-164.

Kincaid, Douglas. 1987. "Peasants into Rebels: Community and Class in Rural El Salvador." *Comparative Studies in Society and History* 29, no. 3: 466-494.

Kirk, John M. 1992. *Politics and the Catholic Church in Nicaragua.* Gainesville: University of Florida Press.

Knight, Alan. 1984. "The Working Class and the Mexican Revolution, c.1900-1920." *Journal of Latin American Studies* 16: 51-79.

Lafeber, Walter. 1984. *Inevitable Revolutions: The United States in Central America.* New York: W.W. Norton.

Lazo, José Francisco. 1987. *El Salvador: Estructura tributaria.* CINAS: Cuaderno de Trabajo 10 (August).

Lenin, Vladimir I. 1905. "Petit-Bourgeois Socialism and Proletarian Socialism." In V.I. Lenin, *The Worker-Peasant Alliance,* pp. 224-231. Moscow: Progress Publishers, 1978.

Leogrande, William M. 1986. "Cuba." In Blackman et al. 1986: 229-255.

Lindenberg, Marc. 1990. "World Economic Cycles and Central American Political Instability." *World Politics* 47, no. 3 (April): 397-421.

Lopez, José Roberto. 1986. *Los orígenes económicos de la crisis en Centroamérica.* San José, ICADIS.

Lovell, W. George. 1988. "Surviving Conquest: The Maya of Guatemala in Historical Perspective." *Latin American Research Review* 23, no. 2: 25-57.

Lundhall, Mats and Wim Pelupessy, eds. 1989. *Crisis económica en Centroamérica y el Caribe.* San José: DEI.

Malloy, James M. and Mitchell Seligson, eds. 1987. *Authoritarians and Democrats: Regime Transition in Latin America.* Pittsburgh: University of Pittsburgh Press.

Marshall, Jonathan et al. 1987. *The Iran-Contra Connection.* Boston: South End Press.

Martinez, Manlio D. et al. 1987. *Cambio tecnológico en la agricultura de Centroamérica.* Tegucigalpa: Guaymuras.

Matamoros, Jorge. 1992. "Las facciones de Yatama y la situación política de la RAAN." *Wani* 13 (November): 1-19.

Mazlish, Bruce. 1991."The Breakdown of Connections and Modern Development," *World Development* 19, no. 1: 31-44.

McClintock, Cynthia. 1984. "Why Peasants Rebel: The Case of Peru's Sendero Luminoso," *World Politics* (October): 48-84.

McClintock, Michael. 1985. *The American Connection: State Terror and Popular Resistance in El Salvador and Guatemala.* 2 vols. London: Zed Books.

McCormick, Gordon et al. 1988. *Nicaraguan Security Policy.* Santa Monica: Rand Corporation.

McCreery, David. 1990. "Hegemony and Repression in Rural Guatemala, 1871-1948." *Peasant Studies* 17, no. 3: 157-177.

Melmed-Sanjak, Jolyne. 1992. "Reformando la estructura: La viabilidad de Empresas de la Reforma Agraria a la luz de los PAE." In Pino and Thorpe 1992: 131-150.

Membreño Cedillo, Sergio. 1985. "25 años de historia de la política del gasto público y del proceso de acumulación de capital em Honduras (1955-1980)." *Revista Centroamericana de Economía* 6, no. 18 (September-December): 81-109.

Menjivar Larin, Rafael. 1985. "Notas sobre el movimiento obrero salvadoreño." In Gonzalez Casanova 1985: vol. 2, 61-127.

Meyer, Jean. 1987. *La Cristiada.* Mexico: Siglo XXI, 1987.

Migdal, Joel. 1974. *Peasants, Politics and Revolutions.* Princeton: Princeton University Press.

Millett, Richard. 1979. *Los guardianes de la dinastía.* San José: EDUCA.

Millman, Joel. 1990. "En El Salvador la corrupción no tiene rival, tras diez años de guerra." *Excélsior* (Mexico), 9 July.

Molina, Uriel. 1981. "El sentido de una experiencia." *Nicaráuac* 5 (April-June): 53-74.

Molina Chocano, Guillermo. 1980. "La formación del estado y el origen minero-mercantil de la burguesía hondureña." *Estudios Sociales Centroamericanos* 25 (January-April): 55-89.

Montes, Segundo. 1988. *El Salvador 1988. Estructura de clases y comportamiento de las fuerzas sociales*. San Salvador: Universidad Centroamericana, Departamento de Sociología y Ciencias Políticas.

Moore, Barrington Jr. 1966. *The Social Origins of Democracy and Dictatorship: Lord and Peasant in the Making of the Modern World*. Boston: Beacon Press.

———. 1978. *Injustice: The Social Basis of Obedience and Revolt*. White Plains, NY: M.E. Sharpe.

Mora, Jorge A. and Angela Arias. 1984. "Estado, planificación y acumulación de capital en Costa Rica, 1974-1982." *Estudios Sociales Centroamericanos* 37 (January-April): 187-209.

Moreno, José A. and Nicholas O. Lardas. 1979. "Integrating International Revolution and Deténte: The Cuban Case." *Latin American Perspectives* 21 (Spring): 36-60.

Moreno Martin, Florentino. 1991. *Infancia y guerra en Centroamérica*. San José: FLACSO.

Mossbrucker, Harald. 1990. *La economía campesina y el concepto "comunidad": Un enfoque crítico*. Lima: Instituto de Estudios Peruanos.

Murga Frasinetti, Antonio. 1985. "Industrialización y formación de clase: El caso de la fracción industrial en Honduras." *Revista Centroamericana de Economía* 6, no. 17 (May-August): 67-87.

Nairn, Allan. 1984. "De Kennedy a Reagan. El Salvador y la disciplina de la muerte." *Nexos* (July).

North, Lisa. 1985. *Bitter Grounds: Roots of Revolt in El Salvador*. Westport, CT: Lawrence Hill.

Nuñez Soto, Orlando. 1980. *El somocismo: Desarrollo y contradicciones del capitalismo agroexportador*. La Habana: Cuadernos del CEA.

Obando y Bravo, Miguel. 1990. *Agonía en el Bunker*. Managua: Comisión de Promoción Social Arquidiocesana.

O'Connor, James. 1964. "On Cuban Political Economy." *Studies on the Left* 4: 97-117.

Association of National Coordinators of Non-Governmental Organizations (NGOs) Working with Refugees, the Displaced and Returnees. 1991. *Las migraciones forzadas en Centroamérica: Una visión regional*. San José: CSUCA.

Opazo Bernales, Andrés. 1987. *Costa Rica. La Iglesia católica y el orden social*. San José: DEI/CSUCA.

Otis, John. 1993. "En peligro de desaparecer a finales del decenio, el dialecto Rama en Nicaragua." *Excélsior*, 7 November.

Paige, Jeffrey. 1975. *Agrarian Revolutions*. New York: The Free Press.

———. 1983. "Social Theory and Peasant Revolution in Vietnam and Guatemala." *Theory and Society* 12, no. 6 (November): 699-737.

———. 1985. "Cotton and Revolution in Nicaragua." In Peter Evans, Dietrich Rueschmeyer, and Evelyne Huber, eds., *States Versus Markets in the World System*, pp. 91-114. Beverly Hills: Sage Publications.

———. 1987. "Coffee and Politics in Central America." In Richard Tardanico, ed., *Crisis in the Caribbean Basin*, pp. 141-190. Beverly Hills: Sage Publications.

Painter, James. 1987. *Guatemala: False Hope, False Freedom*. New York: Latin American Bureau/Distributed by Monthly Review Press.

Paul, Benjamin D. and William J. Demarest. 1991. "Operaciones de un escuadrón de la muerte en San Pedro la Laguna." In Carmack 1991: 203-260.

Pearce, Jenny. 1986. *Promised Land: Peasant Rebellion in Chalatenango, El Salvador*. New York: Latin American Bureau/Distributed by Monthly Review Press.

Pelzer-White, Christine. 1986. "Everyday Resistance, Socialist Revolution and Rural Development: The Vietnamese Case." *Journal of Pesant Studies* 13, no. 2 (January).

Perez, Cristobal. 1986. "Guatemala hacia la pobreza." *Polémica* 21 (September-December): 5-21.

Perez Sainz, Juan Pablo and Rafael Menjivar Larin (coords.). 1991. *Informalidad urbana en Centroamérica. Entre la acumulación y la subsistencia*. Caracas: Nueva Sociedad.

Perez Sainz, Juan Pablo et al. 1992. *...todito, todito es trabajo: Indígenas y empleo en Ciudad de Guatemala*. Guatemala: FLACSO.

Pino, Hugo Noé and Andrew Thorpe (comps.). 1992. *Honduras: El ajuste estructural y la reforma agraria*. Tegucigalpa: CEDOH/POSCAE.

Popkin, Samuel L. 1979. *The Rational Peasant*. Berkeley: University of California Press.

Programa Regional de Empleo de América Latina y el Caribe (PREALC). 1983a. *La evolución de la pobreza rural en Honduras*. Santiago de Chile: OIT/PREALC, Documento de trabajo PREALC/223, March.

————. 1983b. *Producción de alimentos básicos y empleo en el istmo Centroamericano*. Santiago de Chile: OIT/PREALC, Documento de Trabajo PREALC/229, August.

————. 1986. *Cambio y polarización ocupacional en Centroamérica*. San José: EDUCA.

Prosterman, Roy and Jeffrey M. Riedinger. 1987. *Land Reform and Democratic Development*. Baltimore: The Johns Hopkins University Press.

Quiros, Rodolfo. 1973. *Agricultural Development in Central America: Its Origins and Nature*. Madison: University of Wisconsin, Land Tenure Center Research Paper No. 49.

Randall, Margaret. 1980. *Todas estamos despiertas. Testimonios de la mujer nicaragüense de hoy*. Mexico: Siglo XXI.

Recio Adrados, Juan Luis. 1992. "Una cierta clase de política: Las iglesias evangélicas en El Salvador." Paper presented at the 27th LASA International Conference, Los Angeles, September 24-27.

Republica de Costa Rica, Legislative Assembly. 1989a. *Informe de la Comisión sobre el narcotráfico*. San José: UNED.

————. 1989b. *Segundo informe de la Comisión sobre el narcotráfico*. San José: UNED.

Reuben Soto, Sergio. 1982. *Capitalismo y crisis económica en Costa Rica*. San José: Editorial Porvenir.

Reyes, Reynaldo and J.K. Wilson. 1992. *Ráfaga: The Life Story of a Nicaraguan Mískito Comandante*. Norman: Oklahoma University Press.

Reyes Alba, Xabier. 1993. "Un general sin laberinto." *El Día Latinoamericano* 116, 2 August, p.5.

Rivas, David and Guillermo Mejia. 1993. "Los lisiados de guerra en el abandono." *Tendencias* 25 (November): 11-12.

Rodriguez, Ileana. 1990. *Registradas en la historia. Diez años del quehacer feminista en Nicaragua*. Managua: CIAM.

Roeder, Philip G. 1984. "Legitimacy and Peasant Revolution: An Alternative to Moral Economy." *Peasant Studies* 11, no. 3 (Spring): 149-168.

Rosa, Herman. 1992. "El papel de la asistencia de AID en el fortalecimiento de nuevas instituciones del sector privado y en la transformación global de la economía salvadoreña: El caso FUSADES." Paper presented at the 27th Latin American Studies Association Conference, Los Angeles, September.

————. 1993. *AID y las transformaciones estructurales en El Salvador*. Managua: CRIES.

Rosenber, Mark B. 1987. "Political Obstacles to Democracy in Central America." In Malloy and Seligson 1987: 193-215.

Ross, Yazmin. 1992. "El Salvador: Descomposicion del Ejército." *El Financiero*, 14 December.

Ruben, Raúl and Govert Van Oord, eds. 1991. *Más allá del ajuste*. San José: DEI.

Rude, George. 1981. *Revuelta popular y conciencia de clase*. Madrid: Editorial Crítica.

Ruhl, J. Mark. 1984. "Agrarian Structure and Political Stability in Honduras." *Journal of Interamerican Studies and World Affairs* 26, no. 1 (February): 33-68.

Ruiz Granadino, Santiago. 1986. *Crecimiento de la producción agropecuaria y cambios en la estructura social rural*. San José: ICADIS.

Russettt, Bruce M. 1964. "Inequality and Instability: The Relation of Land Tenure to Politics." *World Politics* (April): 442-454.

Sader, Eder. 1988. *Quando novos personagens entraram na cena*. Rio de Janeiro: Paz e Terra.

Saldomando, Angel. 1992. *El retorno de la AID. El caso de Nicaragua: Condicionalidad y reestructuración conservadora*. Managua: CRIES.

Salgado, Ramón. 1992. "Observaciones sobre la situación actual del sector agrícola de Honduras." In *Puntos de Vista: Temas agrarios*, pp. 77-101. Tegucigalpa: CEDOH.

Samandu, Luis E. 1991. "Estrategias evangélicas hacia la población indígena de Guatemala." In Luis E. Samandú, ed., *Protestantismos y procesos sociales en Centroamérica*, pp. 67-114. San José: EDUCA.

———— and Ruud Jansen. 1982. "Nicaragua: Dictadura somocista, movimiento popular e iglesia, 1968-1979." *Estudios Sociales Centroamericanos* 33 (September-December): 189-219.

———— et al. 1990. *Guatemala. Retos de la iglesia católica en una sociedad en crisis*. San José: DEI/CSUCA.

Samaniego, Carlos. 1980. "Movimiento campesino o lucha del proletariado rural en El Salvador?" *Estudios Sociales Centroamericanos* 25 (January-April): 125-144.

Sarti, Carlos. 1991. "Los refugiados centroamericanos y los espacios para la cooperación europea." In Ruben and Van Oord 1991: 307-335.

Schirmer, Jennifer. 1993. "The Seeking of Truth and the Gendering of Consciousness: The CoMadre of El Salvador and the CONAVIGUA Widows of Guatemala." In Sarah A. Radcliffe and Sallie Westwood, eds., *"Viva": Women and Popular Protest in Latin America*, pp. 30-64. London: Routledge.

Schoultz, Lars. 1987. *National Security and United States Policy Toward Latin America*. Princeton: Princeton University Press, 1987.

Scott, James C. 1976. *The Moral Economy of the Peasant: Rebellion and Subsistence in Southeast Asia.* New Haven: Yale University Press.

———. 1977. "Hegemony and the Peasantry." *Politics & Society* 7, no. 3: 267-296.

———. 1985. *Weapons of the Weak: Everyday Forms of Peasant Resistance.* New Haven: Yale University Press.

———. 1986. "Everyday Forms of Peasant Resistance." *Journal of Peasant Studies* 13, no. 2: 5-35.

———. 1990. *Domination and the Art of Resistance: Hidden Transcripts.* New Haven: Yale University Press.

Scott, Peter Dale. 1991. "Cocaine, the Contras and the United States: How the U.S. Government Has Augmented America's Drug Crisis." *Crime, Law and Social Change* 16: 97-131.

——— and Jonathan Marshall. 1991. *Cocaine Politics: Drugs, Armies and the CIA in Central America.* Berkeley: University of California Press.

Serra, Luis. 1985. "Ideology, Religion and Class Struggle in the Nicaraguan Revolution." In Harris and Vilas 1985: 151-174.

———. 1990. *El movimiento campesino: Su participación política durante la revolución sandinista, 1979-1989.* Managua: UCA.

Sevilla, Manuel. 1985. *Visión global de la concentración económica en El Salvador.* CINAS, Cuaderno de Trabajo No. 3.

Sexton, James D. 1978. "Protestantism and Modernization in Two Guatemalan Towns." *American Ethnologist* 5, no. 2: 280-302.

Secretaría Permanente del Tratado General de Integración Económica Centroamericana (SIECA). 1980. *Estadísticas seleccionadas de Centroamérica y Panamá.* Guatemala: SIECA.

———. 1981. *Estadísticas macroeconómicas de Centroamérica, 1970- 1980.* Guatemala, July.

Sierra Pap, Oscar Rolando. 1982. "Iglesia y conflicto social en Guatemala." *Estudios Sociales Centroamericanos* 33 (September-December): 59-91.

Sierra, Oscar and Hans Siebers. 1990. "La iglesia en la sociedad desgarrada." In Samandú 1990: 37-70.

Sigelman, Lee and Miles Simpson. 1977. "A Cross-National Test of the Linkage Between Economic Inequality and Political Violence." *Journal of Conflict Resolution* 21 (March): 105-128.

Sklar, Holly. 1988. *Washington's War on Nicaragua.* Boston: South End Press.

Skocpol, Theda. 1979. *States and Social Revolutions.* Chicago: Chicago University Press.

———. 1982. "What Makes Peasants Revolutionary?" *Comparative Politics* 14, no. 3: 351-375.

Slutzky, Daniel. 1979a. "La agroindustria de la carne en Honduras." *Estudios Sociales Centroamericanos* 22 (January-April): 101-205.

———. 1979b. "Notas sobre empresas transnacionales, agroindustrias y reforma agraria en Honduras." *Estudios Sociales Centroamericanos* 23 (May-August): 35-48.

——— and Esther Alonso. 1980. *Empresas transnacionales y agricultura: El caso del enclave bananero en Honduras.* Tegucigalpa: Editorial Universitaria.

Smith, Carol. 1987. "Culture and Community: The Language of Class in Guatemala." In Mike Davis et al., eds., *The Year Left* 2, pp. 197-217.

210   BETWEEN EARTHQUAKES AND VOLCANOES

———. 1991. "Destrucción de las bases materiales de la cultura indígena: Cambios económicos en Totonicapán." In Carmack 1991: 341-381.

Sojo, Ana. 1984. *Estado empresario y lucha política en Costa Rica*. San José: EDUCA.

Sojo, Carlos. 1991. *La utopía del estado mínimo: Influencia de la AID en Costa Rica en los años ochenta*. Managua: CRIES.

Solorzano Martinez, Mario. 1983. "Centroamérica: Democracias de fachada." *Polémica* 12 (November-December): 40-55.

———. 1984. *El modelo económico guatemalteco: 1954-1982*. San José: ICADIS.

Spalding, Hobart A. 1992-93. "The Two Latin American Foreign Policies of the U.S. Labor Movements: The AFL-CIO Top Brass vs. Rank-and-File." *Science & Society* 56, no. 4 (Winter): 421-439.

Spalding, Rose J. (compiler). 1989. *La economía política de Nicaragua*. Mexico: Fondo de Cultura Económica.

———. 1991. "Capitalists and Revolution: State-Private Sector Relations in Revolutionary Nicaragua (1979-1990)." Paper presented at the 27th International Congress of the Latin American Studies Association, Washington, DC, April.

Stacey, Judith. 1980. "China's Socialist Revolution, Peasant Families and the Uses of the Past." *Theory and Society* 9 (March): 269-281.

Stoll, David. 1990. *Is Latin America Turning Protestant? The Politics of Evangelical Growth*. Los Angeles: University of California Press.

———. 1991. "Evangelistas, guerrilleros y ejército: El triángulo Ixil bajo el poder de Ríos Montt." In Carmack 1991: 155-199.

Stone, Samuel. 1975. *La dinastía de los conquistadores*. San José: EDUCA.

———. 1990. *The Heritage of the Conquistadores*. Lincoln: University of Nebraska Press.

Stonich, Susan C. 1992. "Struggling with Honduran Poverty: The Environmental Consequences of Natural Resource-Based Development and Rural Transformations." *World Development* 20, no. 3: 385-399.

Sujo Wilson, Hugo. 1991. "Historia oral de Bluefields." *Wani* 9 (January-April): 24-31.

Tapia, Gabriel Gaspar. 1989. "Crisis y politización empresarial en Centroamérica." *Polémica* 8 (May-August): 24-34.

———. 1993. "La modernización de las clases dominantes centroamericanas." In Vilas 1993: 51-63.

Taylor, J.R. 1970. "Agricultural Development in the Humid Tropics of Central America." *InterAmerican Economic Affairs* (Summer): 41-49.

Taylor, Lance et al. 1989. *Nicaragua: The Transition from Economic Chaos to Sustainable Growth*. Stockholm: Swedish International Development Agency.

Thielen, Frans. 1989. "Los cambios en la estructura productiva del sector algodonero en Centroamérica." In Lundhall and Pelupessy 1989: 31-53.

———. 1991. "A Comparative Study of the Salvadorean and Nicaraguan Cotton Sectors." In Wim Pelupessy, ed., *Perspectives on the Agro-Export Economy in Central America*, pp. 71-76. Pittsburgh: University of Pittsburgh Press, 1991.

Tilly, Charles. 1978. *From Mobilization to Revolution*. New York: Random House.

Timossi, Gerardo. 1989. *Centroamérica: Deuda externa y ajuste estructural*. San José: CRIES/DEI.

———. 1993. "Crisis y restructuración: El balance centroamericano de los años ochenta." In Vilas 1993: 15-32.

Torres Rivas, Edelberto. 1980. "El Estado contra la sociedad. Las raíces de la revolución nicaragüense." *Estudios Sociales Centroamericanos* 27 (September-December): 79-95.

———. 1982. "Notas para comprender la crisis política centroamericana." In Gert Rosenthal et al., *Centroamérica: Crisis y política internacional*, pp. 39-69. Mexico: Siglo XXI.

———. 1986. "Centroamérica: Guerra, transición y democracia." CINAS: *Cuadernos de Divulgación* 2 (December): 5-25.

———. 1991. "Imágenes, siluetas, formas, en las elecciones centroamericanas: Las lecciones de la década." *Polémica* 14/15 (May-December): 2-21.

———. 1993. "Democracias de baja intensidad." In Casaua Arzu and Castillo Quintana 1993: 73-88.

United Nations. 1980. *Patterns of Urban and Rural Population*. Population Studies No. 68, New York.

———. 1986. *International Trade Statistics Yearbook*. Geneva: UN.

U.S. General Accounting Office. 1990. *Central America. Humanitarian Assistance to the Nicaraguan Democratic Resistance*. Washington DC: GAO/NSIAD-90-92, January.

U.S. Department of State/Department of Defense. 1984a. *Background Paper: Nicaragua's Military Build-Up and Support for Central American Subversion*. Washington DC, 18 July.

———. 1984b. *News Briefing on Intelligence Information on External Support of the Guerrillas in El Salvador*. Washington DC, 8 August.

U.S. Senate, Committee of Foreign Relations, Subcommittee on Terrorism, Narcotics, and International Operations. 1989. *Drugs, Law Enforcement and Foreign Policy*. Washington, DC: U.S. Government Printing Office.

Utting, Peter. 1992. "From Orthodoxy to Reform: Historical Experiences of Post-Revolutionary Societies." *Third World Quarterly* 13, no. 1: 43-65.

Valverde, Jaime. 1987. "Sectarismo religioso y conflicto social." *Polémica* 3 (2ª época) (September-December): 15-25.

Vega Carballo, José Luis. 1984. "Algunas anti-tesis sobre la crisis centroamericana." *Anuario de Estudios Centroamericanos* 10: 23-42.

———. 1989. "Parties, Political Development and Social Conflict in Honduras and Costa Rica: A Comparative Analysis." In Flora and Torres Rivas 1989: 92-111.

Vilas, Carlos M. 1979. "Notas sobre la formación del estado en el Caribe." *Estudios Sociales Centroamericanos* 24 (July-December): 117-177.

———. 1986. *The Sandinista Revolution: National Liberation and Social Transformation in Central America*. New York: Monthly Review Press.

———. 1988. "Popular Insurgency and Social Revolution in Central America." *Latin American Perspectives* 56 (Winter): 55-77.

———. 1989a. *Transición desde el subdesarrollo. Revolución y reforma en la periferia*. Caracas: Nueva Sociedad.

————. 1989b. *State, Class and Ethnicity in Nicaragua*. Boulder and London: Lynne Rienner Publishers.

————. 1990. "Cambio y continuidad en la crisis centramericana." In Marcos Roitman and Carlos Castro-Gil (coords.), *América Latina: Entre los mitos y la utopía*, pp. 119-146. Madrid: Universidad Complutense.

————. 1991a. "Nicaragua: A Revolution that Fell from the Grace of the People." In Ralph Miliband and Leo Panitch, eds., *The Socialist Register 1991*, pp. 300-319. New York: Monthly Review Press.

————. 1991b. "El debate interno sandinista." *Nueva Sociedad* 113 (May-June): 28-36.

————. 1992a. "Family Affairs: Class, Lineage and Politics in Contemporary Nicaragua." *Journal of Latin American Studies* 24, no. 2 (May): 309-341.

————. 1992b. *El proceso de reordenamiento patrimonial del Estado en Nicaragua*. Managua: PNUD, August.

————. 1992-93 "Latin American Populism: A Structural Approach." *Science & Society* 56, no. 4 (Winter): 389-420.

———— (coord.). 1993. *Democracia emergente en Centroamérica*. Mexico: Centro de Investigaciones Interdisciplinarias en Humanidades, UNAM.

Vunderink, Gregg L. 1990-91. "Peasant Participation and Mobilization During Economic Crisis: The Case of Costa Rica." *Studies in Comparative International Development* 25, no. 4 (Winter): 3-34.

Vuskovic Cespedes, Pedro. 1991. "Los actores externos: Presencia y proyectos." In *Cuadernos de CRIES* 19/20. Managua: CRIES.

Walker, Ian. 1991. "El ajuste estructural y el futuro desarrollo de la región centroamericana." *Documento de Trabajo* No. 2. Tegucigalpa: Universidad Nacional Autónoma de Honduras, Posgrado Centroamericano en Economía y Planificación del Desarrollo.

Waller, Douglas. 1993. "Running a 'School for Dictators.'" *Newsweek*, 9 August, pp. 31-33.

Wallerstein, Immanuel. 1980. *The Modern World System II: Mercantilism and the Consolidation of the European World-Economy, 1600-1750*. New York: Academic Press.

Walter, Knut. 1993. *The Regime of Anastasio Somoza, 1936-1956*. Chapel Hill: The University of North Carolina Press.

Walton, John. 1984. *Reluctant Rebels: Comparative Studies of Revolution and Underdevelopment*. New York: Columbia University Press.

Warman, Arturo. 1980. *Ensayos sobre el campesinado en México*. Mexico: Nueva Imagen.

Weeks, John. 1985. *The Economies of Central America*. New York: Holmes & Meier.

————. 1986. "An Interpretation of the Central American Crisis." *Latin American Research Review* 21, no. 3: 31-53.

Wheelock, Jaime. 1976. *Imperialismo y dictadura*. Mexico: Siglo XXI.

White, Richard A. 1984. *The Morass: United States Intervention in Central America*. New York: Harper & Row.

Wickham-Crowly, Timothy P. 1992. *Guerrillas and Revolution in Latin America*. Princeton, NJ: Princeton University Press.

Williams, Robert. 1986. *Export Agriculture and the Crisis in Central America.* Chapel Hill: University of North Carolina Press.

Winocur, Marcos. 1980. *Las clases olvidadas en la revolución cubana.* Barcelona: Grijalbo.

Wolf, Eric. 1972. *Las guerras campesinas del siglo XX.* Mexico: Siglo XXI.

Womack, John Jr. 1969. *Zapata y la revolución mexicana.* Mexico: Siglo XXI.

World Bank. 1988. *World Development Report.* New York: Oxford University Press.

Wynia, Gary. 1972. *Politics and Planners: Economic Development Policy in Central America.* Madison: University of Wisconsin Press.

Index